P25
84
176
177
164

CHARLES R. SWINDOLL

SWINDOLL'S
LIVING
INSIGHTS

NEW TESTAMENT COMMENTARY

1, 2 & 3 JOHN, JUDE

Tyndale House Publishers, Inc.
Carol Stream, Illinois

Swindoll's Living Insights New Testament Commentary, Volume 14

Visit Tyndale online at www.tyndale.com.

Insights on 1, 2 & 3 John, Jude copyright © 2018 by Charles R. Swindoll, Inc.

Cover photograph of table copyright © Pearl-Lightstock.com. All rights reserved.

Photograph of notebook copyright © jcsmilly/Shutterstock. All rights reserved.

Unless otherwise noted, all artwork copyright © Tyndale House Publishers, Inc. All rights reserved.

All images are the property of their respective copyright holders and all rights are reserved.

Maps copyright © 2017 by Tyndale House Publishers, Inc. All rights reserved.

Designed by Nicole Grimes

Published in association with Yates & Yates, LLP (www.yates2.com).

Scripture quotations marked NASB are taken from the New American Standard Bible,® copyright © 1960, 1962, 1963, 1968, 1971, 1972, 1973, 1975, 1977, 1995 by The Lockman Foundation, La Habra, Calif. Used by permission. All rights reserved. For permission to quote information, visit http://www.lockman.org.

Scripture quotations marked NLT are taken from the *Holy Bible,* New Living Translation, copyright © 1996, 2004, 2015 by Tyndale House Foundation. Used by permission of Tyndale House Publishers, Inc., Carol Stream, Illinois 60188. All rights reserved.

Scripture quotations marked RSV are taken from the Revised Standard Version of the Bible, copyright © 1952 [2nd edition, 1971] by the Division of Christian Education of the National Council of the Churches of Christ in the United States of America. Used by permission. All rights reserved.

Scripture quotations marked KJV are taken from the *Holy Bible,* King James Version.

Scripture quotations marked ESV are taken from *The Holy Bible,* English Standard Version® (ESV®), copyright © 2001 by Crossway, a publishing ministry of Good News Publishers. Used by permission. All rights reserved.

Scripture quotations marked MSG are taken from *THE MESSAGE,* copyright © 1993, 1994, 1995, 1996, 2000, 2001, 2002 by Eugene H. Peterson. Used by permission of NavPress. All rights reserved. Represented by Tyndale House Publishers, Inc.

The "NASB," "NAS," "New American Standard Bible," and "New American Standard" trademarks are registered in the United States Patent and Trademark Office by The Lockman Foundation. Use of these trademarks requires the permission of The Lockman Foundation.

TYNDALE, Tyndale's quill logo, *New Living Translation,* and *NLT* are registered trademarks of Tyndale House Publishers, Inc.

ISBN 978-1-4143-9374-2   Hardcover

Printed in China
25   24   23   22   21
7   6   5   4   3

CONTENTS

Author's Preface v
The Strong's Numbering System vii
Introduction: 1, 2 & 3 John 3
A Joyful Life (1 John 1:1-10) 18
   God Is Life (1 John 1:1-4) 20
   God's Light and Our Blight (1 John 1:5-10) 28
A Clean Life (1 John 2:1-17) 37
   Wise Words from a Family Meeting (1 John 2:1-11) 39
   Strong Warnings about the World (1 John 2:12-17) 49
A Discerning Life (1 John 2:18-4:6) 59
   Dealing with Deceivers (1 John 2:18-27) 60
   Living in the Light of the Lord's Return (1 John 2:28-3:3) 72
   Discerning the Works of the Devil (1 John 3:4-10) 79
   Not like Cain, but like Christ! (1 John 3:11-24) 88
   Distinguishing Truth from Error (1 John 4:1-6) 98
A Confident Life (1 John 4:7-5:21) 109
   The Supremacy of Love (1 John 4:7-21) 110
   Believers, Overcomers, Witnesses (1 John 5:1-12) 118
   Absolute Assurance (1 John 5:13-21) 128
Balancing Love and Truth (2 John 1:1-13) 137
Balancing Truth and Love (3 John 1:1-15) 148
Introduction: Jude 161
A Manual for Survival (Jude 1:1-25) 169
   The Acts of the Apostates (Jude 1:1-16) 169
   Get Your Act Together! (Jude 1:17-25) 185
Endnotes 195

List of Features and Images
   Timeline of 1, 2 & 3 John 2
   Map of Western Asia Minor 2
   The Book of 1 John at a Glance 4
   The Book of 2 John at a Glance 4
   The Book of 3 John at a Glance 4
   Authorship of John's Gospel and Letters 7
   Domitian Bust 9
   Quick Facts on 1 John 10
   Quick Facts on 2 John 14
   Quick Facts on 3 John 15
   We Proclaim 24
   The First Heretics' Fleshless Christ 25

Things in the World. 56
Excursus: The Original Counterfeit—Still in Business 63
The Baths in Ephesus 65
Historic Heresies 66
Six Benefits of Truth 67
Excursus: Why Is the Incarnation So Important? 69
Gnostic Hedonism. 84
Cain and Abel 92
Present and Future Antichrists 104
Excursus: Are There Apostles and Prophets Today? 105
Work of the Holy Spirit in the Life of the Believer 115
Three Who Bear Witness in Heaven? 125
A First-Century Handbook on Discernment. 142
From Pioneers to Settlers 153
Timeline of Jude. 160
Map of the Roman World in the Time of the Apostles. 160
The Book of Jude at a Glance 162
The Six "Judes" in the New Testament 164
Quick Facts on Jude. 166
Excursus: Apostates—Defectors from What? 177
Excursus: Angelic Apostates 181
What Was the "Love Feast"? 182
Waterless Cloud and Rootless Tree 183
Triplets in Jude. 191

AUTHOR'S PREFACE

For more than sixty years I have loved the Bible. It was that love for the Scriptures, mixed with a clear call into the gospel ministry during my tour of duty in the Marine Corps, that resulted in my going to Dallas Theological Seminary to prepare for a lifetime of ministry. During those four great years I had the privilege of studying under outstanding men of God, who also loved God's Word. They not only held the inerrant Word of God in high esteem, they taught it carefully, preached it passionately, and modeled it consistently. A week never passes without my giving thanks to God for the grand heritage that has been mine to claim! I am forever indebted to those fine theologians and mentors, who cultivated in me a strong commitment to the understanding, exposition, and application of God's truth.

For more than fifty years I have been engaged in doing just that—*and how I love it!* I confess without hesitation that I am addicted to the examination and the proclamation of the Scriptures. Because of this, books have played a major role in my life for as long as I have been in ministry—especially those volumes that explain the truths and enhance my understanding of what God has written. Through these many years I have collected a large personal library, which has proven invaluable as I have sought to remain a faithful student of the Bible. To the end of my days, my major goal in life is to communicate the Word with accuracy, insight, clarity, and practicality. Without informative and reliable books to turn to, I would have "run dry" decades ago.

Among my favorite and most well-worn volumes are those that have enabled me to get a better grasp of the biblical text. Like most expositors, I am forever searching for literary tools that I can use to hone my gifts and sharpen my skills. For me, that means finding resources that make the complicated simple and easy to understand, that offer insightful comments and word pictures that enable me to see the relevance of sacred truth in light of my twenty-first-century world, and that drive those truths home to my heart in ways I do not easily forget. When I come across such books, they wind up in my hands as I devour them and then place them in my library for further reference . . . and, believe me, I often return to them. What a relief it is to have these resources to turn to when I lack fresh insight, or when I need just the right story or illustration, or when I get stuck in the tangled text and cannot find my way out. For the serious expositor, a library is essential. As a mentor of mine once said, "Where else can you have ten thousand professors at your fingertips?"

In recent years I have discovered there are not nearly enough resources like those I just described. It was such a discovery that prompted me to consider becoming a part of the answer instead of lamenting the problem. But the solution would result in a huge undertaking. A writing project that covers all of the books and letters of the New Testament seemed overwhelming and intimidating. A rush of relief came when I realized that during the past fifty-plus years I've taught and preached through most of the New Testament. In my files were folders filled with notes from those messages that were just lying there, waiting to be brought out of hiding, given a fresh and relevant touch in light of today's needs, and applied to fit into the lives of men and women who long for a fresh word from the Lord. *That did it!* I began to work on plans to turn all of those notes into this commentary on the New Testament.

I must express my gratitude to Mike Svigel for his tireless and devoted efforts, serving as my hands-on, day-to-day editor. He has done superb work as we have walked our way through the verses and chapters of all twenty-seven New Testament books. It has been a pleasure to see how he has taken my original material and helped me shape it into a style that remains true to the text of the Scriptures, at the same time interestingly and creatively developed, and all the while allowing my voice to come through in a natural and easy-to-read manner.

I need to add sincere words of appreciation to the congregations I have served in various parts of these United States for more than five decades. It has been my good fortune to be the recipient of their love, support, encouragement, patience, and frequent words of affirmation as I have fulfilled my calling to stand and deliver God's message year after year. The sheep from all those flocks have endeared themselves to this shepherd in more ways than I can put into words . . . and none more than those I currently serve with delight at Stonebriar Community Church in Frisco, Texas.

Finally, I must thank my wife, Cynthia, for her understanding of my addiction to studying, to preaching, and to writing. Never has she discouraged me from staying at it. Never has she failed to urge me in the pursuit of doing my very best. On the contrary, her affectionate support personally, and her own commitment to excellence in leading Insight for Living for more than three and a half decades, have combined to keep me faithful to my calling "in season and out of season." Without her devotion to me and apart from our mutual partnership throughout our lifetime of ministry together, Swindoll's Living Insights would never have been undertaken.

I am grateful that it has now found its way into your hands and, ultimately, onto the shelves of your library. My continued hope and prayer is that you will find these volumes helpful in your own study and personal application of the Bible. May they help you come to realize, as I have over these many years, that God's Word is as timeless as it is true.

The grass withers, the flower fades,
But the word of our God stands forever. (Isa. 40:8, NASB)

Chuck Swindoll
Frisco, Texas

THE STRONG'S NUMBERING SYSTEM

Swindoll's Living Insights New Testament Commentary uses the Strong's word-study numbering system to give both newer and more advanced Bible students alike quicker, more convenient access to helpful original-language tools (e.g., concordances, lexicons, and theological dictionaries). The Strong's numbering system, made popular by the *Strong's Exhaustive Concordance of the Bible,* is used with the majority of biblical Greek and Hebrew reference works. Those who are unfamiliar with the ancient Hebrew, Aramaic, and Greek alphabets can quickly find information on a given word by looking up the appropriate index number. Advanced students will find the system helpful because it allows them to quickly find the lexical form of obscure conjugations and inflections.

When a Greek word is mentioned in the text, the Strong's number is included in square brackets after the Greek word. So in the example of the Greek word *agapē* [26], "love," the number is used with Greek tools keyed to the Strong's system.

On occasion, a Hebrew word is mentioned in the text. The Strong's Hebrew numbers are completely separate from the Greek numbers, so Hebrew numbers are prefixed with a letter "H." So, for example, the Hebrew word *kapporet* [H3727], "mercy seat," comes from *kopher* [H3722], "to ransom," "to secure favor through a gift."

INSIGHTS ON 1, 2 & 3 JOHN

Here, nearing the end of his life, with clarity

of perspective and singularity of purpose, the

Lord's "beloved disciple" sought to revive the

faith, love, and hope of his younger readers.

He hoped to encourage them to renew an

authentic, contagious walk with Christ.

And his message of right living in a wrong

world is as relevant today as it was then.

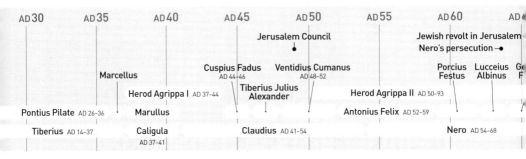

| AD 30 | AD 35 | AD 40 | AD 45 | AD 50 | AD 55 | AD 60 | AD |

Jerusalem Council

Jewish revolt in Jerusalem
Nero's persecution →

Marcellus

Cuspius Fadus
AD 44–46

Ventidius Cumanus
AD 48–52

Porcius
Festus

Lucceius
Albinus

G
F

Herod Agrippa I AD 37–44

Tiberius Julius
Alexander

Herod Agrippa II AD 50–93

Pontius Pilate AD 26–36

Marullus

Antonius Felix AD 52–59

Tiberius AD 14–37

Caligula
AD 37–41

Claudius AD 41–54

Nero AD 54–68

When John wrote these letters, he was most likely living in Ephesus, but he might have sent them while in exile on the island of Patmos. John's most likely recipients were Christians living in the towns and cities in western Asia Minor near Ephesus.

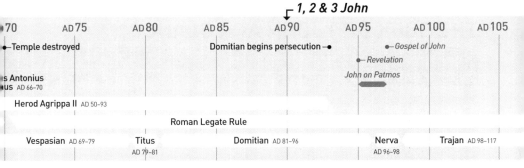

1, 2 & 3 John

70   AD 75   AD 80   AD 85   AD 90   AD 95   AD 100   AD 105

●—Temple destroyed   Domitian begins persecution —●   ●—Gospel of John

●— Revelation

s Antonius   John on Patmos
us AD 66–70

Herod Agrippa II AD 50–93

Roman Legate Rule

Vespasian AD 69–79   Titus   Domitian AD 81–96   Nerva   Trajan AD 98–117
                              AD 79–81   AD 96–98

1, 2 & 3 JOHN
INTRODUCTION

In the twilight of his long life, the apostle John gathered his thoughts, surveyed the landscape of the world around him, and then sat down with parchment and ink to sum up his final words to the churches.

So much had changed since he had walked with Jesus as one of the original Twelve. Those brief but impactful three-plus years John spent with Jesus were followed by six long and painful decades. Erosion had set into the life of the church. In many places, the newness of fresh faith had begun to wane now that the church was in the hands of second- and third-generation Christians. A subtle, lethargic boredom had replaced the excitement modeled by those early followers of Jesus. The initial thrill had subsided, the bright flame of devotion reduced to a flicker.

In a setting like that, the subtle seeds of heresy are easily sown and rapidly grown. Cults feed off complacent churches, where ho-hum indifference replaces dynamic enthusiasm. Also, over the course of time, core values like truth, love, and hospitality can begin to be compromised, misdirected, and abused. Tragically, these scenarios were playing out in the church of John's day—and that's precisely what led him to write these letters.

THE BOOK OF 1 JOHN AT A GLANCE

SECTION	THE JOYFUL LIFE	THE CLEAN LIFE
PASSAGE	1:1-10	2:1-17
THEMES	"These things we write, so that our joy may be made complete." (1:4) • By walking in the light with the Son of God	"I am writing these things to so that you may not sin." (2: • By obeying in love with our Advocate
KEY TERMS	Life Joy Fellowship	Universe Little children Light/darkness Propitiation

THE BOOK OF 2 JOHN AT A GLANCE

SECTION	INTRODUCTION	WALK IN THE TRUTH
PASSAGE	1:1-3	1:4-6
THEMES	Personal greeting	Love one another Walk in obedience
	Encouragement to love and affirm	
KEY TERMS	Truth . . . Children . . . Teaching	

THE BOOK OF 3 JOHN AT A GLANCE

SECTION	CONFIRMATION OF GAIUS	DENUNCIATION OF DIOTREPHES
PASSAGE	1:1-8	1:9-10
THEMES	John commends and encourages Gaius for "walking in the truth" (1:3-4).	John calls out Diotrephes for misdeeds and his arrogance.
KEY TERMS	Beloved . . . Walking	

THE DISCERNING LIFE	THE CONFIDENT LIFE
2:18–4:6	4:7–5:21
ese things I have written to concerning those who are ng to deceive you." (2:26) testing in truth with the Holy One	"These things I have written to you who believe in the name of the Son of God, so that you may know that you have eternal life." (5:13) • By believing in knowledge with our Propitiation
Anointing Abide	Love Conquer

STAND AGAINST ERROR	CONCLUSION
1:7-11	1:12-13
Beware of false teaching Continue in true teaching	Personal farewell
Exhortation to be discerning	

ESTIMONY OF DEMETRIUS	CONCLUSION
1:11-12	1:13-15
sets up Demetrius as a worthy ple and a contrast to Diotrephes.	John wishes to see Gaius "face to face" (1:14) and sends greetings.

1 JOHN

When he wrote the letter known today as 1 John, it's likely that the aged apostle had more years behind him than he had months ahead of him. He was probably somewhere between 88 and 93 years of age. Let's just call him a 90-year-old man. Isn't it remarkable that a man at that age was so in touch with his times? In fact, I would argue that *because* of his age, he saw more clearly than ever. And that's what troubled him enough to write this letter.

Here, nearing the end of his life, with clarity of perspective and singularity of purpose, the Lord's "beloved disciple" sought to revive the faith, love, and hope of his younger readers. He hoped to encourage them to renew an authentic, contagious walk with Christ. And his message of right living in a wrong world is as relevant today as it was then.

THE AUTHOR, PLACE, AND DATE OF 1 JOHN

Although the author of this five-chapter message never names himself, several clues point us to the writer's identity. First, the author clearly places himself as part of a group of apostolic eyewitnesses to the life and ministry of Jesus, noting that "what we have seen and heard we proclaim to you also" (1 Jn. 1:3). This narrows our pool of potential candidates and points us to one of the original disciples of Jesus. But which one?

We are helped by the fact that the language, style, and themes of this letter are similar to those found in the fourth Gospel. Although the author of the fourth Gospel is also unnamed, it doesn't take Sherlock Holmes to narrow the possibilities to one. The author of the fourth Gospel refers to himself indirectly as "the disciple whom Jesus loved" (John 13:23; 19:26; 20:2; 21:7, 20). This is undoubtedly a reference to the apostle John for a few reasons. First, he had to be one of the twelve disciples who had personally witnessed the events about which he wrote. In John 21:24, the author said, "This [disciple whom Jesus loved] is the disciple who is testifying to these things and wrote these things, and we know that his testimony is true." Second, because the description "the disciple whom Jesus loved" implies a close, personal relationship with Jesus, it's most likely that the author was one of the three disciples in Jesus' "inner circle"—Peter, James, or John (Matt. 17:1; Mark 5:37; 14:33). Third, the author couldn't be Peter because he distinguishes himself from Peter (John 20:2), and he couldn't be James because James was martyred too early to have written the Gospel (Acts 12:2). This leaves

Handwritten margin notes: 1. "What we have seen..." 2. Similar language style = Gospel; The disciple whom Jesus loved — Peter? — James?

only one reasonable conclusion for the authorship of the fourth Gospel: John, the son of Zebedee and brother of James (Mark 3:13-17).[1]

Because we have great confidence regarding the authorship of the Gospel of John, we can rely on that knowledge to determine the author of 1 John, which we can then use to determine the authorship of 2 and 3 John. One commentator of yesteryear describes the reasoning this way: "If the Gospel were wanting (faulty), we might be in doubt as to who wrote the Epistles. If the First Epistle were wanting, we might be in doubt as to who wrote the two short Epistles. If the Second Epistle were wanting, we should certainly be in serious doubt as to who wrote the third. But as it is, there is no room for reasonable doubt."[2]

Because of the close relationship between John's Gospel and the first of these three epistles (1 John), we can identify John as the author of this letter as well. And because of the relationship between 2 and 3 John and their common relationship with 1 John, all the puzzles about authorship fall into place.

Authorship

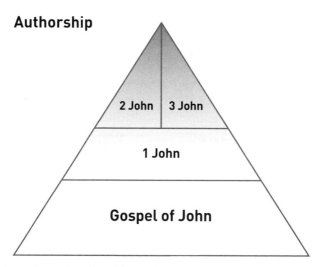

The clarity of the authorship of John's Gospel helps us determine the authorship of 1 John, which in turn helps us determine the authorship of 2 and 3 John.

Besides this evidence, among the earliest Christians there was little doubt that the apostle John wrote the fourth Gospel as well as 1 John. In fact, both of these books are included as authentic works of John in the Muratorian Canon, a list of New Testament books used in the church of Rome in the middle of the second century:

The fourth book of the Gospels [was written by] John, one of the disciples. . . . What marvel therefore if John so firmly sets forth each statement in his Epistle too, saying of himself, "What we have seen with our eyes and heard with our ears and our hands have handled, these things we have written to you"? For so he declared himself not an eyewitness and a hearer only, but a writer of all the marvels of the Lord in order.[3]

Already, in the early second century (around AD 110), one of John's disciples, Polycarp of Smyrna, offered a paraphrase of 1 John 4:2-3, when he wrote, "For everyone who does not confess that Jesus Christ has come in the flesh is an antichrist."[4] In the next generation, Irenaeus of Lyons, a disciple of Polycarp, clearly linked the Gospel of John and 1 John as written by the disciple of that name:

> John, the disciple of the Lord, verifies [this], saying: "But these are written, that ye might believe that Jesus is the Christ, the Son of God, and that believing ye might have eternal life in His name." . . . For this reason also he has thus testified to us in his Epistle: "Little children, it is the last time; and as ye have heard that Antichrist doth come, now have many antichrists appeared; whereby we know that it is the last time."[5]

Not only did John refrain from naming himself as the author of 1 John, but he also declined to name the recipients. It's likely that he intended the letter to be shared among numerous churches with which he was familiar, rather than being written to an individual or a particular local church. This is why the letter has been reckoned among the "Catholic Epistles," where "catholic" means "universal" as opposed to "local."

It may very well be that John originally had this epistle sent to the churches in the immediate vicinity of Ephesus, the city that had become his final home toward the end of his life. This would have included the seven churches mentioned in Revelation 2–3 as well as numerous others dotting the map of western Asia Minor. From there, however, the letter would have spread far and wide until all churches throughout the world were blessed by its profound message.

Just as we can't zero in on the precise location of John's original audience, neither can we triangulate the letter's place of origin. We know that toward the end of John's life, he dwelled in the city of Ephesus in western Asia Minor. But sometime in the early nineties, a persecution against the Christians arose under Emperor Domitian, who reigned from AD 81 to 96. During this persecution, the apostle John was arrested and allegedly thrown into boiling oil, from which he was miraculously preserved.[6] As a "plan B," John was exiled to the tiny island of Patmos in the Aegean Sea, from which he wrote the book of Revelation (Rev. 1:9). After the persecution ended, John returned from exile and continued to minister among the churches of Asia Minor until his death after the crowning of Emperor Trajan around AD 98.[7]

John could have written his first epistle before, during, or after his exile on Patmos. Most likely, 1 John was written around AD 90.

Emperor Domitian reigned from AD 81 to 96. During his persecution against Christians, the apostle John was exiled to Patmos.

© by Sailko/Wikimedia Commons

OCCASION OF 1 JOHN

In his first epistle, the apostle John presents a simple, uncomplicated worldview of right and wrong: Christ versus antichrists, light versus darkness, truth versus falsehood, righteousness versus sin, love of the Father versus love of the world, the Spirit of God versus the spirit of the world, children of God versus children of Satan. In this way, John redraws lines that had begun to fade in the minds of his readers who were beginning to compromise and capitulate in the fog of relativism around them. However, John's hard stand on truth doesn't neglect love. Love for God and for one another is a major theme of the letter (see, e.g., 1 Jn. 4:7). His first epistle thus teaches that while it's important to recognize the lines between truth and error, it must always be done in a spirit of love.

As he did in his Gospel, John stated the purpose of 1 John with clarity. Right up front he informed his audience of the reason for writing to them: "so that you too may have fellowship with us; and indeed our fellowship is with the Father, and with His Son Jesus Christ . . . so that our joy may be made complete" (1:3-4). Later, John added two more purposes for writing: "so that you may not sin" (2:1) and "so that you may know that you have eternal life" (5:13). In short, John wrote to them so they would have fellowship with the Father and the Son and fellowship with one another in the Spirit, resulting in a joyful, clean, discerning, and confident life.

To help them reach those lofty goals, John focused on three issues: the zeal of *entusiasmo* the believers, their ability to stand firm against false teachers, and the reassurance they could have with respect to eternal life. John wrote to churches full of people who had likely struggled with discouragement—whether due to their own sinful failures or the presence of false teachers in their midst. The aging apostle hoped to ignite the zeal of these believers so that they might follow the Lord more closely and stand firm against those who meant to sow discord among the churches. In doing so, they would solidify their relationship with God and gain confidence in His work in their lives.

THE OUTLINE OF 1 JOHN

John wrote this letter to drive home the point that Spirit-enabled fellowship with the Father and the Son produces a joyful life, a clean life, a discerning life, and a confident life. He does this through a four-part outline:

- Fellowship produces *a joyful life* (1:1-10).
- Fellowship produces *a clean life* (2:1-17).
- Fellowship produces *a discerning life* (2:18–4:6).
- Fellowship produces *a confident life* (4:7–5:21).

Fellowship produces a joyful life (1:1-10). The key verse for this section is 1 John 1:4: "These things we write, so that our joy may be made complete." When we have intimate fellowship with God, through His Son, by the power of the Holy Spirit, we have an overflowing joy. Joy comes from walking in the light rather than the darkness. Those who walk in ignorance, sin, and falsehood will reap the misery of anxiety, guilt, and confusion. In our own dark and angry world, the joyful Christian becomes a bright beacon of light. What a refreshing discovery it is for people of the world to witness a group of believers who really enjoy life! Let your joy be full.

Fellowship produces a clean life (2:1-17). In 2:1, John says, "My little children, I am writing these things to you so that you may not sin." When we have a close, personal relationship with God and fellowship with His people, our battles against sin become winnable. We don't have to surrender to temptation. This doesn't mean that temptations vanish or that we won't ever sin, but sin's power is diminished. Even when we do sin, Christ steps in as our Advocate with the Father, making His victory our own (2:1-2). This, in turn, drives us to live a clean life before Him. In our "anything goes" society, the clean Christian is a contagious witness, so let your integrity shine forth.

Fellowship produces a discerning life (2:18–4:6). In 2:26, John writes, "These things I have written to you concerning those who are trying to deceive you." A close relationship with God requires a deep understanding of His truth. Sadly, as Christians grow comfortable and complacent, their ability to discriminate between truth and error, light and darkness, right and wrong, is diminished. So, in this section, the longest of the four, John reinforces the need to beware of "antichrists" (2:18), to "test the spirits" (4:1), and to remember the "anointing" of the Spirit that teaches them the truth (2:20, 27). In a world of falsehood, John emphasizes the need for knowing and applying the truth. In our own deceptive culture the discerning Christian is a convicting presence, so proclaim the truth and conform your life to it.

Fellowship produces a confident life (4:7–5:21). In 5:13, John writes, "These things I have written to you who believe in the name of the Son of God, so that you may know that you have eternal life." Assurance of our eternal, irrevocable salvation is one of the greatest promises we can embrace in the Christian life. Those who lack assurance of salvation fear death, worry about tomorrow, and often view God as an angry drill sergeant ready to pounce whenever they step out of line. Those who have assurance understand that God is the one who saved us by grace alone through faith alone in Christ alone . . . and that He's the one who will keep us through the continuing work of the Holy Spirit in our lives. In an age confused about the future, the Christian is a strong centerpiece of confident expectation. Let the stream of hope flow!

2 JOHN

Only thirteen verses long, the tiny memo that is 2 John would have barely filled a single sheet of papyrus.[8] It's like a note we might write and drop in the mail to a close friend. As a personal letter, it cradles some secrets we as outsiders aren't privy to. Already in the opening line, we're faced with some big questions: Who is the elder? Who is the lady? What's the situation? These are some questions we should try to answer before wrestling with the text itself.

First, who is "the elder"? The Greek term for elder is *presbyteros* [4245], which has the basic meaning "being relatively advanced in age."[9] It can also refer to an official in a civil or religious office—as in an elder of a guild, synagogue, or church.[10] In that instance, the primary focus would have been on the person's office as a community leader, not on his age. However, these two meanings of *presbyteros* aren't mutually exclusive. Generally, the leaders of civic or religious organizations would have been the more senior members of the community.

Whoever "the elder" is in 2 John, he doesn't identify himself by name. However, a little probing helps us solve this first mystery. The same fingerprints of the author of 1 John are all over 2 John, in terms of writing style, themes, and vocabulary. And the book of 1 John likewise shares numerous similarities with the Gospel of John. Because we know the author of the Gospel of John to be the aged disciple of Jesus—John, son of Zebedee—we can identify the author of 2 John as the same person. This is confirmed by the language and style of John that indelibly mark this letter.[11]

Second, who is the "chosen lady"? Two main views have been held from earliest days by commentators on this letter. One sees the phrase "chosen lady and her children" as a reference to a particular church (figuratively called a "chosen lady") and the individual members of the church (figuratively called "her children").[12] However, John switches between the second-person singular ("you") and the second-person plural ("you all") throughout these thirteen verses. If the singular

SECOND-PERSON SINGULAR (YOU)	SECOND-PERSON PLURAL (YOU ALL)
2 John 1:4	2 John 1:6
2 John 1:5	2 John 1:8
2 John 1:13	2 John 1:10
	2 John 1:12

addresses the whole church, whom is the plural addressing? And if the plural addresses all the members of the church, whom is the singular addressing?

Another view, which I have adopted, is that John has a particular person in mind when he uses the term "chosen lady" and employs the second-person singular (1:4, 5, 13). This seems to make the most sense of John's very personal tone in the letter. John's other personal references ("lady" [1:5]; "your house" [1:10]; and "your chosen sister" [1:13]) lead me to this conclusion. Like Lydia in the book of Acts (see Acts 16:14-15, 40), perhaps this lady of 2 John was a gracious hostess who opened her home for the sake of the ministry.

But what's the situation? The specific historical context of the churches in the late first century is important to understanding the letter. At that time, as in some places in the world today where Christianity is an illegal religion, churches were not buildings or big-budget operations. The Christians mostly met in homes and flew under the radar of the Roman authorities and local power holders. So it may very well be that the believers addressed in 2 John met in the house of the "chosen lady."

Also, at the time, there was no complete Bible like we have today. No leather-bound Old and New Testaments. Larger churches would have had access to the Old Testament translated into Greek, the common language. But the New Testament was still being written and compiled. Some of the older and larger churches like the ones at Antioch, Ephesus, and Rome would certainly have had a substantial collection that may have included Gospels, writings of Paul, and perhaps a few other books. But John's works were either brand-new or not even written yet. In any case, the time and expense it took to gather, copy, and distribute a New Testament (when it was complete) would mean that smaller churches and new church-plants would have had to make do with parts and pieces of the Bible for years or even decades.

In a ministry situation in which the New Testament was not yet a complete collection of writings, early Christians had to depend on itinerant prophets and teachers to bring an authoritative message. The prophets of the apostolic era were bearers of divine revelation—just like the prophets of the Old Testament. Their ministry, like that of the apostles, was a temporary, foundational ministry of the church that was needed until the entire Bible was complete and the church had grown to a point of doctrinal stability. (See "Are There Apostles and Prophets Today?" page 105.)

QUICK FACTS ON 2 JOHN

When was it written? Around AD 90
Where was it written? Probably
  Ephesus
Who wrote it? The apostle John,
  son of Zebedee
Why was it written? To balance
  unconditional love with discern-
  ing truth

Small, remote churches welcomed these traveling prophets, providing comfortable lodging, sustaining them, and honoring them as messengers from the Lord. However, the kind of love and respect shown by churches to authentic apostles and prophets began to attract charlatans. As the first century progressed, not all of the roving "reverends" were worthy of their room and board. False prophets and teachers, claiming to be sent by God, would show up occasionally to cash in and lead small, unsuspecting churches astray. Even secular writers attested to their abuses:

> Lucian, the Greek writer, in his work called the *Peregrinus*, draws the picture of a man who had found the easiest possible way of making a living without working. He was an itinerant charlatan who lived on the fat of the land by travelling round the various communities of the Christians, settling down wherever he liked and living luxuriously at their expense.[13]

This kind of threat from false prophets and teachers seems to be the background of John's brief dispatch to the "chosen lady" and "her children." John no doubt caught wind of some of these foul-smelling false teachers and wanted to cut them off at the pass. The dear lady's practice of hospitality demonstrated open-armed love, but in the face of the reality of false prophets and teachers, such hospitality needed to be checked by the important task of protecting doctrinal truth. While affirming her charitable spirit, John sent the "chosen lady" an urgent message: Balance unconditional love with discerning truth.

OVERVIEW OF 2 JOHN

The postcard-sized letter of 2 John urges believers to balance unconditional love and discerning truth. What an important message for us today! Our own twenty-first-century church faces charges of hatred when believers stand for the truth . . . and faces temptations to fudge on doctrinal and moral issues in the name of tolerance and acceptance.

In the introduction (1:1-3), John opens with a personal greeting that sets the affectionate tone of the letter but also introduces the key theme: the balance of love and truth (1:1, 3). The second paragraph urges the lady and her children to continue to walk in the truth (1:4-6) and obey Christ's command to love one another.

The letter then turns somber as John exhorts his readers to stand against error (1:7-11). Because many anti-Christian deceivers are on the prowl, the unconditional love characteristic of obedient Christians must be balanced by watchful discernment. Finally, in the conclusion (1:12-13), John returns to warm affection, expressing his longing to see his readers face-to-face and extending closing greetings.

3 JOHN

Though he isn't named, I have little doubt that the apostle John authored this letter, most likely around the same time and under similar conditions as the letters of 1 and 2 John. Having established the authorship of those works earlier in this volume, the question of the identity of "the elder" (3 Jn. 1:1) has already been answered.[14] The apostle John was an elderly man when he wrote this letter, perhaps in his nineties. He clearly wields great authority and deserves respect; but he writes with kindness, gentleness, and compassion.

COMPARISON BETWEEN 2 JOHN AND 3 JOHN

Second and Third John can be thought of as sibling letters. Both written around the same time by the same person, they have their own unique personalities but also have some striking similarities—much like siblings. If we place them side by side, we can clearly see some of these comparisons and contrasts.

	2 JOHN	3 JOHN
To Whom	To a lady and her children	To a man named Gaius
Occasion	Receiving the wrong kind of travelers	Rejecting the right kind of travelers
Problem	Misplaced hospitality	Missing hospitality
Solution	Truth to balance love	Love to balance truth

John addresses the letter to a particular person but mentions several others in general, and two by name. The recipient of the letter is Gaius, a common name in the Roman Empire, like "John" or "Jim" today. Three other men in the New Testament bore this name: Gaius

QUICK FACTS ON 3 JOHN

When was it written? Around AD 90
Where was it written? Probably Ephesus
Who wrote it? The apostle John, son of Zebedee
Why was it written? To balance truth with love

the Macedonian, who was with Paul at the riot of Ephesus (Acts 19:29); Gaius of Derbe, who transported a collection of money from his church to the suffering Christians in Jerusalem (Acts 20:4); and Gaius of Corinth, who was baptized by Paul and who served as Paul's host (1 Cor. 1:14; Rom. 16:23). Though it's possible that the Gaius of 3 John could be one of these, it's more likely that this particular Gaius was an otherwise unknown convert of John.

Who was Gaius? And what was his role in the church? These questions are best answered by exploring the occasion of the letter, which revolves around a few other individuals. First, there were the "brethren" who were "strangers" to the church (3 Jn. 1:5-8). These missionary workers—endorsed by John—were apparently shown good treatment by Gaius and others in the church, but poor treatment by another individual, Diotrephes, who even rejected the authority of John himself (1:9-10). Diotrephes epitomized wicked behavior, unbecoming of a Christian (1:11). However, another individual, Demetrius, is identified as a positive example to follow (1:11-12).

It seems most reasonable that two of these men—Gaius and Diotrephes—were among the church's leaders, possibly elders. However, Diotrephes appears to have succumbed to personal ambition, arrogance, and pride to the extent that he even set himself up against the authority of the apostle John and the traveling messengers commissioned by John. Instead of working as a team player among equals in the church, he wanted the first place of authority. Part of the purpose of the letter, then, was for John to indirectly urge Diotrephes to repentance through Gaius, backed up by the warning that John will show up in person and, if necessary, cut Diotrephes down to size.

OVERVIEW OF 3 JOHN

The little letter of 3 John breaks down nicely into four sections. First, John articulates a *confirmation of Gaius* (1:1-8), in which Gaius is commended and encouraged for his positive qualities and for doing what is right in the recent church conflict. Second, in his *denunciation of Diotrephes* (1:9-10), John calls out the scoundrel who is the source of the conflict, highlighting some negative attitudes and destructive actions that simply needed to stop. Third, John ends the body of the letter on a positive note, the *testimony of Demetrius* (1:11-12), who serves as an example for others to follow, in contrast to the renegade Diotrephes. Finally, John ends the letter in virtually the same way as he did in 2 John, with a *conclusion* expressing his desire to see Gaius face-to-face (1:13-15).

Times haven't changed much, have they? Church people today—even those who hold the same truth and live according to the same moral principles—still often jostle for recognition, clamber for position, and break fellowship and ruin friendships to get to the top. Thankfully, most leaders do not behave this way. We have many examples of those who reflect good judgment, sound doctrine, and genuine love toward the brethren. The truth we hold must be balanced with genuine love for others.

A JOYFUL LIFE
(1 JOHN 1:1-10)

When I was just a little boy, our family was vacationing at a bay cottage in South Texas near the Gulf of Mexico. One night my father told me, "I'm going to get you up early, Son. We're going out where we've never fished before, but be ready to get up."

It felt like he woke me up just minutes after I had fallen asleep. It must have been two o'clock in the morning. He shook me awake in the pitch dark and said, "Come on, come on. Put your sneakers on, let's go."

I staggered after him through a chilly night to the boathouse. We climbed into a little fishing boat not even sixteen feet long. The 35-horsepower Evinrude motor sounded like a thunderclap as it broke the stillness of the morning, and within moments we were cutting through the slick, moonlit water. There wasn't a ripple on the surface except the shallow wake tailing behind our boat. We eased across the glassy bay and moved out toward the reef. He shut her down, and we slid up over the deep reef.

He slipped the anchor into the water and eased it down until it finally rested at the bottom. I peered across the shiny surface of the bay, which looked like a freshly tarred parking lot slicked with rain. I imagined I could walk on its surface or wade through it like a shallow pond. I dropped the line of my little cane pole into the water and, like the antsy boy that I was, I began to fidget.

My father looked over at me and said, "Sit still, Son. There's big stuff down in there."

I settled down for a minute or two. Maybe I'd catch something a little bigger than my hand. But a few minutes later I'd grown impatient bringing in my line and throwing it back out. As I scratched and shifted and spat in the water, my father just sat there, still as a statue. In the silence of the approaching dawn, he said to me again, "Sit still, Son. Be quiet. *There's big stuff down in there.*"

All of a sudden, as if on cue, a huge Gulf tarpon jumped out of the water, flipped in the air, and splashed back down. It must have been

KEY TERMS IN 1 JOHN 1:1-10

chara (χαρά) [5479] "joy," "cheerfulness," "calm delight," "gladness"
Though only used once in 1 John, the word *chara*, meaning "joy," has a prominent place in the purpose of the letter: "These things we write, so that our joy may be made complete" (1:4). Elsewhere in John's writings, the term refers to the deep joy experienced at a wedding (John 3:29) or at the birth of a child (John 16:21). Lasting, genuine joy comes from a relationship with Jesus Christ, who answers prayer and comforts us in sorrow (John 16:22-24).

koinōnia (κοινωνία) [2842] "fellowship," "communion," "participation"
The word *koinōnia*, frequently translated "fellowship," should be thought of as more than just hanging out with friends, as the word often suggests today. Rather, it indicates "close association involving mutual interests and sharing" and is often used of the marriage relationship in literature outside of the New Testament.[1] Christian *koinōnia* begins with a believer's spiritual union with God, which, in turn, results in a communion of fellow saints through the work of the Holy Spirit (1 Cor. 1:9; 1 Jn. 1:3). In 1 John, this kind of *koinōnia* is the basis for abiding joy (1:3-4).

zōē (ζωή) [2222] "life," especially "spiritual life"
Though this term is related to our English word *zoo*, in the New Testament, *zōē* rarely refers to animal life (cf. Rev. 16:3). Normally the term refers to the eternal life that comes from the Father, through the Son, and by the Holy Spirit. This is how it is used by John (e.g., 1 Jn. 2:25; 3:14; 5:11-13). Elsewhere, Jesus Christ is Himself called the *zōē* (Col. 3:4).

bigger than me. I almost leaped out of the boat, but my dad never budged. Without turning, he muttered under his breath, "Told you there was big stuff down in there."

And right he was! By the end of that little excursion we had caught sixty-four speckled trout. (I've never forgotten that number, because Dad made sure I cleaned all of them!)

The apostle John's unassuming, five-chapter book is like that slick bay we fished on that cold, quiet morning. Judging by a glance across its surface, 1 John looks like it might only be as deep as it is wide—containing a few minnows of truth and a couple of pan-fish principles swimming in a pool of shallow theology. A leisurely boat ride, but not good fishing. But the surface conditions can be misjudged. Despite the simple language and short length of 1 John, *there's big stuff down in there.*

Ask any serious scholar of the Scriptures for their opinion on this letter and you'll hear that it's one of the most challenging of all the New Testament books. And unlike some books, like Romans, 1 Corinthians, or Hebrews, it doesn't have a few "problem passages" in an otherwise straightforward argument; 1 John is complicated from the very beginning. However, this must not stop us from dropping our lines in and pulling out some profound and practical insights.

John wrote this letter with a simple, overarching message in mind: Spirit-enabled fellowship with the Father and the Son produces a joyful life, a clean life, a discerning life, and a confident life. This first section (1:1-10) presents the principle that *fellowship produces a joyful life.* An intimate relationship with God through Jesus Christ will result in close relationships with fellow believers, leading to profound, inexplicable joy. This joy is based on the blessings that come through deep intimacy with the glorious God of the universe. These blessings include eternal life (1:2), right living in a wicked world (1:5-6), and cleansing from the penalty and power of sin (1:7-10).

The apostle John may have been an elderly fisherman-turned-fisher-of-men and may on the surface seem to have been a simplehearted follower of Jesus, but before long, we'll see that what he wrote with just a few dips into his inkwell is profound and deep.

God Is Life
1 JOHN 1:1-4

NASB

¹What was from the beginning, what we have heard, what we have seen with our eyes, what we have looked at and touched with our hands, concerning the Word of Life— ²and the life was manifested, and we have seen and testify and proclaim to you the eternal life, which was with the Father and was manifested to us— ³what we have seen and heard we proclaim to you also, so that you too

NLT

¹We proclaim to you the one who existed from the beginning,* whom we have heard and seen. We saw him with our own eyes and touched him with our own hands. He is the Word of life. ²This one who is life itself was revealed to us, and we have seen him. And now we testify and proclaim to you that he is the one who is eternal life. He was with the Father, and then he was revealed to us. ³We proclaim to you what we ourselves have actually seen and heard

one through whom all things were made. He's the one who, with the Spirit of God, fashioned the heavens and the earth, made light shine in the darkness, and stepped into that creation when "the Word became flesh" (John 1:14).

The term "word" (*logos* [3056]) had a profound significance to both Greeks and Jews in the first century. In Greek philosophy, *logos* referred to the uncreated principle of reason that gave order and structure to the universe.[3] In the Old Testament, the "word" was both God's means of revelation—His message to humanity—and, on occasion, a divine presence that took some kind of physical form, indistinguishable from God (Jer. 1:1-14). In the early first century AD, the Jewish philosopher Philo of Alexandria seemed to merge these Greek and Jewish concepts. One author notes, "Philo of Alexandria puts a great deal of emphasis on the notion of *logos*, making it the mediating principle between God and the world."[4] By the end of the first century AD, when the apostle John was writing, Christians had no doubt about who this one mediator between God and men was—not an immaterial *logos*, but the Word made flesh, "the man Christ Jesus" (1 Tim. 2:5).

John's description of this *logos* is no mere discourse on secondhand information. The aged apostle isn't theologizing or speculating when he talks about the Word. He claims to have literally *experienced*, firsthand, the incarnate Word. The next three relative clauses, still referring to the same subject of his proclamation, emphasize this fact. John was among those few people still alive late in the first century who had heard and seen with their own ears and eyes the incarnate God-man, Jesus Christ. John made this same claim in his Gospel when he referred to events of the Crucifixion. Speaking of himself in the third person, he wrote, "And he who has seen has testified, and his testimony is true; and he knows that he is telling the truth, so that you also may believe" (John 19:35).

It was vital for John that he had been an original earwitness of Christ's teachings and eyewitness of His life, miracles, death, and resurrection. In fact, when referring to the time he caught his first glimpse of the empty tomb, John wrote of himself (again in the third person), "So the other disciple who had first come to the tomb then also entered, and he saw and believed" (John 20:8).

John had also been present with the rest of the disciples when "doubting Thomas" obstinately declared, "Unless I see in His hands the imprint of the nails, and put my finger into the place of the nails, and put my hand into His side, I will not believe" (John 20:25). Eight days later, the resurrected Lord Jesus called that same doubter to put

We Proclaim

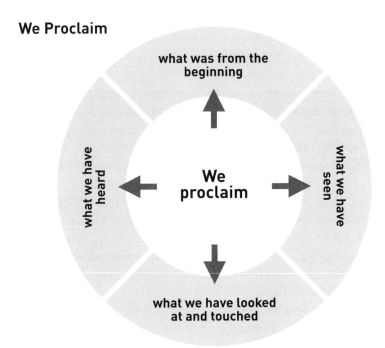

what was from the
beginning

what we have
heard

**We
proclaim**

what we have
seen

what we have looked
at and touched

his finger in His hands and side and to feel for himself that He had indeed risen bodily from the dead (John 20:26-27). Because they were eyewitnesses, John and his fellow disciples could confidently confess to Jesus Christ, as Thomas had, "My Lord and my God!" (John 20:28).

With this background, the apostle John added in his letter that he and the other disciples had "looked at and touched" the incarnate God both during His earthly ministry and in His resurrected state (1 Jn. 1:1). Why does John say that he had "looked at" the Word of Life after he already said that he had seen Him with his eyes? The term "looked at" is the Greek word *theaomai* [2300], which conveys more attentiveness than mere observation. It means "to have an intent look" or to perceive "above and beyond what is merely seen with the eye."[5] John also emphasized the fact that he and his companions had "touched" the Word of Life "with [their] hands" (1:1).

What a powerful testimony at a time when heretics were on the rise spreading a false doctrine of a fleshless, phantom Christ (4:2-3; 2 Jn. 1:7; see "The First Heretics' Fleshless Christ," page 25). One commentator sums up John's testimony well: "John's experience was both a mysterious perception of the living Lord and yet it was also very basic and down to earth. Jesus was no phantom of the spiritual realm but He was Jesus of Nazareth."[6]

sisters in Christ (1 Cor. 1:9; 1 Jn. 1:3). As believers have this intimate communion "with the Father, and with His Son Jesus Christ," they will have the same kind of deep communion with one another through the work of the Holy Spirit. John proclaimed the Word of Life so his readers could have this kind of fellowship.

Second, John's proclamation concerning the Word of Life is to result in full joy (1:4). Just as the word "fellowship" has suffered from flippancy, so has "joy." When we hear the word "joy" we immediately begin to think of the emotion we feel when we find out we're getting money back on our tax return . . . or when we pass a big exam . . . or when the person we've fallen for says, "I love you." That's joy, right? Wrong! Martyn Lloyd-Jones proposes this definition of biblical joy—

> Joy is something very deep and profound, something that affects the whole and entire personality. . . . It comes to this; there is only one thing that can give true joy and that is a contemplation of the Lord Jesus Christ. He satisfies my mind; He satisfies my emotions; He satisfies my every desire. He and His great salvation include the whole personality and nothing less, and in Him I am complete. Joy, in other words, is the response and the reaction of the soul to a knowledge of the Lord Jesus Christ.[10]

In 1:3-4, the purposes of true fellowship and full joy are closely related. In order for the apostle's joy to be full, he needs to have a true intimate relationship with his fellow believers based on their mutual relationship with God through Jesus Christ. Authentic, lasting joy is inseparably linked to the Word of Life whom we worship and adore. In this joy, shared by those who have fellowship with God and with one another, we are fully accepted as we grow together in the Word of Life.

APPLICATION: 1 JOHN 1:1-4

A Practical Response to a Profound Prologue

In just four verses, making up only two sentences, the apostle John has packed a lifetime's worth of practical principles we should never forget. I wouldn't be exaggerating if I said we could spend the rest of our Christian lives meditating on and living out these few verses. The truths expressed by this passage are fundamental to Christian faith and life.

Let me help us begin to ponder its truths by putting these four verses into a loose paraphrase that I hope catches the essence of the passage:

> From the very first time we disciples laid our eyes on Him, taking it all in—hearing with our own ears, seeing with our own eyes, staring at and studying Him over the years . . . actually *touching* Him with these hands—we saw it all happen before our very eyes, literally, and we're now declaring what we witnessed: incredibly, the infinite life of God Himself who took shape before us! And now I'm writing about it so all of you can experience what has transformed our lives: intimate communion with the Heavenly Father and His Son, Jesus Christ . . . and the same satisfying joy we've known since we began walking with Him. That's why I'm writing you this letter today.

The Word of Life, Jesus Christ the God-man, paid the complete price for your sins—His death for your life. He did it for you. All you have to do to enter into this deep communion and to experience this full joy is to accept the gift that God offers through faith in His Son. You can pray a prayer like this, in your own words, from your heart, to take the first step into that relationship with Him:

> Lord Jesus, I accept you now. I want to know this life. I want to know this deep communion with God and with others. I want to experience this life of joy. I admit I've lost my way. Thank you for giving Jesus to die for my sins and to rise again to be my living Savior and to give me new life—His life—through the power of the Holy Spirit who comes to live in those who believe. I believe.

If you haven't accepted Christ before, do so now. Enter into communion with God and with all of us who have already done so. If you do, our joy—yours and mine—will be full.

God's Light and Our Blight
1 JOHN 1:5-10

NASB

[5] This is the message we have heard from Him and announce to you, that God is Light, and in Him there is no darkness at all. [6] If we say that

NLT

[5] This is the message we heard from Jesus* and now declare to you: God is light, and there is no darkness in him at all. [6] So we are lying if we say

we have fellowship with Him and *yet* walk in the darkness, we lie and do not practice the truth; ⁷but if we walk in the Light as He Himself is in the Light, we have fellowship with one another, and the blood of Jesus His Son cleanses us from all sin. ⁸If we say that we have no sin, we are deceiving ourselves and the truth is not in us. ⁹If we confess our sins, He is faithful and righteous to forgive us our sins and to cleanse us from all unrighteousness. ¹⁰If we say that we have not sinned, we make Him a liar and His word is not in us.

we have fellowship with God but go on living in spiritual darkness; we are not practicing the truth. ⁷But if we are living in the light, as God is in the light, then we have fellowship with each other, and the blood of Jesus, his Son, cleanses us from all sin.

⁸If we claim we have no sin, we are only fooling ourselves and not living in the truth. ⁹But if we confess our sins to him, he is faithful and just to forgive us our sins and to cleanse us from all wickedness. ¹⁰If we claim we have not sinned, we are calling God a liar and showing that his word has no place in our hearts.

1:5 Greek *from him.*

At some point in each of our lives, we transition from childhood to adulthood, from student to teacher, from mentee to mentor. I vividly remember when I was on my way out of the house for the last time. My parents did all they could to raise me right, to instill in me solid values, words of wisdom, and examples to follow. When I had to cross the threshold of the house that marked the moment of my transition from dependent child to independent adult, my mother said to me, "I've told you all I know to tell you. Now you're on your own."

I may have been on my own physically, at least for a season—until I began to build my own family and emulate the wisdom and lessons my parents had taught me. But I wasn't on my own spiritually. The words and examples of my parents were always there, becoming increasingly relevant and meaningful as I faced my own real-life situations. As I continued to mature as an adult, I can't remember how many times the words of my mom or dad came back to me, and I thought, "That's what they meant!" They also left me a priceless spiritual legacy, introducing me to the Lord Jesus, a respect for God's Word, and a love for His church.

I imagine something similar happened with Jesus' original disciples. They continued to mature in their understanding of the faith after the Lord Jesus pushed His disciples out of the nest and sent them into the world. He didn't completely abandon them, though. He sent His Spirit to abide with them, to comfort them, to teach them, and to lead them into all truth (John 14:16-17, 25-26; 15:26-27; 16:5-15). He sent the Spirit not only to teach the disciples new things but also, as Jesus promised them, to "bring to your remembrance all that I said to you" (John 14:26).

In the letter of 1 John, the aged apostle is memorializing with paper and ink the wisdom imparted to him from Christ after decades of real-life reflection and teaching by the Spirit of God. The memory of Christ's teaching had not faded over the years but had become more pronounced, more meaningful, and more practical as he not only learned it but lived it and imparted it to others. In 1 John 1:5-10, John casts the message he had received from Jesus in the simple terms of light and darkness.

The principles of 1:5-10 are clear and straightforward:

- God's character is holy and pure (1:5).
- Our nature is dark and depraved (1:6).
- Our hope is in confessing and cleansing (1:7-10).

We can learn and even memorize these words in a matter of minutes, but it will take a lifetime of walking in the light to come to terms with the depth of their significance.

—1:5—

Many biblical authors tell us a lot about what God *does*. The Old Testament largely recounts His mighty deeds from Creation to the eve of the coming of the Messiah. The New Testament also presents numerous blow-by-blow accounts of the Savior's actions and the Spirit's deeds through the apostles.

The apostle John has left us an account—in the Gospel of John and the book of Revelation—of what Christ has done and will do. But he has also focused a lot on who God is, and much of this focus comes through in 1 John. While others write of God's power, God's work, God's will, and God's way, John keeps bringing us back to who God is in His very nature. And because the infinite depths of God's nature are veiled to us, John uses images and metaphors to help us catch a glimpse of His essence and character.

In the opening sentence of this letter, John tells us that God is life, manifested to us through Jesus Christ (1:1-2). He is the One who originates life, who gives eternal life, and who made Himself known as the Word of Life. While exulting in the memory of having seen Him, heard Him, and touched Him, the elderly apostle states that it's this incarnate Word whom "we proclaim to you" (1:3).

All of this prompts him to announce "the message" he wanted his readers never to forget—that God is Light (1:5). "Light" is a single term that captures the essence of God's nature. It represents the holiness and purity of God. In John's metaphor, God isn't simply a source of light, a being brilliantly illumined by light, or a reflector of light. God *is* Light. As such, there's no possibility of even a trace of darkness with Him. God is ALL LIGHT, ZERO DARKNESS.

What does this mean? It means that God is all good, with nothing bad. He is all pure, with nothing impure. He is all clean, with nothing dirty. He is all right, with nothing wrong. He is all truth, with nothing false. What a profound statement to make in a culture in which many of the numerous "gods" of the Greeks and Romans were simply imperfect, cruel, vindictive supermen—like twisted and troublesome humans . . . only bigger, stronger, and immortal.

False gods, past or present, pale in comparison to the one true God, who is Light. This is vitally important because without His light of purity and holiness in our lives, we dwell in constant spiritual darkness. It is a simple fact that in the physical world, as well as in the spiritual world, darkness can't continue when it encounters light. Light always dispels darkness.

—1:6-7—

In contrast to God's nature as light, our human nature in its fallen condition is dark and depraved. I know this isn't a popular topic for polite preachers today. Television's beaming, it's-all-about-you pastors downplay our spiritual darkness and make it sound as if the key to success is to simply get in touch with our inner light of optimism, motivation, or purpose. Other preachers are subtler. They simply avoid seemingly harsh language and concepts that allude to moral or spiritual darkness.

In 1:6, John begins a series of three "if we say" clauses that take us to the end of the chapter. The problem throughout these verses is a contradiction between a believer's profession of faith and their lifestyle. In the first of these, John (1) sets up the claim, (2) describes the contradiction, and (3) draws a reasonable conclusion. In this way, he leads his readers through a self-evaluation of the very real issue of sin in a believer's life.

CLAIM	CONTRADICTION	CONCLUSION
"If we say that we have fellowship with Him"	"and yet walk in the darkness"	"we lie and do not practice the truth."

This is the situation of those who ignore their sinfulness while claiming to have an intimate relationship with God. Their words are nothing more than that—words. When there is such a stark contradiction be-tween our claim of closeness to the Light and our lifestyle of darkness, the only conclusion that can be drawn is that we're lying. If we say we have fellowship with God and gawk at pornography, we're liars. If we say we enjoy intimacy with God but are verbally or physically abusive toward our spouses and children, we lie. If we claim to be close with God but stir up trouble at church through murmuring, complain-ing, and gossiping, we're not practicing the truth.

What's the solution to a life of total contradiction between what we say and what we do? Verse 7 gives the contrast. If we walk in the Light, as God dwells in Light, two things happen. First, we enjoy inti-mate fellowship with our fellow believers who are walking in the Light. Second, we experience continual cleansing of our lives through our intimate fellowship with God.

But what does it mean, practically, to "walk in the Light?" The Greek word translated "walk" (*peripateō* [4043]) literally means "to walk around" (Matt. 4:18). However, it had a common idiomatic usage refer-ring to a person's lifestyle or pattern of behavior (Rom. 6:4; Eph. 4:1). It doesn't refer to a single, isolated action—either positively or nega-tively. A single action might be called a "step in the right direction" or a "step down the wrong path." However, the image of "*walking* in the light" or "*walking* in the darkness" implies step after step in the same direction—a pattern of living.

So, when we "walk in the Light," we adapt our thinking and be-havior to His. We allow Him to take control of our urges. We stay in close contact with Him, reading His Word, praying, and assembling with fellow believers. And we participate in these things continually, not sporadically . . . frequently, not occasionally.

—1:8-10—

In verses 8 and 10 we see the second and third contradictions, this time of a different kind, but just as false and damaging to a right walk in fellowship with God.

CLAIM	CONCLUSION
"If we say that we have no sin,"	"we are deceiving ourselves and the truth is not in us."
"If we say that we have not sinned,"	"we make Him a liar and His word is not in us."

You probably noticed that there is no explicit contradiction stated in these "if we say" clauses. The reason for this is that the contradiction is patently obvious to anybody who dwells in this mortal, fallen flesh. The truth is, we do have sin. And because of this sin nature, we commit actual sins, even as believers. The root cause of the abiding sin in our lives is often called "total depravity." The doctrine of total depravity can be defined this way:

> Because of the fall, humans are spiritually dead—essentially and unchangeably bad apart from divine grace. Their guilt before God is *total*. Total depravity doesn't mean everyone is as evil as they could possibly be, but that everyone absolutely needs the grace of God to even understand the gospel and choose to accept it.[11]

As uncomfortable as this doctrine may be to a postmodern "I'm okay, you're okay" mind-set, it's clearly and repeatedly taught in Scripture. Let me share just three verses that establish the fact that we are as bad off as we can be with regard to our own righteousness and right standing with God.

> "There is not a righteous man on earth who continually does good and who never sins." (Eccl. 7:20)

> "As it is written, 'THERE IS NONE RIGHTEOUS, NOT EVEN ONE; THERE IS NONE WHO UNDERSTANDS, THERE IS NONE WHO SEEKS FOR GOD; ALL HAVE TURNED ASIDE, TOGETHER THEY HAVE BECOME USELESS; THERE IS NONE WHO DOES GOOD, THERE IS NOT EVEN ONE.'" (Rom. 3:10-12)

> "And you were dead in your trespasses and sins, in which you formerly walked according to the course of this world, according to the prince of the power of the air, of the spirit that is now working in the sons of disobedience. Among them we too all formerly lived in the lusts of our flesh, indulging the desires of the flesh and of the mind, and were by nature children of wrath, even as the rest." (Eph. 2:1-3)

The doctrine of depravity and our resulting sinfulness is so clear in Scripture it's no wonder John declares that if we claim we haven't sinned, "we make Him a liar and His word is not in us" (1 Jn. 1:10).

While there is no darkness in God because He is Light (1:5), there is no light of holiness and purity in fallen, unsaved humanity apart from the light of God's grace. Try as we may, we humans cannot, without

God's help, produce a single spark of genuine righteousness that would be pleasing to God and move us one step closer to Christlikeness. Sin mars us within, down to the core of our being, down to the fount of our motives. We may attempt to hide it, try to deny it, or dogmatically reject it. But fallen humanity's stain of sin and guilt has blighted all of us through and through.

This condition of our sinfulness stands behind John's discussion of the believer's relationship to light and darkness. By casting God's light and our blight in black-and-white terms, the apostle gets his readers to take seriously not only God's holiness but also their own sinfulness. Because our God is Light (holy, pure, and righteous), He wants His children to walk not in darkness but in light.

John could have easily amassed a flood of verses, countless biblical examples, and a slew of personal experiences to prove that anybody claiming to be sinless is simply self-deceived! Sadly, more and more people in our world are falling into this deception, denying or downplaying the reality of their own sinfulness.

John MacArthur puts it well:

> People today minimize and redefine sin, often alleging that the "failures" of their lives and certain "disorders" exist because of how others have treated them. The victim mentality reigns supreme as popular culture comforts itself in affirming that people are basically good and whatever may be wrong is not really wrong, but merely a preference of personal freedom. Instead of accepting responsibility for their behavior, people demand to be accepted as they are.[12]

The antidote to denying our sin is to do exactly the opposite: confess it. John assures us in 1:9 that our loving God offers us a glorious promise of mercy and grace. If we "confess our sins," God will be faithful to His promise of cleansing through the blood of Christ, releasing us from the relationship-bruising effects of our actions and working in us by the Spirit to wash away our unrighteousness. The term translated "confess" is *homologeō* [3670], a compound word that literally means "to say the same thing." To confess our sins is to "concede that something is factual or true."[13] We agree with what God says about our sinfulness, not what we would prefer to be true or what the world says.

When we sin, we must take responsibility for it. We don't blame others, our family history, our genes, our environment, or our circumstances. We don't blame the devil or God. We admit that we are sinners in need of God's forgiveness and restoration. When we do this—simply confess our sinfulness to God—He cleanses us from all unrighteousness and restores us to intimate fellowship with Him. What a great promise of ever-present, always-available grace and mercy!

However, I want to warn against making this single verse, 1 John 1:9, stand all alone. God's promise to forgive us when we confess our sins should never be interpreted as an invitation to an all-you-can-sin smorgasbord for which Jesus paid the check. It isn't an infinite supply of instant sin sanitizer you simply squirt on your wicked deeds as you continually get your hands grubbed up in unrighteousness. This verse is embedded in a context that puts it in its proper perspective.

The God who is Light wants us to walk in the Light, not in darkness. He wants us to have constant closeness with Him. In our intimate relationship with Him and with fellow believers, God wants us to be aware of our sinfulness, to speak the truth about our condition, to walk in the light of His Word, and to strive for righteousness by His Spirit. But when we do inevitably sin, He wants us to go to Him for cleansing so we can maintain our fellowship with Him.

APPLICATION: 1 JOHN 1:5-10

God's Light Each Day

As we begin to think about how to apply 1 John 1:5-10, let me give you a statement I don't want you to ever forget: *Intimacy is rooted in honesty.* Because it's never too late to do what's right, acknowledging wrong is the first step toward a recovery of intimacy with God and communion with fellow believers. This is why confession plays such a vital role in both. Without an attitude of confession, we'll begin to stockpile sin and guilt, which will turn to worry and shame, which will drive us farther from the light of God's purity, holiness, righteousness, and truth.

Each day we need to do what it takes to walk in the Light and let His grace and mercy drive out the darkness. Over the years, I have worked up a simple plan for putting this into practice. If we commit to this plan, or something like it, we'll experience more victories over darkness than defeats.

First, I begin each morning determined to walk all day in the Light. I commit to it. In my morning prayers, I pray something like "Lord, I don't know what the hours in front of me will hold. I have no idea the people I'll encounter, the challenges I'll face, the temptations I'll need to overcome. I don't know what tragedies, trials, or triumphs I'll experience. I don't know what my health will be like by the end of the day. But You know. So today, I determine before You to walk in the Light by Your power. As I come to forks in the road throughout the day—choices between darkness and light—guide me to the Light. I know that I'm a sinner, and in my own strength I can do nothing to make this happen. So, I ask for Your power to walk in the Light."

Then, as I continue each day, I try to remain aware of my own dark nature. I must never forget that I can, at any point, take a step toward the darkness. In fact, there's never a day that goes by in which I haven't entertained a stray thought, a bad attitude, a careless glance, a foolish word, or an offensive remark. But when I do, I confess it. I say the same thing God says about me: I'm a sinner. And I call it what it is: sin. By confessing it, I'm keeping short accounts with God.

Finally, as the sun sets and the day draws to a close, I never forget to thank Him for seeing me through. It's not my own might or power, or some clever method or trick I've discovered, that gets me through the day. It's only through His powerful, transforming grace—His Light that guides me deeper into the Light.

A CLEAN LIFE
(1 JOHN 2:1-17)

I've been to a lot of museums in my day. Some small, some large. Some focused on just a slice of history, like the Civil War . . . others focused on the entire history of a part of the world, like the Holy Land. Some museums are organized according to a strict linear path—usually with a sign on one entry that says "Entrance" and another that says "Exit." You never wonder where to go; you just follow the flow of the exhibits and eventually come out on the other side. The only way you can miss something at a museum like that is if you close your eyes or leave through a fire escape!

Other museums, though, are arranged so as to have connected chambers or clusters of exhibits. No straight line. No single entrance or exit. You sort of wander from hall to hall, ascend or descend stairs, and browse collections at your leisure. If you like Egyptian mummies, you spend your time on the west side of the third floor. If you like Italian Renaissance art, you head for the south wing of the annex connected by a skywalk. You know you're done when you get hungry or bored or the museum closes. Of course, in a nonlinear museum, you'll probably miss something. You spend so much time ogling the mineral collection that you never even visit the hall with the bones of a woolly mammoth!

Books of the Bible are a little like museums. Some are large, focused on a number of themes treated in a logical, linear manner. Others are small, narrowing in on one particular topic. The book of 1 John is a moderately long letter and follows a meandering path around a number of themes that are on display. The apostle John, our personal tour guide through these topics, may lead us first to the matter of walking in the light, then to confession of sin, back to light, then to love, then to sin again, then to truth, back to light, and so on. For the more linear thinkers, it can get a little bewildering. But if we realize that John is actually taking us on a journey of transformation, we can trust that we won't leave the museum having missed something important. We can enjoy the journey.

Because of the winding nature of the book, it helps to periodically step back and remind ourselves of the big picture: John wanted to communicate to his readers that Spirit-enabled fellowship with the Father and Son produces a joyful life, a clean life, a discerning life, and a confident life.

We've already visited the first section, which focused on the joy that comes from intimate fellowship with God and others by walking in the Light. In this second section, John develops the truth that fellowship produces a clean life (2:1-17). Here, the tone becomes more personal. He addresses his readers with familial terms that suggest a close, endearing communion between them. When we share this kind of intimate relationship with God and fellow believers, it has obvious effects on our spiritual lives. We begin winning battles against sin. And we begin loving others with the love of heaven—an unconditional, self-sacrificial love. Both of these help us experience what it means to truly walk in the Light.

KEY TERMS IN 1 JOHN 2:1-17

teknion (τεκνίον) [5040] "little children"
Several times in this letter, John addresses his readers directly as "little children" (2:1, 12, 28; 3:7, 18; 4:4; 5:21). A "familiar, loving address,"[1] *teknion* is the diminutive form of the word for "child" (*teknon* [5043]; see 3:1, 2, 10; 5:2). John uses *teknion* only in the vocative case (direct address) to illustrate the believers' relationship with God. By addressing his readers as *teknion*, John set a parental, gentle, and loving tone.

kosmos (κόσμος) [2889] "orderly arrangement," "universe," "sinful world"
In its most general sense, *kosmos* can refer to all that exists, i.e., the universe. However, the apostle John uses the term in a more limited, technical, and theological sense to refer to the system of this present age before the return of Christ. The "world" in this narrow sense is in the clutches of Satan and is characterized by wickedness (2:15-17; 3:1, 13; 4:4-5, 17; 5:4-5). John does not intend to suggest that physical creation itself is evil, but that in its current condition, it stands in opposition to God.

phōs (φῶς) [5457] "light"
    skotos (σκότος) [4655] "darkness"
In the opening lines of this letter, John introduces the principle that "God is Light, and in Him there is no darkness at all" (1:5). In this second section, John uses the same contrast to make a clear distinction between the wickedness of this dark world and the lives of genuine believers who are "in the Light" (2:8-9). In the ancient world, without the ability to flip on a switch and produce light, unseen and unknown hazards lingered in the

darkness. Paul portrays those who are apart from Christ as actually *being* "darkness" in contrast to being "Light in the Lord" (Eph. 5:8). And in John's Gospel, the Light of Christ is repeatedly contrasted with the darkness of this present world (John 1:5; 3:19; 8:12; 12:35, 46).

hilasmos (ἱλασμός) [2434] "propitiation," "atoning sacrifice"

[handwritten: → the act of gaining or regaining the favor or goodwill of someone or something. Synonyms: appease, conciliate, pacify. Antonyms: provoke, harass, agitate]

[handwritten: redención - expiación]

Used only twice in the New Testament (both in 1 John and both in reference to Christ's death), *hilasmos* has an Old Testament background in sacrificial atonement imagery. It is used to refer to the "ram of atonement" in Numbers 5:8 and to a "sin offering" in Ezekiel 44:27. When John calls Jesus Christ the "propitiation for our sins" in 1 John 2:2, he means that Christ's death turned away God's wrath toward us and fully satisfies the debt we have toward Him.

[handwritten: conciliate, pacify, placate / propiciar, facilitar]

Wise Words from a Family Meeting
1 JOHN 2:1-11

NASB

¹My little children, I am writing these things to you so that you may not sin. And if anyone sins, we have an ᵃAdvocate with the Father, Jesus Christ the righteous; ²and He Himself is the ᵃpropitiation for our sins; and not for ours only, but also for *those of* the whole world.

³By this we know that we have come to know Him, if we keep His commandments. ⁴The one who says, "I have come to know Him," and does not keep His commandments, is a liar, and the truth is not in him; ⁵but whoever keeps His word, in him the love of God has truly been perfected. By this we know that we are in Him: ⁶the one who says he abides in Him ought himself to walk in the same manner as He walked.

⁷Beloved, I am not writing a new commandment to you, but an old commandment which you have had from the beginning; the old commandment is the word which you have heard. ⁸ᵃOn the other hand,

NLT

¹My dear children, I am writing this to you so that you will not sin. But if anyone does sin, we have an advocate who pleads our case before the Father. He is Jesus Christ, the one who is truly righteous. ²He himself is the sacrifice that atones for our sins—and not only our sins but the sins of all the world.

³And we can be sure that we know him if we obey his commandments. ⁴If someone claims, "I know God," but doesn't obey God's commandments, that person is a liar and is not living in the truth. ⁵But those who obey God's word truly show how completely they love him. That is how we know we are living in him. ⁶Those who say they live in God should live their lives as Jesus did.

⁷Dear friends, I am not writing a new commandment for you; rather it is an old one you have had from the very beginning. This old commandment—to love one another—is the same message you heard before. ⁸Yet it is also new. Jesus lived the

[handwritten lower left: ...acción, eliminación del pecado o la culpa. Propiciación; tiene que ver con aplacar la ira de Dios]

39

NASB

I am writing a new commandment to you, which is true in Him and in you, because the darkness is passing away and the true Light is already shining. ⁹The one who says he is in the Light and *yet* hates his brother is in the darkness until now. ¹⁰The one who loves his brother abides in the Light and there is no cause for stumbling in him. ¹¹But the one who hates his brother is in the darkness and walks in the darkness, and does not know where he is going because the darkness has blinded his eyes.

2:1 ªGr *Paracletos*, one called alongside to help; or *Intercessor* 2:2 ªOr *satisfaction* 2:8 ªLit *Again*

NLT

truth of this commandment, and you also are living it. For the darkness is disappearing, and the true light is already shining. ⁹If anyone claims, "I am living in the light," but hates a fellow believer,* that person is still living in darkness. ¹⁰Anyone who loves a fellow believer* is living in the light and does not cause others to stumble. ¹¹But anyone who hates a fellow believer is still living and walking in darkness. Such a person does not know the way to go, having been blinded by the darkness.

2:9 Greek *hates his brother;* also in 2:11. 2:10 Greek *loves his brother.*

Back in the 1980s, a best-selling book by Robert Fulghum delighted the world with a surprisingly simple thesis: *All I Really Need to Know I Learned in Kindergarten.*[2] In the opening pages of that book, Fulghum asserts, "Wisdom was not at the top of the graduate-school mountain, but there in the sandpile at Sunday School."[3] Some of his basic rules of life are "share everything," "play fair," "don't hit people," "clean up your own mess," and "say you're sorry when you hurt somebody."[4] Those simple rules resonate with us not only because they make good sense but also because we tend to forget them. I'm convinced that the more we return to the basics, the easier we'll be to live with.

As we get deeper into our study of 1 John, it becomes obvious that John is taking his readers back to the basics—not in a condescending way, but in an endearing way. He addresses them sincerely as members of a spiritual family—little children, fathers, young men (2:12-14). This is a "family meeting," in which his readers are sitting at their spiritual grandfather's feet and gleaning timeless wisdom. When he opens his mouth, his words aren't meant to impress or to chide. This isn't a rebuke or a scolding. These are words of loving instruction and concerned warning. This isn't lofty sophistry but loving wisdom.

Hearing these wise words from a family meeting should change how we see ourselves. If John is placing himself in the role of family patriarch, we, too, should receive these words as his spiritual children, members of the same spiritual family. Don't think of John as a crotchety killjoy, even though some of his language may be firm and convicting.

He isn't a puritanical curmudgeon. Remember, his words of exhortation and warning at this family meeting are meant to bring true fellowship and joy!

Let me present my notes from John's family meeting in the form of "family rules for little children." I see at least seven straightforward, basic principles in these eleven verses—six in 2:1-6 and the foundational command in 2:7-11.

—2:1-6—

John addresses his readers for the first time as "my little children" in 2:1. The Greek term is *teknion*, a diminutive form of the word for "child." In English, the diminutive form of "bird" is "birdie"; the diminutive of "dog" is "doggy." Clearly, John wants to communicate close, loving affection, like a grandfather addressing small children. Because of this, as I outline what I see as John's basic list of family wisdom, I'm going to follow his lead and present these principles as I would to a child. In fact, if I could write them in crayon, I would.

Rule 1: Don't ever mess with stuff that gets you into trouble. That's the gist of John's opening words: "I am writing these things to you so that you may not sin" (2:1). Remember, John has just mentioned in the previous chapter that God will be faithful to forgive us our sins if we confess them to Him (1:9) and that all of us have sinned (1:10). The reality of ever-present sin in our lives and of God's ever-ready forgiveness must never become an excuse to sin like there's no tomorrow! John pulls up that weed of misunderstanding before it gets a chance to sprout. He's not giving us an excuse to sin, but urging us to avoid it. Why? Because it's dangerous.

Rule 2: When you foul things up, remember you have Someone who's always in your corner. No matter what happens, we're never alone. No matter how far we might stray into the murky waters of temptation and disobedience, no matter how wrong the action or how severe the consequences, "we have an Advocate with the Father, Jesus Christ the righteous" (2:1). This is the second time that John has made this point. Back in 1:9 he stated that if we confess our sins, God is ready to forgive us and cleanse us of our unrighteousness.

The word translated "Advocate" is *paraklētos* [3875], the same Greek word used of the Holy Spirit in John 14:16 (translated there as "Helper")—"I will ask the Father, and He will give you another Helper, that He may be with you forever." It refers to "one who appears in another's behalf" as a mediator, intercessor, or helper.[5] Warren Wiersbe

41

puts it well: "Christ is our Representative. He defends us at the Father's throne. Satan may stand there as the accuser of the brethren (Zech. 3; Rev. 12:10), but Christ stands there as our Advocate—He pleads on our behalf! Continuing forgiveness, in response to His prayers, is God's answer to our sinfulness."[6]

Like a defense attorney, Christ constantly pleads our case before the heavenly court. But a couple of key differences distinguish our divine Advocate from an earthly attorney. An attorney tries to defend a client's innocence. Our Savior comes to our aid as we acknowledge our guilt. An attorney works within the law, arguing the merits of our case and trying to persuade a judge or jury. Our Savior came to our aid by becoming "the propitiation for our sins" (1 Jn. 2:2). He paid the penalty for the sins of humanity. As the one perfect God-man, He took the place of all humanity through His atoning sacrifice on the cross. The term "propitiation" can be defined as an "offering that turns away (or satisfies) divine wrath against us."[7] When Christ steps in for the believer who confesses their sin, the divine Judge responds to our Advocate who has paid the price for the sins of the world, saying, in effect, "I'm satisfied. Case dismissed."

Rule 3: Behave like a member of the family. The best proof that "we have come to know Him" and therefore are members of God's family is a life of obedience to Him (2:3). How many of us have heard an obstinate child look defiantly at an adult and shout, "You're not my dad!" If children try that with their real fathers, though, there'll be consequences! We obey God as our heavenly Father. And our obedience should come out of love and respect, not constant fear.

I wonder if John was reaching back in his memory to the Last Supper, where Jesus drove home this point: "If you love Me, you will keep My commandments. . . . He who has My commandments and keeps them is the one who loves Me; and he who loves Me will be loved by My Father, and I will love him and will disclose Myself to him. . . . If anyone loves Me, he will keep My word; and My Father will love him, and We will come to him and make Our abode with him" (John 14:15-23). With each statement, the relationship the believer has with the Father and Son becomes deeper, more intimate, more personal. Members of God's family obey their Father.

Rule 4: No matter what you say, your actions tell the real truth. The old adage is true: Actions speak louder than words. Here's another one: Talk is cheap. Anyone who announces, "I've come to know Jesus," but doesn't take a single step into the light or lift a finger to do what He

There's Danger behind Me

1 JOHN 2:1

Back in 1976, during the United States Bicentennial celebration, Cynthia and I joined some friends for a bus tour from Jamestown to Boston. By the time we got to New York City, we were all "bussed out" and wanted to stretch our legs. About half a dozen of us decided to do a self-guided walking tour around Manhattan. Now, back in '76, there were still parts of Manhattan where you didn't even want to stop at red lights. But what did we know? That day, we were just naive West Coast tourists biting off more of the Big Apple than we could chew.

After wandering a few blocks in this or that direction and taking in some historic sights, we ran into one of New York's finest. A polite but firm police officer held out his hand and said, "Hold it. You guys ain't from New York, are you?"

"Um, no, officer. California."

The policeman nodded and said sternly, "You don't wanna go any farther. There's danger behind me. Don't go there."

That officer wasn't trying to take away our fun, keep us from the best tourist attractions, or flaunt the authority of his NYPD badge. He was concerned for our safety. His warnings were for our good. He knew best. Danger lurked behind him.

The same is true of John's stern warnings to his readers. He stands at the threshold of sin, holds out his hand, and says to his spiritual children, "Don't go there. There's danger behind me."

We would do well to heed his warning.

commands is a hypocrite. John's language in 1 John 2:4 is even stronger: That person is "a liar, and the truth is not in him." This is true of all our relationships. Imagine a man who says he loves his wife but constantly does things that hurt her—treating her disrespectfully, unfairly, or abusively. His actions say, "I don't love my wife." A man who truly loves his wife will treat her with dignity, respect, faithfulness, and kindness.

Now, before you misunderstand, this isn't referring to someone who blows it occasionally. We all do that. We all snap at our spouses, shout at our kids, or neglect our families at times. That doesn't mean we don't love them. It means we're frail, fallen, finite humans. The same is true of our relationship with Christ. The verb translated "does not keep" in 2:4 is a present participle, which reflects a constant or habitual practice (in this case, disobedience). This is not simply a person who loves the Lord but occasionally fails to keep His commands. This is a person who says they love the Lord but is characterized by a constant sinful lifestyle.[8]

Rule 5: Always remember that your obedience reveals how much you respect your Father. Whereas in 2:4, John draws the conclusion that a person who is constantly breaking God's commandments lies about having come to know Christ, in 2:5, he looks positively at a person who habitually keeps God's word. Even if we haven't heard that person's verbal profession of their relationship with Christ, we can see from their life itself how much love and respect they have for God.

When we see a woman constantly loving her neighbor as herself, turning the other cheek when wronged, giving sacrificially to those in need, showing hospitality to Christian workers, and contributing faithfully to her local church, we wouldn't take her aside and ask, "Listen, do you really love and respect your heavenly Father?" Our question is answered before we even ask it—not by her words but by her deeds. Compare this to a man who treats others with disrespect, neglects the needs of others, and stirs up strife in the church. That man is rightly challenged regarding the depth of his relationship with the Lord. And if he says, "Oh, Jesus and I are tight. Like two peas in a pod. Super close," we're justified in our skepticism.

Rule 6: When you're looking for an example to follow, choose Jesus. Another sure sign of a person who has spiritual family ties with the Lord is that he or she walks "in the same manner as He walked" (2:5-6). If you're looking for a hero to follow, take your eyes off the sports star, the powerful politician, the high-rolling entrepreneur, or even the megachurch preacher. Turn your focus to Jesus. Put your feet in His footprints, take your cues from His life, study His ways, learn from His example, and emulate His actions. This means getting to know Him through a careful reading of, and reflection on, the Gospels. It also means falling so in love with the Savior that you can't help but spend time with Him . . . and you spend so much time with Him, that you can't help but act like Him.

—2:7-11—

Rule 7: Love your brothers and sisters. I can't imagine what it would be like to grow up in a family in which no one ever said "I love you." Or to live in a family that never showed affection through hugs, appreciation through gifts, or commitment through staying faithful in thick and thin. But such families are certainly out there. Maybe some of you reading these words grew up in one of those families, and for your whole life you've longed to hear those three words we all want to hear.

The truth is, we never outgrow these words, never get tired of them, never find a substitute for them. We say, "I love you," and demonstrate our love in many different ways. Expressions of love are the lifeblood of relationships. Without love, a marriage or a family will shrivel and die.

In communicating these seven basic rules for spiritual family life, the apostle John focuses several verses on what is without question the most central principle: Love your brothers and sisters. No doubt, John emphasizes this rule because Jesus had driven the same point so deeply into His disciples' memories decades earlier, not only in words, but also in deeds. John recorded this in the thirteenth chapter of his Gospel. He began with a profound statement concerning Jesus' own love for His disciples: "Having loved His own who were in the world, He loved them to the end" (John 13:1). Jesus demonstrated this unending love when He washed the feet of His disciples (John 13:1-17). He modeled self-sacrificial, humble, other-centered actions as a sign of authentic love: "If I then, the Lord and the Teacher, washed your feet, you also ought to wash one another's feet. For I gave you an example that you also should do as I did to you" (John 13:14-15). *Washing feet.*

That experience likely changed the apostle John's heart, mind, and actions, and he was probably never the same. At that moment, love was demonstrated to John. And when Jesus followed up His profound actions with clear words, the lesson would be etched into John's soul forever. Jesus said, "A new commandment I give to you, that you love one another, even as I have loved you, that you also love one another. By this all men will know that you are My disciples, if you have love for one another" (John 13:34-35).

45

Now, I'm sure at least some of the disciples—steeped in the teaching of the Old Testament—would have known that the command to "love one another" wasn't really "new." It went back to the Law of Moses, where God says, "You shall not take vengeance, nor bear any grudge against the sons of your people, but you shall love your neighbor as yourself" (Lev. 19:18). So, that part was "old." Yet, look more closely at Jesus' words: "Even as I have loved you, . . . you also love one another" (John 13:34). In the New Testament, the quality of the love for one another is increased to an unsurpassable level. Jesus' perfect, self-sacrificial love for His disciples demonstrates the new form of the old command!

All of this is no doubt in John's mind when he describes the final family rule. In 1 John 2:7, he calls his readers "beloved," a special term of endearment. Though the command he's about to describe is, in a sense, not new because they had heard it "from the beginning," it has taken on new life. In light of Christ's example and because of their spiritual union with Him and with one another, the command "is true in Him and in you" (2:8). James Montgomery Boice explains this language: "In this verse 'true' . . . means 'genuine,' and the point is that the true or genuine love, like genuine righteousness, is now being seen not only in Jesus but in those who are made alive in him as well."[9]

This "new" command is modeled on selflessness and sacrifice—unconditional love expressed by followers of Christ regardless of the response of the other person. Christ models this kind of love (3:16), and the Holy Spirit enables it (see Gal. 5:22). Although we all have a long way to go, believers can already demonstrate that "the darkness is passing away and the true Light is already shining" (1 Jn. 2:8).

Because of the dawning of this new light, the life of the genuine Christ-follower should reveal and drive out the darkness of hatred (2:9). Something's wrong when a person claims to be in the Light, having become a true child of God through faith in the Lord Jesus, but then they still seethe with enmity, hostility, bitterness, and prejudice against fellow believers in the body of Christ. That person still lives in the realm of darkness. John seems to leave no room for "neutral ground" or a "gray area." It's either light or dark . . . love or hate.

The believer who genuinely loves their brothers and sisters in Christ enjoys a walk without stumbling. Such believers can see where they're going (2:10). They're in step with the Lord, enjoying His enabling power, joy, and effectiveness. They're making progress in their growth toward mature Christlikeness.

On the other hand, those who grope about in darkness, fumbling and bumbling, bring harm to themselves and to others (2:11). Their hatred brings blindness. Their powers of judgment are obscured. Personal prejudice colors their responses, poisons their relationships, and transforms them into forces of destruction in the church. This impedes the growth of others in the church. Conflicts and controversies ensue.

John's point is clear. The distinguishing mark of a Christian, the sign that sets you apart from the world and demonstrates that you're a member of God's family, is not a gold cross hanging around your neck. It's not a fish sticker stuck to the back of your car. It's not a well-worn Bible tucked under your arm or a wall full of Christian-camp trophies at home. It's not your baptismal certificate or seminary degree. The distinguishing mark of a Christian is that he or she has Christlike love for others.

APPLICATION: 1 JOHN 2:1-11

Dear Children . . . Grow Up!

It doesn't matter how old you are according to your driver's license. Or how many years have elapsed since a pastor signed your baptismal certificate. We're never too old to sit at the feet of John in a spiritual family meeting and hear him review his basic family rules.

We need these rules. Truth be told, we all have messes that need to be cleaned up. We all have fractured relationships that need mending. We all have obligations we've been neglecting for far too long. We all have sins we've been hiding even from those we've invited into our lives to provide accountability. We all have pots we've been stirring in church—murmuring, gossiping, criticizing, and complaining.

To provide an opportunity to reflect on our own failure and to put these family rules into practice, let's restate each of them and think through some personal questions.

Rule 1: Don't ever mess with stuff that gets you into trouble. Are you nurturing secret, unconfessed sins? Are there things you're doing that you need to stop? Consider the long-term negative effects on both yourself and others if you let these things go on and allow them to grow.

Rule 2: When you foul things up, remember you have Someone who's always in your corner. Does your guilt and shame prevent you from bringing your struggles and conflicts to God for forgiveness? Having been forgiven, what steps do you take to break free from the habit? Are you relying on your own strength for this, or taking it to Christ, who alone can provide deliverance?

Rule 3: Behave like a member of the family. What specific commands of Christ have you been rejecting or neglecting? Do you spend time with Him in prayer and Bible reading? Do you regularly gather together with fellow believers for support and encouragement? Are you striving to walk in the Spirit and to cultivate His fruit in your life, or are you caught in the muck of the deeds of the flesh?

Rule 4: No matter what you say, your actions tell the real truth. If someone were to place your public words beside your private actions, would they see contradiction or harmony? In what areas might you be guilty of hypocrisy—saying one thing but doing another? How is this kind of contradiction affecting your witness for Christ in your family, in your church, or in your neighborhood?

Rule 5: Always remember that your obedience reveals how much you respect your Father. If you were to remove all outward signs of your Christian faith except your actions, would people know you're a follower of Christ? What evidence could you give that you respect His lordship over your life? Are there areas of your life in which Christ is not Master? If so, what are they? Bring these to Him in prayer now.

Rule 6: When you're looking for an example to follow, choose Jesus. Do you strive after role models that reflect the character of Christ or the values and priorities of the world? What personal heroes or examples have the most influence on you through their writings, music, personal interactions, teachings, or behavior? If you could be just like those people, would you be more or less Christlike? What are you doing every day to get to know Jesus better and to become more like Him?

Rule 7: Love your brothers and sisters. If you were put on trial for hating your brothers and sisters in Christ, what evidence do you fear your accusers might produce to prove you guilty? What evidence could you produce in your defense? How would you describe the quality of your love for fellow believers? Is it wilting, half-hearted love? Or selfless, Christlike love?

All of us have strengths and weaknesses that we bring as we emerge from the darkness into a strong and steady walk in the Light. Being aware of these—and seeking help from others in those areas that are particular problems—demonstrates that we are genuine members of God's family, growing up into the likeness of the One who is Light.

Strong Warnings about the World
1 JOHN 2:12-17

NASB

¹²I am writing to you, little children, because your sins have been forgiven you for His name's sake. ¹³I am writing to you, fathers, because you know Him who has been from the beginning. I am writing to you, young men, because you have overcome the evil one. I have written to you, children, because you know the Father. ¹⁴I have written to you, fathers, because you know Him who has been from the beginning. I have written to you, young men, because you are strong, and the word of God abides in you, and you have overcome the evil one.

¹⁵Do not love the world nor the things in the world. If anyone loves the world, the love of the Father is not in him. ¹⁶For all that is in the world, the lust of the flesh and the lust of the eyes and the boastful pride of life, is not from the Father, but is from the world. ¹⁷The world is passing away, and *also* its lusts; but the one who does the will of God lives forever.

NLT

¹² I am writing to you who are God's children
because your sins have been forgiven through Jesus.*
¹³ I am writing to you who are mature in the faith*
because you know Christ, who existed from the beginning.
I am writing to you who are young in the faith
because you have won your battle with the evil one.
¹⁴ I have written to you who are God's children
because you know the Father.
I have written to you who are mature in the faith
because you know Christ, who existed from the beginning.
I have written to you who are young in the faith
because you are strong.
God's word lives in your hearts, and you have won your battle with the evil one.

¹⁵Do not love this world nor the things it offers you, for when you love the world, you do not have the love of the Father in you. ¹⁶For the world offers only a craving for physical pleasure, a craving for everything we see, and pride in our achievements and possessions. These are not from the Father, but are from this world. ¹⁷And this world is fading away, along with everything that people crave. But anyone who does what pleases God will live forever.

2:12 Greek *through his name.* **2:13** Or *to you fathers;* also in 2:14.

When danger draws near, a warning is in order. And the greater the danger, the more vital the warning.

When I think of warnings, my mind goes back over fifty years to when I found myself standing on the deck of a massive troopship, seeing the city of Yokohama, Japan, in the distance, just across the Tokyo Bay. Our ship was slowly snaking its way through the bay because there were still some naval mines lurking beneath those waters—leftovers from World War II. As the pilot was guiding us carefully, a full colonel called some thirty-five hundred Marines to an assembly.

He called us together to give us a warning. Great danger drew near. Not the physical danger of the naval mines. Those could be easily navigated. He had other dangers in mind . . . dangers lurking not in Tokyo Bay but in the streets of Yokohama, where thousands of pent-up Marines were about to be unleashed.

"All of you, listen up," he said. "For many of you, you will be the foreigner for the first time in your lives. You're going to be walking in an area you've never walked before. You'll be among people who speak a language you've never spoken before. You'll be in the midst of a culture you don't understand. So, I have a few words of warning for all of you. First, a message to every one of you: You'll be wearing your uniform. It's the uniform of the United States Marine Corps. You're representing your country while you're on this land. Don't bring reproach to our land and our country. Behave yourselves."

And then the colonel went into some particulars as he addressed some specific categories of personnel. "Some of you," he said, "are older men. You've traveled abroad before. You know better what to expect. But you're not safe any more than the younger men among us."

Then he said to those of us who were younger: "Most of you have never been out of your own country, so you hardly know where the danger lies. Let me say to all of you: Remember these things today. Less than two days from now, at 1100 hours, we will be leaving this dock, and I want all of you back on this ship. Between now and then, you're going to find yourself among great crowds of people. Watch out for pickpockets. Be careful what you eat . . . and where you eat. Don't buy any food off the street. In some parts of the city, there's open prostitution. Don't be stupid. The bars would love to see you come in. And they'd love to see your face flat on the floor. And when you wake up, you'll have nothing of value that belonged to you before. So, discipline yourself."

After several other similar warnings, he concluded, "Again, we're leaving this dock at 1100 hours in less than forty-eight hours. I want all of you back on the ship, in uniform, on your feet, ready to make your way down to Okinawa."

I hardly need to tell you that there were some who promptly forgot the warnings. It wasn't long before some had their pockets picked. Some got back on the ship with temporary food poisoning, others with long-term diseases they picked up from streetwalkers. A number of them were still inebriated or nursing hangovers. And, yes, a handful even missed the ship! I'll never forget when we were leaving the dock at 1100 hours sharp. A few guys were running toward the ship waving their ties and yelling, "Wait! Wait! Wait!" The ship didn't delay its departure for them. It just sailed right out of the harbor as planned.

Many of those men—young and old alike—didn't take the colonel's warnings seriously. Maybe they thought he was just killing time while the ship weaved around the naval mines. Maybe they thought the "old man" was simply obligated to go through that litany of do-nots as part of an official "cover our behinds" policy. But he was serious. These were real warnings from an older, seasoned Marine who wanted to impart wisdom to those under his charge. But because many failed to take heed, they became victims of the dangers. And they paid the price.

My mind immediately returns to that scene on the ship decades ago as I turn to 1 John 2:12-17. I can picture the apostle John, seasoned by years of trials and tragedy, made wise by years of testing and triumph. Like that veteran colonel imparting wisdom to a ship of Marines young and old alike, John was leaning into his audience—not to tell them things they wanted to hear, but to tell them things they needed to hear. Whether they were older men and women or younger men and women, whether they had been believers for a few days or a few decades, John needed to impart to them strong warnings about the real world.

—2:12-14—

John precedes his strong warnings by again addressing his readers with that term of grandfatherly affection that underscores their close family relationship: "I am writing to you, *little children*" (2:12). I understand this as a general address to all his readers, as it is throughout this letter (see 2:1, 28; 3:7, 18; 4:4; 5:21).

However, included among his spiritual children are "fathers," "young men," and even "children" (2:13-14). The term "fathers" is probably used in the same sense as in 1 Timothy 5:1, where Paul says, "Do not sharply rebuke an older man, but rather appeal to him as a father."

John is addressing the older members of the church, perhaps even the church's leaders.[10] In this case, the "young men" would be a reference to those under the mentorship of the older members. Finally, the word translated "children" in 1 John 2:13 is not *teknion*, as in 2:12, but rather the word *paidion* [3813], which usually refers to a preteen who is still under the tutelage of teachers. In any case, the term likely refers to the youngest members of the church, especially those who are still very early in their spiritual formation.

Like that colonel of my own youth who addressed his warning about Yokohama to both battle-hardened veterans and wide-eyed novices, the apostle John calls to attention every generation at every level of spiritual maturity. In my lifetime of ministry, I've learned that some are so young in age and so new to the faith that they have no idea how dangerous the world can be to their spiritual lives. On the other hand, some are so old and mature in the faith that they begin to believe they've outgrown the power of temptation. These older types fittingly fall under Paul's warning: "Let him who thinks he stands take heed that he does not fall" (1 Cor. 10:12). The truth is, we all need these warnings about the world.

Before launching into his warnings in 1 John 2:15-17, John reminds his readers of the spiritual blessings they have in their permanent family relationship with Christ. Though different blessings are associated with different groups within the church, these are general qualities that apply to all believers. He first reaffirms the complete forgiveness of their sins (2:12). These believers are children of the eternal God, not because of their own merit or something special they have done or achieved. They are forgiven "for His name's sake," purely by the grace of God through Jesus Christ. This is the permanent condition in which they stand.

These forgiven ones "know Him who has been from the beginning" (2:13-14). It may seem strange that John repeats this statement virtually word for word in these two verses. The only difference is that in the first instance John says, "I am writing to you, fathers" (2:13), while in the second he says, "I have written to you, fathers" (2:14). Bible scholars have puzzled over the reason for John's repetition and change of tense in these two statements, and it's probably impossible to sort out exactly what John's doing.[11]

Perhaps his reference to writing in the present tense refers to 1 John, while his reference to writing in the past refers to the Gospel of John. In that case, John would be emphasizing the fact that knowing Christ "who has been from the beginning" is a significant theme in his writings, life, and ministry. In John 20:31, he made his purpose in writing the Gospel clear: "These have been written so that you may believe that Jesus is the Christ, the Son of God; and that believing you may have life in His name."

However, it may be that John is simply using the past tense as an "epistolary aorist," which means the author is referring to the writing of his letter in terms of the time frame that the audience reads it (i.e., the past tense). As such, this would be a reference to the letter of 1 John only, and the repetition would be stylistic, used to emphasize the importance of their personal relationship with Christ.[12] In that case, John clearly wants to underscore the importance of knowing Christ, who is "from the beginning." This description of Christ, emphasizing His eternal deity, recalls the opening words of the letter: "What was from the beginning, what we have heard, what we have seen with our eyes, what we have looked at and touched with our hands, concerning the Word of Life" (1 Jn. 1:1).

Because of their permanent, personal relationship with the Lord Jesus, the "young men" have "overcome the evil one" (2:13). This blessing is also repeated, with a couple of important additions, in 2:14: "You are strong, and the word of God abides in you, and you have overcome the evil one." Our relationship with Christ results in the indwelling of the Spirit and the empowering of His word. As Jesus taught:

I will ask the Father, and He will give you another Helper, that He may be with you forever; that is the Spirit of truth, whom the world cannot receive, because it does not see Him or know Him, but you know Him because He abides with you and will be in you. . . . In that day you will know that I am in My Father, and you in Me, and I in you. (John 14:16-17, 20)

This indwelling presence of the Spirit is what gives believers strength, which results in an ability to stand firm against the spiritual wickedness of the world.

And to the "children," John offers a reminder to them that they "know the Father" (1 Jn. 2:13). To know Jesus, who is "from the beginning," is to know the Father. Jesus Himself said, "If you had known Me, you would have known My Father also; from now on you know Him, and have seen Him" (John 14:7). John writes later in this letter, "The one who confesses the Son has the Father also" (1 Jn. 2:23); and he writes in 2 John, "The one who abides in the teaching, he has both the Father and the Son" (2 Jn. 1:9).

Because of the reality of the triune God in the lives of all believers—young and old alike—believers are able to take a stand against the world.

—2:15-17—

Having firmly established the believers' irrevocable position of power and victory because of the forgiveness of their sins and their relationship with the Father, Son, and Spirit (1 Jn. 2:12-14), John levels some strong warnings about the world.

What does John mean by "the world"? In his usage here, the Greek term *kosmos* [2889] refers to the system of this present age before the return of Christ. This world is led by Satan, who works against Christ and His people. It's therefore hostile to righteousness. The world magnifies humanity, celebrates depravity, and rejects God's word. In this negative sense, the world's values, pleasures, pastimes, aspirations, and even attitudes have no room for God, no respect for Christ, and no regard for His followers. John uses the term *kosmos* in this sense throughout the letter, but in 2:15-17 alone, he uses the term six times as part of his strong warning.

John begins his warning with a straightforward, simple command: "Do not love the world nor the things in the world" (2:15). But wait! Doesn't John 3:16 say "For God so loved the world"? And didn't God send Jesus into the world "that the world might be saved through Him" (John 3:17)? Why does John seem to tell believers not to love what God clearly loves?

The answer is found in the two different senses of the word "world" and the two different senses of the term "love." While John's warning in 1 John 2:15-17 is primarily concerned with the wicked, fallen world system, the "world" that is the object of the self-sacrificial love of Christ is the world of humanity in desperate need of a Savior, just as John said earlier in this letter: "He Himself is the propitiation for our sins; and not for ours only, but also for those of the whole world" (2:2). Also, the word "love" here is used with the meaning "to have high esteem for or satisfaction with" or to "take pleasure in" something.[13] What are the things in which a lover of the world takes pleasure? In 2:16, John describes them as "the lust of the flesh and the lust of the eyes and the boastful pride of life."

Let's take a closer look at these things of the world. The first is "the lust of the flesh." The term "lust" refers to a craving or a passionate desire. This is more than a person who is hungry and desires food. It's more like an alcoholic who longs for a drink . . . or a drug addict who'll do anything for another hit.

The term *sarx* (4561), translated "flesh," refers most basically to physical things, particularly the material nature of the body. In that neutral sense, "flesh" is not essentially evil but can be used as a vessel of holiness to glorify God (2 Cor. 4:11). However, the term can also be used in a negative sense, as in 1 John 2:16. This is similar to the way the apostle Paul often used the term "flesh" in reference to our sinful, rebellious manner of thought and deed that reveres the world system, perverted since the Fall. *Sarx* is that part of our fallen state that opposes God and is in conflict with the Spirit's work of instilling attitudes and promoting actions that counter the world and its values.

The "lust of the flesh," then, appears to be self-generated. It's our internal sinful tendencies taking shape and looking for something to satiate our carnal desires. This includes selfish ambitions and self-serving objectives—the all-powerful triumvirate of me, myself, and I. It finds its focus in self: my comfort, my possessions, my money, my future, my career, my hopes. The lust of the flesh starts with me, ends with me, and keeps me in the middle of it all.

John next refers to the "lust of the eyes" (2:16). This includes sinful cravings triggered by what we see, leading to covetousness and envy. We may be perfectly content with what we have, but then we see what somebody else has. Suddenly our own house, car, spouse, family, job, clothes, or church just isn't enough anymore. The lust of the eyes can also be our symbols of success: titles, positions, degrees, or added pages to our résumés. The lust of the eyes suddenly makes us desperately "need" something we never knew we didn't have!

Finally, John refers to "the boastful pride of life" (2:16). The lust of the flesh comes from our sinful hearts. The lust of the eyes comes from the sinful world around us. And the boastful pride of life comes from our lips. The arrogant words. The prideful claims. The exaggerated tales that make us look greater than we are, usually at the cost of tearing other people down. We see this kind of boasting flowing from many sports heroes, slick politicians, and strutting rock stars.

Those are the things of the world: the lust of the flesh, the lust of the eyes, and the boastful pride of life. This cocktail of cravings is not a nourishing spiritual drink served up by the Father of Light, but a toxic poison pushed and promoted by the father of lies through the means of

The Things in the World

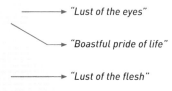

"Lust of the eyes"

"Boastful pride of life"

"Lust of the flesh"

The "things in the world" include the "lust of the flesh," which energizes us from within, the "lust of the eyes," which entices us from without, and "the boastful pride of life," which erupts from our lips.

a wicked world. The point of John's admonition in 2:15-16 is clear: The object of a Christian's unconditional devotion and commitment should be God and His people, not the sinful world and all of its delights. To embrace the wicked world system with the same kind of boundless love we should have for God is to demonstrate that "the love of the Father is not in [us]" (2:15). When we fall in love with the world, we fall out of love with God.

As if we didn't already have enough reason to avoid a love affair with the world, John gives us one more warning in 2:17: The world with all its lusts "is passing away." These sinful delights have no part to play in eternity. Those who embrace the world system embrace what is temporal. But when you do God's will—believing in His Son and living by the power of the Spirit—you embrace the eternal.

APPLICATION: 1 JOHN 2:12-17

Overcoming the Things of the World

John's warning to believers is clear: Don't get tangled up with the world or the things of the world. If you do, you'll be like those late-arriving Marines stranded at the dock, shouting and waving their arms as the ship pulled away and left them behind. They were so wrapped up in the pleasures of Yokohama that they had forgotten the colonel's warning. The dangers were real, and the consequences put permanent marks on their military records. I don't know exactly what the colonel said later to those Marines when he confronted them, but I know I wouldn't be able to use those words here!

We need to heed John's strong warnings about the world. And we need to be sensible and practical when it comes to putting these warnings into action. I know it's easy to jump to extremes. Back on that ship, I could have walked out of the colonel's assembly, headed to my bunk, and hid under the covers for forty-eight hours. That would have definitely kept me safe from the pickpockets, pork products, and prostitutes of Yokohama! But I would have gone to an unnecessary extreme.

Similarly, some Christians respond to the lust of the flesh, the lust of the eyes, and the boastful pride of life by resorting to radical isolation—"HIDE YOURSELF!" Their list of "don'ts" would include things like: Don't own a television! Don't go to the movies! No computer! No smart phone! Stay away from worldly people! Don't watch sports! Don't ever dress up or drive a decent car! Keep your life plain and drab and colorless.

But Jesus clearly stated in John 17:15, "I do not ask You to take them out of the world, but to keep them from the evil one." God's will for believers is not *isolation*, but *insulation*—to be living in the world but not as part of the world. We're to be salt and light, witnesses in the world. How are we to do that if we completely disengage, hide ourselves, or seek shelter in what amounts to a Christianized ghetto?

At the other extreme, some Christians may engage in radical provocation—"ASSERT YOURSELF!" Their rules of engagement would include things like: Everywhere you go, openly insult those who embrace "the things of the world." Broadcast your moral convictions in ways that not only shame sinners but also anger them. Be obnoxious about your displeasure with the world. Go out of your way to insult people who disagree with you. Put down those who are more liberal than you or less faithful than you. In short, openly judge them!

But Paul said, "I wrote you in my letter not to associate with immoral people; I did not at all mean with the immoral people of this world, or with the covetous and swindlers, or with idolaters, for then you would have to go out of the world" (1 Cor. 5:9-10). In fact, he takes it much further: "What have I to do with judging outsiders? . . . Those who are outside, God judges" (1 Cor. 5:12-13). Our presence in this wicked world should be winsome and gracious. We stand firm on our convictions, but we respond to outsiders with kindness, not condescension. Peter puts it best: "Sanctify Christ as Lord in your hearts, always being ready to make a defense to everyone who asks you to give an account for the hope that is in you, yet with gentleness and reverence" (1 Pet. 3:15).

That's balance—not isolation or provocation, but insulation and proclamation!

A DISCERNING LIFE
(1 JOHN 2:18-4:6)

As we press on in John's first letter, the tone begins to shift from serious to severe. The warnings against sin and the world in the previous section now give way to portents of spiritual dangers—often invisible—that can lure unbelievers to hell and send a Christian's faith skidding into the ditch. John is not trying to unduly alarm stable, mature believers, who are taught by the Spirit and kept by His power. But he has grave concern both for those standing on the verge of faith who could confuse the true gospel for a counterfeit and for immature believers who could spend a season in doctrinal and moral fog because of hazy teaching.

The specter of spiritual deception doesn't have to win. Just as Spirit-enabled fellowship with the Father and Son produces a joyful life (1:1-10) and a clean life (2:1-17), it also produces a discerning life (2:18-4:6). A close relationship with God requires understanding His truth. All too often, though, even seemingly mature Christians have a hard time discerning between true doctrine and false teaching, between right and wrong, between walking in the light and walking in darkness.

In this third section, John warns about the coming of "antichrists" (2:18), urges his readers to diligently "test the spirits" (4:1), and reminds them of the "anointing" of the Spirit that seals them with deep-down conviction of the essential truths of the Christian faith (2:20, 27). In our deceptive world, filled with demon-led deceivers, discerning Christians must stand together in fellowship around the truth.

KEY TERMS IN 1 JOHN 2:18-4:6

chrisma (χρῖσμα) [5545] "anointing," "unction," "consecrating oil"

Related to the title "Christ" (the "anointed one"), the term *chrisma* appears in the New Testament only in 1 John 2:20 and 2:27. However, it appears a handful of times in the Septuagint, the Greek translation of the

Old Testament, in reference to the anointing oil for the consecration of the high priest and Levites (Exod. 29:7; 40:15) as well as the tabernacle and its furnishings (Exod. 40:9). In 1 John, the term is used figuratively of the Holy Spirit's special work of setting apart a person for holiness in doctrine and life. Just as Christ was "anointed" by the Holy Spirit (Luke 4:18), so too those who are "in Christ" are anointed with the same power.

menō (μένω) [3306] "abide," "remain," "stay," "live"

In its normal, everyday use, this verb means to "remain" in one place for a period of time—settling down in the same city, residing in the same home, or staying married to the same person. John uses the term frequently in his Gospel to refer to the permanent, life-giving relationship disciples are to have with their Lord (John 15:4, 7, 10). In 1 John the same meaning is employed. As believers abide in God's word, they will "abide in the Son and in the Father" (1 Jn. 2:24) And they will live by the power of the Holy Spirit, who abides in them (2:27).

Dealing with Deceivers
1 JOHN 2:18-27

NASB

18 Children, it is the last hour; and just as you heard that antichrist is coming, even now many antichrists have appeared; from this we know that it is the last hour. 19 They went out from us, but they were not *really* of us; for if they had been of us, they would have remained with us; but *they went out,* so that ªit would be shown that they all are not of us. 20ªBut you have an anointing from the Holy One, and you all know. 21 I have not written to you because you do not know the truth, but because you do know it, and ªbecause no lie is of the truth. 22 Who is the liar but the one who denies that Jesus is the ªChrist? This is the antichrist, the one who denies the Father and the Son. 23 Whoever denies the Son does not have the Father; the one who confesses the Son has the Father also. 24 As for you, let that abide in you which you heard from the

NLT

18 Dear children, the last hour is here. You have heard that the Antichrist is coming, and already many such antichrists have appeared. From this we know that the last hour has come. 19 These people left our churches, but they never really belonged with us; otherwise they would have stayed with us. When they left, it proved that they did not belong with us. 20 But you are not like that, for the Holy One has given you his Spirit,* and all of you know the truth. 21 So I am writing to you not because you don't know the truth but because you know the difference between truth and lies. 22 And who is a liar? Anyone who says that Jesus is not the Christ.* Anyone who denies the Father and the Son is an antichrist.* 23 Anyone who denies the Son doesn't have the Father, either. But anyone who acknowledges the Son has the Father also.

24 So you must remain faithful to

beginning. If what you heard from the beginning abides in you, you also will abide in the Son and in the Father.

²⁵This is the promise which He Himself ᵃmade to us: eternal life.

²⁶These things I have written to you concerning those who are trying to deceive you. ²⁷As for you, the anointing which you received from Him abides in you, and you have no need for anyone to teach you; but as His anointing teaches you about all things, and is true and is not a lie, and just as it has taught you, ᵃyou abide in Him.

2:19 ᵃLit *they would be revealed* 2:20 ᵃLit *And*
2:21 ᵃOr know *that* 2:22 ᵃI.e. Messiah 2:25 ᵃLit *promised us* 2:27 ᵃOr *abide in Him;* Gr command

what you have been taught from the beginning. If you do, you will remain in fellowship with the Son and with the Father. ²⁵And in this fellowship we enjoy the eternal life he promised us.

²⁶I am writing these things to warn you about those who want to lead you astray. ²⁷But you have received the Holy Spirit,* and he lives within you, so you don't need anyone to teach you what is true. For the Spirit* teaches you everything you need to know, and what he teaches is true—it is not a lie. So just as he has taught you, remain in fellowship with Christ.

2:20 Greek *But you have an anointing from the Holy One.* 2:22a Or *not the Messiah.* 2:22b Or *the antichrist.* 2:27a Greek *the anointing from him.* 2:27b Greek *the anointing.*

Think about a time in your life when you were deceived. Some of you might think back to a time when you were deceived by someone close to you. A friend, a family member, a long-term boyfriend or girlfriend, a spouse, or a business partner proved to be someone other than who you thought they were. And the pain of living with that deception is almost more than you can bear to think about even today.

Maybe you have been deceived by a marketing or sales scam. That happens all the time. Sometimes people get cheated out of just a few bucks; other times, people lose their entire life savings to smooth-talking charlatans who get fat and rich by swindling hundreds of people. Sometimes you buy something you think is genuine only to learn later that it's a cheap knockoff. The "great deal" you thought you got turned out to be a total rip-off.

Then there's spiritual or religious deception. This is the worst kind. Any kind of deception can break your heart, mind, and bank, but this kind can crush your soul. A hypocritical pastor . . . an abusive church . . . or an outright cult—these can cause long-term psychological and spiritual damage in a person's life. Such toxic deception can even lead to a disavowal of all religion, a rejection of God, and a hatred for His authentic people. How tragic!

First John 2:18-27 introduces a new set of sinister figures in the world of spiritual darkness. False teachers called "antichrists," who foreshadow an ultimate end-times "Antichrist," were already on the prowl in John's day. This was a sure sign that God's final countdown toward judgment had begun. Now, more than ever, believers must live with their eyes wide open to the wiles of the devil and their feet firmly fixed on the solid rock of God's truth. Only then will they be equipped for dealing with deceivers.

—2:18-19—

I'm speculating here, but if we could have caught a glimpse of the goings-on in the spiritual world as John dipped his stylus in his ink-well and scratched out the words of 1 John 2:18-19, my guess is we'd see a host of demons going from rattled to panicked. Why? Deceivers *hate* to be exposed. They love to operate under the radar, spreading false doctrines, twisting the truth, and exploiting the spiritually weak. But the apostle John boldly launches a tell-all exposé of the devil's cunning strategies of deception.

John begins by reminding believers that with the coming of false teachers, dawn is on the horizon because, as he said in 2:8, "the darkness is passing away and the true Light is already shining." John can thus say in 2:18, "Children, it is the last hour." Warren Wiersbe explains the image of the "last hour" well:

> All of Old Testament history prepared the way for the work of Christ on the Cross. All history since that time is merely preparation for "the end," when Jesus will come and establish His kingdom. . . . "The last hour" began back in John's day *and has been growing in intensity ever since.* There were ungodly false teachers in John's day and during the intervening centuries they have increased both in number and in influence. "The last hour" or "the last times" are phrases that describe a *kind* of time, not a *duration* of time. . . . In other words, Christians have *always* been living in "the last time"—in crisis days.[1]

According to John, this "last hour" between Christ's first and second comings is like an inky predawn inhabited by shadowy agents of evil. He calls these figures "antichrists" (2:18). The Greek term *antichristos* [500], used here for the first time in Christian literature, is a compound of two words: *anti* [473], meaning "in place of" or "against," and *christos* [5547], "Messiah" or "Christ." The ambiguity may be purposeful. While all "antichrists" are opposed to Christ and His teachings, some antichrists go so far as to claim to be a messiah, thus opposing the true Christ by seeking to replace Him.

—2:20-21—

On the heels of his warning about antichrists ohn suddenly shifts attention to their opposites: true believers. By ining the light on those who "have an anointing from the Holy One" :20), John shows what it takes to deal with deceivers. What does he sa about genuine believers? *Genuine*

First, genuine believers have the Holy S rit. The metaphor of "an *Believers!* anointing from the Holy One" most likely fers to the gift of the Holy Spirit given to those who are truly saved Acts 10:38 says that "God anointed [Jesus] with the Holy Spirit and ith power." Similarly, Jesus said to the disciples regarding the baptis of the Holy Spirit, "You will receive power when the Holy Spirit has c ne upon you" (Acts 1:8). And in 2 Corinthians 1:21, Paul writes, "He v io establishes us with you in Christ and anointed us is God." The sa ie Spirit who anointed Christ (literally, "the anointed one") anoints   iristians by the baptism of the Holy Spirit. It is this permanent anoir ng of the Holy Spirit that antichrists lack.

Second genuine believers know od's saving truth. In the upper room prior to His arrest, Jesus prom ed His disciples, "When He, the Spirit of truth, comes, He will guide ou into all the truth" (John 16:13). Ephesians 1:13 says, "In Him, you   so, after listening to the message of truth, the gospel of your salvati n—having also believed, you were sealed in Him with the Holy Spiri of promise." So, it's clear that the presence of the Spirit brings a permanent spiritual knowledge and discernment concerning the key tenets of the gospel of salvation, the "message of truth."

Notice that 1 John 2:20 doesn't say that the true believers know everything there is to know, but that they "all know." And even when John later refers to the anointing that teaches "about all things" (2:27), we should not take this to mean that each believer knows everything there is to know about spiritual things. The context here refers to the

SIX BENEFITS OF TRUTH

1. Truth gives stability to our faith.

2. Truth strengthens us when we're tested.

3. Truth enables us to understand the Bible accurately.

4. Truth equips us to detect and confront error.

5. Truth allows us to live with confidence.

6. Truth releases us from fears and superstition.

foundational, saving truth of the gospel of Jesus Christ. The fact remains that even now, with the Spirit, believers only "know in part" (1 Cor. 13:9, 12). However, this knowledge, though not exhaustive, is sufficient, as Peter said, "His divine power has granted to us everything pertaining to life and godliness, through the true knowledge of Him who called us by His own glory and excellence" (2 Pet. 1:3). It is this true knowledge of the gospel that antichrists reject.

Third, genuine believers are able to discern lies. Because the Spirit has impressed the gospel of the person and work of Christ upon our hearts and minds, He enables us to tell the difference between truth and error. The Spirit prepares our minds for discernment as we dig deeply into the Word of God, which was inspired by the Holy Spirit (2 Tim. 3:16), and as we abide in the body of Christ, the church, which is indwelled by the Holy Spirit (Eph. 2:21-22). Those who abide in Christ, in His Word and in His body, "know the truth" and know that "no lie is of the truth" (1 Jn. 2:21). This is language of discernment. Their truth detectors are fine-tuned to discriminate between fact and fiction.

Have you ever found yourself catching some kind of preacher or teacher on the television spewing nonsense, and you think, "How could anybody believe this?" Then the camera pans across the audience with a wide shot and you see an arena-sized building packed with people nodding, smiling, clapping their hands, and shouting "Amen!" Your right response in that situation is to thank God that His Spirit has given you discernment through His Word. Antichrists target people who lack this kind of discernment. And how do you respond with regard to those who have fallen prey to false teachers? Pray that the Spirit would open their eyes to the deception and give them discernment. And if you personally know anybody who has been hooked and reeled in by the lure of spiritual deception, never underestimate the power of lovingly sharing the word of truth, which is able to set them free (John 8:32).

—2:22-23—

In 1 John 2:18-19, the spotlight was shone on the antichrists. In 2:20-21, John illuminated the true believers. Now, John shifts back to the antichrists in 2:22-23. He adds to his description of the antichrists, providing more detail about their doctrinal deviations. Allow me to pick up again our earlier discussion with another characteristic of false teachers.

Fourth, false teachers deny who Jesus really is—the incarnate God-man. John says they deny that "Jesus is the Christ" (2:22). In doing so, they deny "the Father and the Son" because to confess the Son is to have the Father, but to deny the Son is to deny the Father (2:23). Notice that these false teachers are not only denying that Jesus of Nazareth is the long-expected Messiah, but they are also denying the essential *sonship* of Jesus in His personal, eternal relationship to the Father (see John 10:30). In another letter, John would note that these antichrists "do not acknowledge Jesus Christ as coming in the flesh" (2 Jn. 1:7).

EXCURSUS: WHY IS THE INCARNATION SO IMPORTANT?

1 JOHN 2:23

In light of the clear teaching of Scripture, the ancient Council of Chalcedon in AD 451 described Jesus Christ (in relation to his incarnation) as "perfect both in deity and also in humanness . . . actually God and actually man."[6] This careful statement reflects the beliefs of orthodox Christians from the time of the apostles all the way to the present day (see John 1:1-3, 14; Rom. 1:3-4; Phil. 2:6-8). True Christians understand and embrace this doctrine of the two natures of Christ as an essential, central, foundational truth of the Christian faith. Jesus is both God and man.

Why is this truth so important? Think about it. If Christ were only God, He would have been unable to die in the place of sinful humanity and pay the price for our salvation. If He were only a man, the death He died would have had no eternal benefit for those who are saved. However, because He died in His incarnate humanity as the perfect sacrifice for sin, and because He was raised to live forever in the power of His indestructible life, He has authority to give eternal life to all who believe in Him. This doctrine of the Incarnation is no mere theological conundrum; it forms the very bedrock of salvation!

The truth of the deity and humanity of Christ also has an impact on our daily Christian lives. If Christ were only God, He would have remained separated from our human experiences of suffering and unable to participate in our desperate plight. If Christ were only man, His death would have been simply the martyrdom of a good man—nothing more than an inspirational example to follow. He would have been simply a victim of human tragedy, unable to conquer death, powerless to triumph over the grave.

But praise God! Christ is fully God and fully man, undiminished deity and true humanity. We can take comfort in the fact that the Eternal One chose to dwell in time with us, that the infinite and untouchable God can be touched by our finite fingers, met by our finite minds. The writer of Hebrews put it beautifully:

Therefore, since we have a great high priest who has passed through the heavens, Jesus the Son of God, let us hold fast our confession. For we do not have a high priest who cannot sympathize with our weaknesses, but One who has been tempted in all things as we are, yet without sin. Therefore let us draw near with confidence to the throne of grace, so that we may receive mercy and find grace to help in time of need. (Heb. 4:14-16)

This denial of the full deity and full humanity of Christ shows a failure of the fundamental test of the genuineness of a person's claim to be a true Christian. Whoever "denies the Son" by rejecting His identity as the Messiah who is God incarnate "does not have the Father" (1 Jn. 2:23). There's no margin for error here. On the other hand, those who place their faith in the true Jesus—the God-man who died and rose again—are united through Him to the Father by the power of the Holy Spirit.

—2:24-27—

Once again, John shifts the spotlight from the antichrists to the true believers, demonstrating the black-and-white difference between the two groups. The repetition of "as for you" in 2:24 and 2:27 indicates that John wants his readers to know they have nothing in common with the deceivers—those anti-Christian false teachers who dwell in the darkness and spout nothing but lies about Jesus. John wants to set up two guardrails against the influence that false teachers have on the spiritual stability of true believers.

The first guardrail is to stick with the truth of sound doctrine. John instructs his readers to "let that abide in you which you heard from the beginning" so that they "will abide in the Son and in the Father" (2:24). In addition to this, he reminds his readers that only through adherence to this sound doctrine do we have the promise of "eternal life" (2:25). We should recall the opening words of John's letter: "What was from the beginning, what we have heard, what we have seen with our eyes, what we have looked at and touched with our hands, concerning the Word of Life—and the life was manifested, and we have seen and testify and proclaim to you the eternal life, which was with the Father and was manifested to us" (1:1-2). If we stick with the truth about Christ as revealed in Holy Scriptures, continually proclaimed in the church, and always believed by orthodox Christians throughout history, we will never be lured away by false teachers—"those who are trying to deceive you" (2:26).

At first glance, this may sound like it's somehow up to us to keep hold of our salvation by staying true to sound doctrine and thus achieving eternal life. But the second guardrail rules out that false understanding. The second guardrail is to rely on the Holy Spirit's power to abide in Christ. The anointing of the Holy Spirit "abides in you," John says (2:27). Note the dynamic interplay between the several senses of "abiding." In 2:24, John says, "Let that abide in you which you heard from the beginning" so that "you also will abide in the Son." Then, in

2:27, he says, "The anointing which you received from Him abides in you," which empowers the truly saved to "abide in Him."

The idea that God's Spirit accomplishes through us all that God asks from us is not unique to John. Paul also taught this notion in Philippians 2:12-13: "So then, my beloved, just as you have always obeyed, not as in my presence only, but now much more in my absence, work out your salvation with fear and trembling; for it is God who is at work in you, both to will and to work for His good pleasure." Yes, we obey, will, and work, but we must also remember that we do so by the power of God working in us through the Holy Spirit.

Because of this anointing of the Holy Spirit abiding in us, we have no need of false teachers peddling their newfangled doctrines, their "new and improved" scriptures, or their unheard-of gospel. The original anointing we received when we accepted Christ as the God-man who died and rose again—the true gospel that gives eternal life— teaches us everything we need for life and godliness (2 Pet. 1:3).

APPLICATION: 1 JOHN 2:18-27
Triumphing against False Teachers

No doubt, the world has lost its way. Teachers, preachers, churches, and even whole denominations have followed suit. How can we walk in triumph, overcoming the numerous antichrists that have been unleashed in this "last hour"? Let me present you with three simple principles that will keep you from tottering and enable you to strengthen the faith of others.

First, *spend time in God's Word*. I know you've been told this over and over again, but that's because it's vital. The devil would like nothing better than for you to say, "I've been reading my Bible year after year. I'm tired of it. Give me something new to do." Don't let the sun set on any day without spending some time reading His Word. Those inspired writings aren't just words of men long dead; they're the living Word of the Holy Spirit, the same Spirit who abides in you and enables you to abide in Him. Think of your Scripture reading as filling your tank with fuel so you're able to reach your destination without running dry. It'll enable you to discern between truth and falsehood. It'll give you direction for decisions you need to make—not just moral choices but also everyday, practical decisions. You'll find hope in its promises and inspiration in its examples. Renew your commitment to the Scriptures.

Second, *stand firm in your convictions*. When false teachers come your way, stand strong. Don't flinch. Continue to confess the God-man who died and rose again . . . the deity of the Father, Son, and Holy Spirit . . . the salvation that comes by grace alone through faith alone in Christ alone—all the essential truths of the Christian faith. Of course, if you stand firm, you'll stand out, like a light shining in a dark place. So be ready to give voice to the gospel. Don't be shy about it. Be gracious and loving, but don't be shy. Tell the truth. Stand up and be heard.

Third, *stay focused on Christ*. We're called to be followers of one Shepherd, disciples of one Master, servants of one Lord. Let your mind, like a laser, be pointed wholly and solely on Christ as Savior. Examine His life, obey His teachings, follow His examples, meditate on His person and work, and proclaim Him far and wide. Yes, antichrists will try to convince you that a focus on Jesus is far too narrow. They'll try to distract you from "the simplicity and purity of devotion to Christ" (2 Cor. 11:3). Don't let them. Remind yourself every day that Jesus is the center.

Do these things—not in your own power, but always dependent on the Holy Spirit. Then you'll be able to triumph over false teachers.

Living in the Light of the Lord's Return
1 JOHN 2:28–3:3

NASB

28 Now, little children, abide in Him, so that when He appears, we may have confidence and not ᵃshrink away from Him in shame ᵇat His coming. 29 If you know that He is righteous, you know that everyone also who practices righteousness is ᵃborn of Him.

3:1 See ᵃhow great a love the Father has bestowed on us, that we would be called children of God; and *such* we are. For this reason the world does not know us, because it did not know Him. 2 Beloved, now we

NLT

28 And now, dear children, remain in fellowship with Christ so that when he returns, you will be full of courage and not shrink back from him in shame.

29 Since we know that Christ is righteous, we also know that all who do what is right are God's children.

3:1 See how very much our Father loves us, for he calls us his children, and that is what we are! But the people who belong to this world don't recognize that we are God's children because they don't know him. 2 Dear are children of God, and it has not appeared as yet what we will be. We know that when He appears, we will be like Him, because we will see Him just as He is. ³And everyone who has this hope *fixed* on Him purifies himself, just as He is pure.

2:28 ªLit *be put to shame from Him* ᵇOr *in His presence* 2:29 ªOr *begotten* 3:1 ªLit *what kind of love*

friends, we are already God's children, but he has not yet shown us what we will be like when Christ appears. But we do know that we will be like him, for we will see him as he really is. ³And all who have this eager expectation will keep themselves pure, just as he is pure.

The doctrine known as the Second Coming (or the return of Christ) either attracts mockery, strikes fear, or brings comfort. From early on, the proclamation of Christ's return was met by scoffers "following after their own lusts and saying, 'Where is the promise of His coming?'" (2 Pet. 3:3-4). Sadly, stubborn scoffers will one day be blindsided by "the day of judgment and destruction of ungodly men" (2 Pet. 3:7).

Then there are those who fear the coming of Christ. Many men and women were raised with a respect for the Bible or were brought up in the church but never fully grasped the gospel of salvation by grace alone through faith alone in Christ alone. As such, they hear about the coming of Christ to judge the living and the dead . . . and it brings dread. Perhaps there are also some true believers who have strayed so far from the right path that they fear the coming of the Savior as the day they must give an account for their lives of unfaithfulness to the Lord. In both cases, the Second Coming is associated with fear or shame.

Finally, many believers long for their Lord's return with hope and anticipation. They know and believe with longing the words of Paul:

For the Lord Himself will descend from heaven with a shout, with the voice of the archangel and with the trumpet of God, and the dead in Christ will rise first. Then we who are alive and remain will be caught up together with them in the clouds to meet the Lord in the air, and so we shall always be with the Lord. Therefore comfort one another with these words. (1 Thes. 4:16-18)

Invariably, when I have the privilege of serving people who have lost loved ones, I remind them of this very passage of Scripture. It's the event grieving believers can look forward to—the return of Christ, the resurrection of the dead, and a great "family reunion" with all those who have gone before us!

The doctrine of the return of Christ is no fairy tale to get children to behave, no soothsaying fantasy to get people through a dismal world, and no fad invented to sell books to people worried about the future. On the contrary, the second coming of Christ is part of the body of truth taught not only by Jesus Himself but also by His apostles, the early church, and every generation of true believers throughout the last two millennia.

In 1 John 2:28–3:3, John refers twice to the moment "when He appears" (2:28; 3:2). It's clear that he's urging all of us, his readers, to think and plan ahead, to realize that the Lord's return is an inescapable reality which we can face with assurance, not shame. In light of Christ's coming, we're to be filled with hopeful anticipation, knowing that "we will see Him just as He is" (3:2).

—2:28-29—

Christ is coming back one day. It may be today. It may be next week. It may be years, decades, even centuries from now. Nobody knows when (Mark 13:32). But His future coming *from* heaven is as certain as His past ascension *to* heaven (Acts 1:9-11). The fulfillment of this prophecy, based on the unbreakable promise of God, is certain. But the responses of believers to the coming of Christ vary. For those who are ready, it brings comfort and promotes purity. For those who are unprepared, it strikes fear and shame. How should we live in light of Christ's return?

John begins this section with a straightforward command: "Now, little children, abide in Him" (1 Jn. 2:28). This is the same Greek term (*menō* [3306]) that was used in the previous section regarding our response to false teachers. We're to "abide in the Son and in the Father" by letting God's word abide in us (2:24). And we "abide in Him" by the power of the Holy Spirit, our Teacher, who abides in us (2:27). When John tells his readers to "abide in Him" in 2:28, we know this involves walking in the light, keeping God's Word, attending to the foundational truths of the faith, avoiding deception by false teachers, and living lives in conformity with Christ's example—all by the power of the indwelling Spirit. The verb "abide" is in the present tense, which implies an ongoing activity, not a one-time event. We're to continually abide in Him.

This important command to continue abiding in Christ is followed by a reassuring reminder. The result of abiding in Christ is that we will anticipate His return with confidence, not being put to shame by His appearance (2:28). The Greek word translated "coming" is *parousia* [3952], which in this context refers to Christ's "Messianic Advent in glory to judge the world at the end of this age."[7] By abiding now, we'll have confidence then. But the opposite is also true: By failing to abide in fellowship with Him—walking in the Spirit—we'll shrink back in shame when He appears!

Because we know that the coming Son of God "is righteous" (2:29), we also know that He will judge righteously. Acts 17:31 says, "He has fixed a day in which He will judge the world in righteousness through a Man whom He has appointed, having furnished proof to all men by raising Him from the dead." So, for those who have walked in the Spirit and strived to serve Him with their lives, the righteous Judge will reward justly, as Paul wrote: "In the future there is laid up for me the crown of righteousness, which the Lord, the righteous Judge, will award to me on that day; and not only to me, but also to all who have loved His appearing" (2 Tim. 4:8). Paul makes this point crystal clear when he refers to the judgment seat of Christ, where each believer must appear—not to determine whether we are worthy of salvation, but to be rewarded for our faithfulness in our life of service to Him (1 Cor. 3:12-15; 2 Cor. 5:9-10). This should prompt all those who are "born of Him" to practice righteousness (1 Jn. 2:29).

But John's point goes even deeper. Those who are "born of Him" are those who have genuinely experienced regeneration by grace through faith. They are thus declared righteous and are spiritually united to Christ by the Holy Spirit. Stephen Smalley notes, "It is only by being 'born again' (through Christ) that the believer can be properly related to God. . . . Moreover, only as the believer is firmly related to God through Christ, and by the Spirit, is it possible to 'abide in him' and 'act rightly.'"[8] By the righteousness of Christ, God has provided two things:

- *the internal ability*—spiritual union with Him that declares us righteous in Him and enables us to live rightly
- *the external motivation*—the fact that we must give an account to Christ as a righteous Judge who will reward us for our faithfulness

—3:1-3—

The regenerating work of Christ freely grants believers a right standing *before* Him and enables them to live rightly *for* Him. In light of this truth, John caps off his exhortation to live in light of Christ's return with an outburst of wonder (3:1), a glorious promise (3:2), and a fixed hope (3:3).

The King James Version translates the first word of chapter 3 not with a weak "see" but a more dramatic "behold." I think that captures the wonder in John's words better than "see" or "look." John is gushing with excitement at the splendor of salvation, "that we would be called children of God" (3:1). And just to be perfectly clear that we aren't merely called something we're not, John adds, "and such we are."

As Christ is by nature the Son of God, our union with Him places us in a position of "adoption as [children]" of God (Rom. 8:15, 23; 9:4; Gal. 4:5; Eph. 1:5). This is a great blessing to be reckoned as one with Him and to be ushered—purely by grace—into the family of God. But there is also a more sobering side to this: Just as the world does not know Christ and does not rightly relate to Him, so the world does not know us as we really are (1 Jn. 3:1). This will inevitably lead to misunderstanding and discord between the believer and the world.

However, this dissonance between the world and the family of believers is only temporary. Everything will change when Christ returns and sets this world straight. John's outburst of wonder leads to a glorious promise related to the Second Coming. Though we don't fully understand many of the details about the future life after the return of Christ and our glorious resurrection, we do know this: "When He appears, we will be like Him, because we will see Him just as He is" (3:2). The notion that "we will be like Him" is clarified by Paul's words in Philippians 3:20-21: "Our citizenship is in heaven, from which also we eagerly wait for a Savior, the Lord Jesus Christ; who will transform the body of our humble state into conformity with the body of His glory."

But what does John mean by the explanatory clause "because we will see Him just as He is"? How does seeing Jesus "as is" affect what we will become? In order for those of us who are believers to actually see Jesus in His glorious nature, we ourselves will first need to be changed. We will need to be made capable of perceiving not only the physical realm as it really is, but also the spiritual realm. Then, what Paul describes in 1 Corinthians 13:12 will be fulfilled: "For now we see in a mirror dimly, but then face to face; now I know in part, but then I will know fully just as I also have been fully known."

Only a miraculous transformation to a glorious condition will allow us to see Him "as He is." Paul describes our transformation in this way:

> Behold, I tell you a mystery; we will not all sleep, but we will all be changed, in a moment, in the twinkling of an eye, at the last trumpet; for the trumpet will sound, and the dead will be raised imperishable, and we will be changed. For this perishable must put on the imperishable, and this mortal must put on immortality. (1 Cor. 15:51-53)

This transformation, in turn, will only deepen and intensify the spiritual union we have with Christ, which itself will lead to greater conformity to Him. One commentator explains:

> At His appearing, believers will see Jesus in His true nature because their spiritual as well as physical eyes will be fully open. This vision of Christ will change each one. We will become like Him in terms of what we see in Him and in ourselves. What we will come to recognize fully is that Jesus is morally pure, absolutely righteous. At that moment, we too will become so.[9]

But that's yet future. Perhaps in the near future, perhaps in the distant future. Maybe the trumpet of God will usher our souls from heaven to be reunited with our glorious bodies, or maybe we'll still be alive and experience an instant transformation from mortality to immortality. Whatever is in store for us, this resurrection and glorification is still to come.

So, what do we do in the meantime as we wait eagerly for the Second Coming and long for our transformation? John answers this in the next verse: "Everyone who has this hope fixed on Him purifies himself, just as He is pure" (1 Jn. 3:3). With this one line, John's soaring, out-of-this-world theology lands in the center of the personal and the practical. Every Christian who places their confident expectation in Christ's return, yearning to see Him face-to-face, to be changed from the inside out, and to spend eternity basking in His glory, should experience an internal cleansing in the here and now.

This isn't a ceremonial cleansing. And it isn't a mere declaration of cleansing. This is sanctification, in which we are set apart to live in a way that's pleasing to Him, becoming more and more like Him even in this life. By setting our hearts and minds on His imminent and certain return, a purification occurs that cleanses us from the things that would otherwise drag us down. We're saved from the power of sin over our lives and empowered to live a life pleasing to Him.

What a series of verses! This section starts with a command to abide in Him (2:28). It includes a word of reassurance (2:28-29), and it reaches a zenith with the wonder of the Father's saving love by which He adopts us as His children (3:1). At the top of this peak, John reminds us of the promise that, in our future state, we will be like Christ (3:2). And he concludes this section with a note on the purifying purpose of a hope fixed on Christ's second coming (3:3).

APPLICATION: 1 JOHN 2:28–3:3

Christ Is Coming . . . Now What?

Very seldom do I hear "prophecy experts"—with their detailed charts and confident arguments—spend a lot of time on how the Second Coming should affect the way we live today. They go on and on about what God will be doing *then* . . . and they leave us wondering what we're supposed to be doing *now*. But not the biblical authors. All inspired Scripture—even prophecy of future events—is given to us "for teaching, for reproof, for correction, for training in righteousness; so that the man of God may be adequate, equipped for every good work" (2 Tim. 3:16-17).

So what should we be doing now as we wait for the return of Christ? Let me answer this "Now what?" question with three principles to keep in mind.

First, *we should purify our lives*. All of us have sin in our lives. The apostle John has already made this patently clear (1 Jn. 1:8). Even the most seasoned saint has some daily spiritual hygiene to take care of or they'll start to stink. We should occasionally peruse Paul's lists of "deeds of the flesh" and "fruit of the Spirit" (Gal. 5:19-23) as a way to remind ourselves of some of the blemishes in our character and behavior. Or read repeatedly and deeply through the Proverbs to help expose areas of folly in our lives. Or study intently the life of Christ as a standard of holiness to which none of us measure up. Then we need to go to God to confess our sins, asking Him to "cleanse us from all unrighteousness" (1 Jn. 1:9). In this way, as we await Christ's return, we will be striving to purify ourselves, just as He is pure (3:3).

Second, *we should focus on the future*. We humans are so easily weighed down by the gravity of this present age. We forget that this world system is temporary and that at His future return, Christ will usher in an eternal kingdom. Knowing this truth, do we live like it? Do we spend our time and money investing in eternal things that will contribute to the proclamation of the gospel and the growth of the body of Christ? Or are we stockpiling perishable treasures in this life that serve only to distract us from heavenly things? A glance at your bank statement will reveal the answer!

Let me suggest a periodic review of your spending habits and your calendar, taking a close look at where your time and treasures are going.

Is there an imbalance between what you spend on things like entertainment and leisure versus things like evangelism and missions—things that will contribute to eternity? Think of specific ways you may need to adjust your budget and your schedule to focus on the future.

Finally, *we should share Christ while there's still time.* The day will come when we will no longer be able to proclaim the good news of salvation to the lost. If you knew for sure Jesus was coming back tomorrow, whom would you share the gospel with today? It's not an irrelevant question, because He could return even sooner than that!

Remember that simple faith in the person and work of Jesus Christ is all that's needed for a lost soul to be ushered into the glorious promises of salvation in Christ. But they need to hear that good news in order to believe it. It's time to get off the sidelines and get into the game. Lovingly share the truth. They may not listen. They may even mock you. But maybe you'll be the last voice in a series of evangelists, the one who will be there when the Spirit penetrates that sinner's heart and eternity adds another soul to its roster. There is such a thing as procrastinating so long that it's too late!

Discerning the Works of the Devil
1 JOHN 3:4-10

NASB

⁴Everyone who practices sin also practices lawlessness; and sin is lawlessness. ⁵You know that He appeared in order to take away sins; and in Him there is no sin. ⁶No one who abides in Him sins; no one who sins has seen Him or ᵃknows Him. ⁷Little children, make sure no one deceives you; the one who practices righteousness is righteous, just as He is righteous; ⁸the one who practices sin is of the devil; for the devil ᵃhas sinned from the beginning. The Son of God appeared for this purpose, to destroy the works of the devil. ⁹No one who is ᵃborn of God practices

NLT

⁴Everyone who sins is breaking God's law, for all sin is contrary to the law of God. ⁵And you know that Jesus came to take away our sins, and there is no sin in him. ⁶Anyone who continues to live in him will not sin. But anyone who keeps on sinning does not know him or understand who he is.

⁷Dear children, don't let anyone deceive you about this: When people do what is right, it shows that they are righteous, even as Christ is righteous. ⁸But when people keep on sinning, it shows that they belong to the devil, who has been sinning since the beginning. But the Son of God came to destroy the works of the devil. ⁹Those who have been

NASB

sin, because His seed abides in him; and he cannot sin, because he is ªborn of God. ¹⁰By this the children of God and the children of the devil are obvious: ªanyone who does not practice righteousness is not of God, nor the one who does not love his brother.

3:6 ªOr *has known* 3:8 ªLit *sins* 3:9 ªOr *begotten*
3:10 ªLit *everyone*

NLT

born into God's family do not make a practice of sinning, because God's life* is in them. So they can't keep on sinning, because they are children of God. ¹⁰So now we can tell who are children of God and who are children of the devil. Anyone who does not live righteously and does not love other believers* does not belong to God.

3:9 Greek *because his seed.* 3:10 Greek *does not love his brother.*

When a person today hears the phrase "What you're doing is a sin," they probably won't hear it as "I love you enough to point out that destructive behavior in your life." Instead, they hear something like, "I'm judging you." The idea of loving sinners enough to help them deal with their sin is lost on a world that has increasingly downplayed that three-letter word.

Whatever happened to sin? When did it get deleted from our cultural lexicon? Why have we been told that it's now one of those "politically incorrect" terms? The word *sin* is obviously no longer *in*. Today it's been replaced by words like error, mistake, tragedy, addiction, sickness, misdeed, faux pas, failure, weakness, or fault. And on that last one, more often than not, it's someone else's fault!

But the Bible sets forth a completely different message regarding sin. The entrance, presence, and consequences of sin are major plot points in the drama of God's story of creation, fall, and redemption. Romans 5:12 sums it up nicely: "Just as through one man sin entered into the world, and death through sin, and so death spread to all men, because all sinned." Adam was the figure by whom sin made its first appearance on the stage of human history. The consequence of death followed. And from that point forward, the entire story was marred by sin, which spread universally to all humans and brought suffering and corruption to all creation (Rom. 8:18-22).

However, we're not left in this desperate plight of bondage to sin and death. The hero of the story of redemption appears on stage, providing a way of escape for all of us enslaved by sin: "For as through the one man's disobedience the many were made sinners, even so through the obedience of the One the many will be made righteous" (Rom. 5:19). Jesus Christ is that life-bringing hero who bore our sin on the cross and rose again: "For if by the transgression of the one, death reigned through the one, much more those who receive the abundance of grace and of the gift of righteousness will reign in life through the One, Jesus Christ" (Rom. 5:17).

Nevertheless, the drama isn't over. The curtain hasn't dropped. In the present act, we still await the return of Christ, when He will utterly vanquish sin and death. In the meantime, the old sin nature remains, still subject to disobedience, corruption, and death. The result is a spiritual conflict between the power of Christ's righteousness dwelling in those who are saved and sealed by the Holy Spirit and the old tendency toward sin, which Paul calls "the flesh." Paul depicts this constant melee in Romans 7:18-21:

> For I know that nothing good dwells in me, that is, in my flesh; for the willing is present in me, but the doing of the good is not. For the good that I want, I do not do, but I practice the very evil that I do not want. But if I am doing the very thing I do not want, I am no longer the one doing it, but sin which dwells in me. I find then the principle that evil is present in me, the one who wants to do good.

What, then, should be the normal expectation of holiness in the Christian life? Constant victory? Constant drudgery? Frequent defeat? Slow but steady progress? The apostle John helps us begin to answer this question in 1 John 3:4-10. We have to be careful here, though. If we don't pay close attention to the specific words and the way John uses them, we might come away unsure of our salvation and wondering whether we're saved by more than just faith alone. Let me assure you that John's purpose is not to cast doubt on the truly saved but to call pretenders to conversion and straying believers to faithfulness.

—3:4—

With his opening words of this section, John refers to "everyone who practices sin." Stop there. Understanding this phrase correctly will make the difference between good theology and bad theology, right application and wrong application. The Greek term translated "practices," *poiōn* (from *poieō* [4160]), is a present active participle. John has in mind a person who commits sin continually, persistently, habitually—as a lifestyle, not an occasional sin. Daniel Akin notes, "The word *poiōn* is used frequently in this section . . . to imply a continual practice of sin as well as a realization of sin's completeness. In other words, it is a willful, habitual action."[10] So, John is talking about a lost person who has no power of the Spirit to wage warfare against the flesh, no recourse to forgiveness from Christ. Their lifestyle is characterized by sinfulness.

The lost person who habitually sins "also practices lawlessness; and sin is lawlessness." What's the difference between "practicing sin" and "practicing lawlessness"? Smalley suggests that the second phrase "is forceful; it suggests a deliberate act of law-breaking on the part of any sinner."[11] However, in the broader context, John just referred to genuine children of God as those who purify themselves and live holy lives in light of Christ's imminent return (3:3). This stands in stark contrast to the antichrists and false teachers whose lives are characterized by lawlessness. In this sense, then, "lawlessness" can be defined as "a rebellious alignment with the devil, rather than with God in Christ. . . . It implies not merely breaking God's law, but flagrantly opposing him (in Satanic fashion) by so doing."[12]

In short, the kind of person described in 1 John 3:4 is the antithesis of the Spirit-indwelled child of God. This person who "practices sin/lawlessness" is the opposite of the true believer mentioned in 2:29—the person who "practices righteousness."

—3:5-6—

Christ's mission in His first coming was to "take away sins" (3:5). Christ came "in the likeness of sinful flesh" (Rom. 8:3) as the incarnate God-man, lived a sinless life, died to pay for the sins of others, and rose again because sin had no power over Him. Paul wrote, "He made Him who knew no sin to be sin on our behalf, so that we might become the righteousness of God in Him" (2 Cor. 5:21). Christ could only accomplish this self-sacrificial, substitutionary act if He was perfectly righteous, without sin. When we place our trust in Him and become children of God, the righteousness of Christ enables us to be declared righteous (positionally) and begins working within us to produce righteousness (experientially). The result for the believer is an all-day, everyday struggle against the power of sin. Because of the Spirit of God living in us, the battle is palpable and righteous living is possible. But the unbeliever, devoid of the Spirit of God and the righteousness of Christ, will be characterized by "practicing sin."

In 1 John 3:6, John hammers this point even harder. Nobody who abides in Christ—that is, true believers in fellowship with Him—lives in sinfulness habitually and persistently. And the opposite is also true:

of the devil" (1 Jn. 3:8), it stands to reason that the group who is doing the works of the devil can't possibly be on the side of Christ.

What wise words! One of the best tests you can apply to any ministry is to weigh the importance it gives to balancing doctrine with duty, loving the Lord alongside loving one another, believing and doing. If you're not seeing both, something's wrong. It may be a cult or at least a fertile seedbed for false teaching.

—3:9-10—

1 John 3:9 can appear to be a contradiction of 1:8-10 if we forget our careful definitions of terms as discussed in relation to 3:4. In 3:9, John says: "Whosoever is born of God doth not commit sin . . . and he cannot sin, because he is born of God" (KJV). But in 1:8 and 10, John says, "If we say that we have no sin, we are deceiving ourselves, and the truth is not in us. . . . If we say that we have not sinned, we make Him a liar." So which is it? Does the person born of God "not commit sin"—even being unable to sin—or is such a claim to be without sin a lie?

Here the different tenses in Greek help clear things up. Nigel Turner notes:

> John used the present tense (*hamartanein*); it is a verb of which the present stem means "to be a sinner," that is, it expresses a state rather than an action. . . . The apostle affirms that a Christian believer can never be a sinner. He will start to be one, will take the first . . . step by committing this or that sin, but he stops short of the condition of being "a sinner." To be "in Christ" is not to be at once perfect, but whenever such a one disgraces himself, his actions never permanently remove him from that mystical union which is unbreakable. Sin will not have dominion over him.[13]

The New American Standard Bible properly translates the first part of 3:9 as "No one who is born of God practices sin." And the inability to continually practice sin is a direct result of being "born of God" (3:9). This expression is a reference to the new birth of regeneration resulting in the abiding presence and internal working of the Holy Spirit. The "seed" that abides in the one who has been born again is a reference to the Spirit, though the work of the Spirit is always connected to the planting and sprouting of the Word of God (Matt. 13:1-23).[14]

In 3:10, this section concludes with a final test to discern between the teachers of righteousness and the teachers of falsehood. The children of God live lifestyles of righteousness and love their brothers and sisters in Christ, whereas the children of the devil do not live righteous lifestyles and do not love the brethren.

What a stark difference John expects from the children of God and the children of the devil!

APPLICATION: 1 JOHN 3:4-10
Blotting Out Sin

To help you blot out sin, let me give you three simple statements. For most of us, these are reminders of very basic biblical truths. But I want to add some important practical implications to each of them.

First, *we're all sinners.* Some of us are saved sinners and others are lost sinners. But since the events of Genesis 3, all humanity is in sin because sinning is in our nature. The lost often don't accept that they're lost . . . and often don't regard themselves as sinners or call their actions "sin." Some have so resisted the inner conviction of the conscience that they have little or no remorse for the things they do (see Rom. 2:15; 1 Tim. 4:2). Such people are in persistent rebellion, usually antagonistic to God and the Christian faith. On the other hand, those of us who are saved sinners, who have acknowledged the truths of Genesis 3 and Romans 3, *are still sinners*; but we have a different understanding. We call it what it is: sin. And we have a new desire to align our lives with Christ. The Spirit bears witness to our consciences that engaging in thoughts and actions contrary to the will of God is dishonoring to Him and destructive to ourselves.

Remember that each one of us saved sinners, before coming to know Christ's salvation, was a lost sinner. We need to have compassion for the lost, showing mercy and kindness as we offer to them what someone once offered to us: forgiveness from the guilt of sin and a new start. Don't be surprised when lost sinners persist in sin, make fun of spiritual things, or find silly your own struggle against sin for the sake of Christ. But when those who claim to be believers in Christ embrace a sinful lifestyle, you have every right to question and challenge this contradiction. Read 1 Corinthians 5:9-13 for Paul's perspective on how we should approach lost sinners and saved sinners.

Second, *God loves sinners.* He loves lost sinners enough to send His

DISCERNING THE WORKS OF THE DEVIL | 1 JOHN 3:4-10

Son to die for them (John 3:16; Rom. 5:8). He loves lost sinners enough to send His Spirit into the world to "convict the world concerning sin and righteousness and judgment" (John 16:8). At every moment, God bids the lost sinner to come home. God also loves saved sinners enough to send the Holy Spirit into their lives (Rom. 5:5). His love compels us to live self-sacrificial lives (2 Cor. 5:14-15; 1 Jn. 3:16; 4:9-11). And His love for us through the Son keeps us in a permanent relationship of salvation (Rom. 8:35-39). He never leaves us nor forsakes us (Heb. 13:5).

As believers—sinners saved by grace—our response to both the lost and the saved should reflect this basic truth of the love of God. Just as God loves the lost enough to reach down from heaven through the Son and the Spirit, we, too, as the body of Christ indwelled by the Spirit, must reach out to the lost across the street and around the world. If the perfectly holy God loves lost sinners, what excuse can saved sinners like us possibly have to reject the lost as unworthy of the gospel? How are you involved in proclaiming the love of God to the lost? And regarding fellow believers, who are recipients of the saving and sanctifying love of God, we're called to love each other enough to aid in each other's spiritual growth toward Christlikeness. Hebrews 10:24-25 says, "Let us consider how to stimulate one another to love and good deeds, not forsaking our own assembling together, as is the habit of some, but encouraging one another." How are you involved in encouraging the saved toward greater maturity?

Third, *the devil confuses sinners*. Satan can confuse lost sinners in many ways. One way is to confuse them about sin itself—either denying its reality or its seriousness. Another way is to confuse them about whether there's a God who loves them and a Savior who died for them. But there's another, more subtle way to confuse the lost: convince them that they're saved when they're not. He points them to their good works, their church membership, the legacy of their parents' faith, or other things that are not the gospel of salvation by grace alone through faith alone in Christ alone.

For saved sinners, Satan often attempts the opposite: He tries to convince them that they're lost. He draws their attention not to their good works, but to their sinful acts. He distracts them from the promise of the grace and mercy of God and gets them to focus instead on their own inadequacies. And he lures them away from fellow saved sinners in the community of faith—those who could encourage the confused Christian in their hour of doubt and despair.

With lost sinners who think they're not lost, we need to help them realize they're lost. That is, we need to show them clearly that the first of our three simple statements is true: We are all sinners. Prayerfully sharing Romans 3:9-18 is a good place to start. And sober, honest conversations about the state of the world and the failure of every person to live up even to their own consciences can help rattle lost sinners into the reality of their sin and their need for a savior.

But what do we say to saved sinners who have become doubtful about their salvation because of sin in their lives? We need to help them get their focus off their own works and back onto the work of Christ. We need to reassure them that salvation is by grace through faith, not by their good works (Eph. 2:8-9). But we also need to help them in their struggle against the power of sin in their lives so they can begin experiencing the abundant life of righteousness, fruitfulness, and joy. (This will take a lot of grace!) The less they are wallowing in sin, the less Satan will be able to accuse them.

Not like Cain, but like Christ!
1 JOHN 3:11-24

NASB

11 For this is the message which you have heard from the beginning, that we should love one another; 12 not as Cain, *who* was of the evil one and slew his brother. And for what reason did he slay him? Because his deeds were evil, and his brother's were righteous.

13 Do not be surprised, brethren, if the world hates you. 14 We know that we have passed out of death into life, because we love the brethren. He who does not love abides in death. 15 Everyone who hates his brother is a murderer; and you know that no murderer has eternal life abiding in him. 16 We know love by this, that He laid down His life for us; and we ought to lay down our lives for

NLT

11 This is the message you have heard from the beginning: We should love one another. 12 We must not be like Cain, who belonged to the evil one and killed his brother. And why did he kill him? Because Cain had been doing what was evil, and his brother had been doing what was righteous.

13 So don't be surprised, dear brothers and sisters,* if the world hates you.

14 If we love our brothers and sisters,* it proves that we have passed from death to life. But a person who has no love is still dead. 15 Anyone who hates another brother or sister* is really a murderer at heart. And you know that murderers don't have eternal life within them.

16 We know what real love is because Jesus gave up his life for us. So we also ought to give up our lives for our brothers and sisters. 17 If someone

the brethren. ¹⁷But whoever has the world's goods, and sees his brother in need and closes his ᵃheart ᵇagainst him, how does the love of God abide in him? ¹⁸Little children, let us not love with word or with tongue, but in deed and truth. ¹⁹We will know by this that we are of the truth, and will ᵃassure our heart before Him ²⁰ᵃin whatever our heart condemns us; for God is greater than our heart and knows all things. ²¹Beloved, if our heart does not condemn us, we have confidence ᵃbefore God; ²²and whatever we ask we receive from Him, because we keep His commandments and do the things that are pleasing in His sight.

²³This is His commandment, that we ᵃbelieve in the name of His Son Jesus Christ, and love one another, just as He ᵇcommanded us. ²⁴The one who keeps His commandments abides in Him, and He in him. We know by this that He abides in us, by the Spirit whom He has given us.

3:17 ᵃLit *inward parts* ᵇLit *from* 3:19 ᵃLit *persuade* 3:20 ᵃOr *that if our heart condemns us, that God...* 3:21 ᵃLit *toward* 3:23 ᵃOr *believe the name* ᵇLit *gave us a commandment*

has enough money to live well and sees a brother or sister* in need but shows no compassion—how can God's love be in that person?

¹⁸Dear children, let's not merely say that we love each other; let us show the truth by our actions. ¹⁹Our actions will show that we belong to the truth, so we will be confident when we stand before God. ²⁰Even if we feel guilty, God is greater than our feelings, and he knows everything. ²¹Dear friends, if we don't feel guilty, we can come to God with bold confidence. ²²And we will receive from him whatever we ask because we obey him and do the things that please him.

²³And this is his commandment: We must believe in the name of his Son, Jesus Christ, and love one another, just as he commanded us. ²⁴Those who obey God's commandments remain in fellowship with him, and he with them. And we know he lives in us because the Spirit he gave us lives in us.

3:13 Greek *brothers*. 3:14 Greek *the brothers*; similarly in 3:16. 3:15 Greek *hates his brother*. 3:17 Greek *sees his brother*.

Over and over again, John urges his readers to love God and to love one another (1 Jn. 2:10; 3:10-11, 14, 23; 4:7, 11-12, 20-21; 5:2). He warns them against loving the world (2:15-16). And he underscores the danger of embracing a sinful lifestyle (3:10). All of these subjects begin to wear on the consciences of Christians who desire to be like Christ but constantly fall short. If we allow the full impact of these words to weigh on us, it'll make us squirm because all of us fall short of the perfect standard of love given to us in Jesus Christ.

In light of these convicting truths, some believers might even begin to think, "Am I even saved? Have I loved the world too much? Have I not loved my brother or sister in Christ enough? Are there people in my life whom I hate?" Because these questions naturally begin pestering the consciences of believers who take God's commands seriously, John applies a soothing balm to calm the disquieted conscience: the balm of grace.

—3:11—

John begins this section with a very familiar message. It's a message that serves as a hinge on which much of the book of 1 John turns: "Love one another." When Jesus spoke that simple command decades earlier at the Last Supper (John 13:34-35), John got the message. He never forgot it. That command filled John's mind and heart and took hold of his actions.

It's not the first time John's readers had heard the command. John had already mentioned a variation of it to them in 1 John 2:10. And no doubt the "love one another" theme was a frequent refrain in John's teaching and preaching over the years. The recipients of 1 John, in fact, had heard this message "from the beginning" of their life as believers in Christ.

It's clear, then, that loving one another is the heart of the Christian life. Along with loving God, it sums up what it means to observe the commandments (Matt. 22:36-40). It is a theme that emerges throughout the New Testament (e.g., Rom. 13:8; 1 Thes. 4:9; 1 Pet. 1:22). And it's a distinguishing mark of the authenticity of the disciples of Jesus (John 13:35).

But what does this love of the brethren look like?

—3:12-18—

If you haven't noticed already, the apostle John loves using contrasts to drive home his points:

- truth vs. lies
- love vs. hate
- righteousness vs. wickedness
- obedience vs. disobedience
- light vs. darkness
- children of God vs. children of the devil

Not surprisingly, in these verses John provides two contrasting examples to put flesh on the bones of the command to "love one another." The first example illustrates the extreme opposite of loving our brother or sister in Christ (1 Jn. 3:12-15). The second example illustrates the extreme ideal of love (3:16-18). By placing believers in the middle of these two examples, John tries to urge them away from the one and toward the other.

In giving an example of brotherly hatred rather than brotherly love, John takes us all the way back to the original saga of sibling rivalry: the account of Cain's murder of his brother Abel (3:12). Cain, John says, was "of the evil one." This phrase parallels the phrase "of the devil" in 3:8:

| 1 John 3:8 | "The one who practices sin | is | of the devil." |
| 1 John 3:12 | "Cain . . . who slew his brother | was | of the evil one." |

John sets Cain up as the original example of a "child of the devil," providing a smooth transition in his argument from 3:10 ("By this the children of God and the children of the devil are obvious: anyone who does not practice righteousness is not of God, nor the one who does not love his brother"). Cain is a perfect illustration of this category of person. Not only did he disobey God's commands and fail to heed God's warnings, but he also harbored hatred in his heart and took it to its extreme conclusion: the murder of his own brother Abel.

John uses a graphic term to describe Cain's actions: *sphazō* [4969], which means "to butcher or slaughter."[15] It implies brutality, savagery, and hatred on the part of Cain toward his brother. This was no tragic, accidental death in which a fistfight of wrangling brothers went too far. Cain's attack on Abel was violent, premeditated murder.

But why? John asks this question: "For what reason did he slay him?" What stirred up so much hatred, anger, rage, and violence in Cain? Had Abel made Cain's life miserable by constantly bullying his brother until he finally snapped? Did Cain have some sort of deep-seated derangement that made him delusional, believing he was doing what was right? The answer John gives should shock us: Cain killed Abel "because his deeds were evil, and his brother's were righteous" (3:12).

To understand what John means by this, we need to look back at the original account of the slaying in Genesis 4. The narrative reveals that Cain, the firstborn, was "a tiller of the ground" while Abel, his younger brother, was "a keeper of flocks" (Gen. 4:2). In other words, Cain was a farmer, Abel a shepherd. But something happened that provoked Cain to envy, jealousy, and rage. Cain brought an offering to God—"the fruit of the ground" (Gen. 4:3). Abel, meanwhile, brought the very best specimens of his flock to offer as sacrifices (Gen. 4:4). On Abel's offering of blood, God looked favorably; but for Cain's offering of veggies, God had no regard (Gen. 4:4-5). _es fuerzo_

But why? Didn't each brother bring an offering from the toil of his own hands? Why would God accept Abel's animal sacrifice but reject Cain's produce from the earth? The passage doesn't clearly give a reason, but we can make a few observations. Both Cain and Abel likely knew what kind of sacrifice God required as an appropriate offering. It might be that a requirement of animal sacrifice was made clear immediately after the sin of Adam and Eve when God Himself "made garments of skin for Adam and his wife, and clothed them" (Gen. 3:21). Think about it. In order to make coverings for Adam and Eve out of animal skins, several animals had to die.

A depiction of Cain and Abel, crafted around AD 1084 on an ivory panel in the Cathedral of Salerno, Italy. It is now housed at the Louvre Museum in Paris.

If Cain and Abel had God's own sacrifice of animals as an example, they may also have had specific instructions from their parents regarding the need for animal sacrifice (see Lev. 17:11; Heb. 9:22). The sacrifice of a living thing and the shedding of its blood ultimately looked forward to the atoning death of Christ, who "put away sin by the sacrifice of Himself" (Heb. 9:26). If Cain knew that only the shedding of blood was an acceptable sacrifice to God and instead chose to do it his own way by offering fruits or vegetables, this would reveal not a spirit of genuine faith and obedience, but of rebellion and self-reliance.

But there's another, related dimension to Cain's rejected offering. Hebrews 11:4 says, "By faith Abel offered to God a better sacrifice than Cain, through which he obtained the testimony that he was righteous." Abel presented his offering "by faith." He trusted God at His word, and he believed that His demands were right, that He knew best, and that He deserved full obedience. Cain, on the other hand, apparently thought the sweat of his labor was good enough and that he didn't have to follow God's specific requirements as long as he offered something.

What would it have taken for Cain to offer a sacrifice in faith and obedience? Some effort to capture an animal worthy of sacrifice to the Lord? Or a barter with his brother Abel, trading the produce of his fields for animals from Abel's flock? Perhaps he could have joined his brother Abel in offering animals together. In any case, Cain revealed a self-centered, faithless, disobedient heart that was already predisposed to a sour relationship with his brother.

We know the rest of the story. Cain became angry, and he didn't hide it (Gen. 4:5-6). God Himself confronted Cain with a choice at that pivotal moment in his life: "If you do well, will not your countenance be lifted up? And if you do not do well, sin is crouching at the door; and its desire is for you, but you must master it" (Gen. 4:7). Instead of heeding God's plea for repentance while the cauldron of anger in his heart had not yet reached the boiling point, Cain slaughtered his brother in the field (Gen. 4:8)! By slaying his brother with bloody violence, it was as if he were thumbing his nose at God and saying, in effect, "You want blood? Here's your blood!"

This episode vividly illustrates that Cain was "of the evil one," and this association determined his movement from what he saw (his brother's deeds were righteous) to what he did (killed his brother). The implication for John's readers in the first century (and for us today) is clear: There are many people in the world who are "of the evil one" just like Cain. Even when confronted with the truth, they will continue down the path of wickedness. John states: "Do not be surprised, brethren, if the world hates you" (1 Jn. 3:13).

Though this horrific episode sheds light on the kind of wickedness John meant when he spoke of those who were "of the devil" and "of the evil one," this example also communicates an important point about the true believer's situation. In what follows, John sets up another contrast, between those who "love the brethren" and the person who "hates his brother" (3:14-15). A person who hates the brethren "abides in death" (3:14), meaning they do not truly possess eternal life by grace through faith (3:15). This person is also a murderer because, as in the case of Cain, murder is the ultimate end of unchecked hatred (Matt. 5:21-22; 15:19).

John's purpose, though, is not to cast doubt on his readers' salvation. Rather, unlike those who hate other believers and lack salvation, "we know that we have passed out of death into life" (1 Jn. 3:14). How do we know this? Because we love the brothers and sisters. John's intention is that, as his readers consider the disposition and murderous actions of Cain, they will not see themselves as being like him. Just the opposite. Instead of behaving like Cain, who slew his brother to satiate his own anger, children of God ought to follow Christ's extreme example of self-sacrificial love (3:16). Just as Christ laid down His life for us because of His love, we should love the brethren by laying down our lives for them.

Does John mean for us to take this literally—searching for ways to shed our own blood or sacrifice ourselves to somehow benefit our fellow believers? Surely, if the situation ever arose, it would be Christlike to die as martyrs for the sake of our spiritual family. But John had something much more practical in mind: providing for the material needs of a brother or sister in Christ (3:17). If we have material blessings in this life but fail to provide for fellow believers' real needs, "how does the love of God abide in [us]?" Clearly, John's answer is, "It doesn't." To follow Christ's example, we must love our brothers and sisters not simply in the words we say but "in deed and truth" (3:18).

—3:19-24—

Right now, you may be wondering where you stand. None of us lives perfectly like Christ. None of us exhibits continual self-sacrificial love for our brothers and sisters in Christ. All of us have moments when we mistreat the brethren by our actions—neglecting them in time of need, lashing out at them with our words, failing to minister to them as fellow members of the body. We may not be shedding blood like Cain did to Abel, but we frequently find ourselves failing to love the brethren as Christ loved us.

John knows that all of us are in this predicament, in which we know the good we ought to do but we just fail to do it. This is why he includes the important words of encouragement in these verses. Genuine believers who waffle between Cain and Christ need to remember that they're not made righteous by their works, but by faith in the name of the Son of God.

John says, "We will know by this that we are of the truth" (3:19). By *what*? By loving our brothers and sisters in Christ in deed and truth. When we love as He loved, we demonstrate that a new nature dwells in us from above. However, when sin inevitably finds its way into our thoughts, words, and actions, we can still have assurance before God, who is greater than our self-condemning hearts. He knows us. He knows the genuineness of our faith and love. He knows all about our bouts with evil and our struggles against habitual sins. And He provides the strength to overcome them by His Spirit.

John's desire is to strengthen our assurance.

"You're not like Cain!" he says.

A doubter might respond, "But you can't see my heart, John. Last week I was really, really angry at one of the elders. And his wife!"

"No, no, no," John responds. "Look at the totality of your life. You kept the faith even when you were challenged by false teaching. You've consistently provided for the poor in the church, opened your home to the hurting, and reached out to the lost—all motivated by your faith in Christ and love for others."

"But I punched that deacon in the mouth yesterday!"

John shakes his head, "Look, the fact that you feel remorse for these things means you're definitely *not* like Cain. You're not a child of the devil. The Spirit is prodding your conscience. You just need to respond to it. Confess your sins against God. Reconcile with your brothers and sisters. Sacrifice your pride and make amends."

That's John's main point in 3:19-24. He's not trying to make true children of God doubt their salvation because of their sins, but to motivate them to return immediately to the way of righteousness and truth whenever they find themselves beginning to take even small steps in Cain's direction.

In this process, John uses positive encouragement rather than negative warnings. He spells out the benefits of a life lived in such a way that such doubts aren't able to creep into the believer's heart. When we have a clean conscience before God because we keep His commands and please Him, we can have confidence before Him that our prayers will be answered (3:21-22). The term "confidence" is the same word John used back in 2:28—"Abide in Him, so that when He appears, we may have confidence and not shrink away from Him in shame at His coming." This term conveys the notion of boldness.

Because of this confidence brought on by a life of obedience, we don't shy away from prayer. We don't skulk in the margins while others go to God with their requests. Few things keep people from genuine prayer to their heavenly Father more than unconfessed sin and a resulting guilty conscience. Shame is a barrier to fellowship with God. But when we confess our sins, clear the air, and walk in the light, we find ourselves going to God constantly and confidently, thanking Him, sharing with Him, worshiping and praising Him, and letting our requests be known.

Finally, John turns our attention from our own hearts and good works to Jesus Christ and the Spirit. Ultimately, the lasting assurance of our salvation must come from God. Yes, we are urged to abide in Christ and to walk in His commandments, but John again reminds us that the only reason we're willing and able to abide in Him is because

He abides in us! By works? By good intentions? By a life purified by constant discipline? No, *Christ abides in us by faith alone.* John writes, "This is His commandment, that we believe in the name of His Son Jesus Christ" (3:23). That's the first step, because "without faith it is impossible to please Him" (Heb. 11:6).

Genuine, saving faith that unites us to Christ also results in the permanent indwelling of the Holy Spirit. By the power of the Spirit we're able to keep His commandment to "love one another" (1 Jn. 3:23). And this mutual abiding—He in us and we in Him—produces an internal assurance that can't be quantified. It can only be known by those who have an authentic saving relationship with the Lord Jesus Christ. John writes, "We know by this that He abides in us, by the Spirit whom He has given us" (3:24). This Spirit produces in us assurance and confidence—faith in the goodness of the Father, the perfect and complete work of the Son, and the ongoing empowerment of the Spirit. The Holy Spirit inspires us to confess Christ. He empowers us to live righteously. He prompts us to love others. He teaches us all truth. He convicts us of our sin. He comforts us through trials.

And, thanks be to God, He holds us secure in the gift of eternal life!

APPLICATION: 1 JOHN 3:11-24
You and Your Conscience

Who of us hasn't looked at our lives at a low point and seen a little more Cain than Christ? This understandably leads many people to start questioning the genuineness of their faith and the prospect of their eternal life. "If I'm really saved," they think, "why am I thinking and talking and acting like a lost person?" All of us have similar battles with a guilty conscience—especially those of us with very sensitive consciences or those of us who were raised in an environment that was big on guilt, shame, and holding our mistakes against us.

On the other hand, most of us have also felt the reassurance of a clear conscience, when we've reached "cruising altitude" in our Christian life and readily feel the Spirit working through us. Sometimes we turn away from temptations that normally drag us down . . . or we find ourselves saying and doing Christlike things in a way that surprises us . . . or we demonstrate a love for others we didn't know we had in us!

Most of the time, though, the normal Christian life is lived somewhere in between soaring in the clouds of spiritual triumph and dragging along the ground of spiritual defeat. It's in this middle space that nagging doubts creep in, making us wonder whether we're more like Cain or more like Christ. What do we do when we begin to have doubts about our salvation? How do we minister to others who lack assurance because of sin in their lives? Let me offer three thoughts in response to 1 John 3:12-24 to help us or those we know to have assurance.

First, *when your conscience accuses you, look back and ask why*. You're going along pretty well and suddenly your inner alarm goes off and says, "Stop right there. That wasn't right." Don't just ignore that pricking of the conscience. It's given to you as a gift, not to cause you to doubt your salvation, but to live out the salvation you have in a way that pleases God. When the alarm of your conscience is tripped, deal with it. Maybe you spoke impatiently with a brother or sister in Christ, and you need to mend that relationship. Maybe you made a decision motivated by pride, greed, or envy, and you need to reconsider. Maybe you've been drifting from a close fellowship with God and His people, and your conscience is raising a red flag, prompting you to reflect on your priorities. Whatever the case may be, rather than ignoring your conscience, ask why. Let your conscience drive you to Christ. Your response should be confession and repentance.

Second, *when your heart affirms you, look around and see why*. You might see fellow believers in Christ who care for you and share with you. You might see those to whom you've ministered become fellow children of God. Or perhaps you'll notice the blessings that are often easy to overlook: family, friends, a good job, a great church, health, and happiness. God answers prayer and keeps His promises. Your response should be praise and thanksgiving.

Third, *when the Spirit assures you, look within and know why*. The Spirit indwells you. This isn't metaphorical language. He is truly present, imparting to you His life and producing in you the fruit of the Spirit: love, joy, peace, patience, kindness, goodness, faithfulness, gentleness, and self-control (Gal. 5:22-23). The Christian faith is not merely intellectual, consisting of a list of propositional truths we affirm. It is also a living faith, in which our experiences can't always be reduced to words. We have a mystical union with God through Christ by the indwelling Spirit. And the Holy Spirit speaks into the souls of His beloved children to say, "You are my precious child" (see Rom. 8:16). Your response to this supernatural assurance should be wonder and awe.

Distinguishing Truth from Error
1 JOHN 4:1-6

NASB

¹Beloved, do not believe every spirit, but test the spirits to see whether they are from God, because many false prophets have gone out into the world. ²By this you know the Spirit of God: every spirit that confesses that Jesus Christ has come in the flesh is from God; ³and every spirit that does not confess Jesus is not from God; this is the *spirit* of the antichrist, of which you have heard that it is coming, and now it is already in the world. ⁴You are from God, little children, and have overcome them; because greater is He who is in you than he who is in the world. ⁵They are from the world; therefore they speak *as* from the world, and the world listens to them. ⁶We are from God; he who knows God listens to us; he who is not from God does not listen to us. By this we know the spirit of truth and the spirit of error.

NLT

¹Dear friends, do not believe everyone who claims to speak by the Spirit. You must test them to see if the spirit they have comes from God. For there are many false prophets in the world. ²This is how we know if they have the Spirit of God: If a person claiming to be a prophet* acknowledges that Jesus Christ came in a real body, that person has the Spirit of God. ³But if someone claims to be a prophet and does not acknowledge the truth about Jesus, that person is not from God. Such a person has the spirit of the Antichrist, which you heard is coming into the world and indeed is already here.

⁴But you belong to God, my dear children. You have already won a victory over those people, because the Spirit who lives in you is greater than the spirit who lives in the world. ⁵Those people belong to this world, so they speak from the world's viewpoint, and the world listens to them. ⁶But we belong to God, and those who know God listen to us. If they do not belong to God, they do not listen to us. That is how we know if someone has the Spirit of truth or the spirit of deception.

4:2 Greek *If a spirit;* similarly in 4:3.

Some statements of Scripture haunt me. If I were to dwell on them too long, meditate on them too deeply, or obsess over them too frequently, they would keep me awake at night. They warn of impending trouble for believers and alarming developments for the church. These passages together paint a pretty bleak picture of the deteriorating world around us:

- "You will be hated by all nations because of My name." (Matt. 24:9)

- "Many false prophets will arise and will mislead many." (Matt. 24:11)
- "Because lawlessness is increased, most people's love will grow cold." (Matt. 24:12)
- "False Christs and false prophets will arise and will show great signs and wonders, so as to mislead, if possible, even the elect." (Matt. 24:24)
- "An hour is coming for everyone who kills you to think that he is offering service to God." (John 16:2)
- "In the world you have tribulation." (John 16:33)
- "The Spirit explicitly says that in later times some will fall away from the faith, paying attention to deceitful spirits and doctrines of demons." (1 Tim. 4:1)
- "The time will come when they will not endure sound doctrine; but wanting to have their ears tickled, they will accumulate for themselves teachers in accordance to their own desires, and will turn away their ears from the truth and will turn aside to myths." (2 Tim. 4:3-4)
- "Do not be surprised at the fiery ordeal among you, which comes upon you for your testing, as though some strange thing were happening to you." (1 Pet. 4:12)

I'm often asked by believers who are alarmed at the spiritual, moral, and cultural decline today, "What in the world is going on? What's happening to our families? To our churches? To our schools . . . our country . . . our world?" In light of those haunting Scriptures, I have a quick and simple answer: *exactly what was predicted.*

In his meandering discussion of the Christian life, the apostle John returns to a theme he already introduced in the very beginning of this section: the contrast between truth and error, between deceiving "antichrists" and trustworthy teachers. In this particular passage, John focuses on the responsibility not of the teachers but of the hearers—our responsibility to distinguish truth from error.

—4:1—

John begins expressing his concern for the doctrinal purity of his readers by issuing two serious commands. He commands these things because he cares for his readers deeply—they are his "beloved" children in Christ. John has already written to these believers about the importance of loving one another and not loving the world (1 Jn. 2:15; 3:23). Our love must be discriminating, discerning, distinguishing love.

Similarly, as John discusses the doctrines we embrace as Christians, it becomes clear that our faith must be discriminating, discerning, distinguishing faith. To that end, John issues these two commands—the first is negative, the second positive—"Do not believe every spirit" and "Test the spirits" (4:1).

The term translated "spirit" here is *pneuma* [4151], which most basically means "breath" or "wind." It's also used to describe an immaterial, nonphysical nature, either divine, angelic, or human.[16] In 1 John 4:1, as Smalley notes, "The term . . . signifies a human person who is inspired by the spirit of truth or the spirit of error."[17]

The fact is, every human teacher—whether true or false in their teaching—is motivated and empowered by something that is often hidden behind the scenes. This may be a spirit of wickedness, falsehood, self-interest, and carnality . . . or a spirit of righteousness, truth, love, and holiness. Ultimately, we know that teachers blown about by the winds of error are under the influence of satanic deception, whether they know it or not. And teachers driven by the winds of truth are empowered by the Holy Spirit.

John uses his characteristic this-or-that method of setting forth the truth in his no-nonsense, cut-to-the-chase manner. Everyone who teaches is either the mouthpiece of the spirit of truth, speaking for God . . . or the mouthpiece of the spirit of error, speaking for Satan. His first command is, essentially, "Don't be gullible." Don't believe everything you hear. Look before you leap! You need to look beyond the outward and discern the spiritual reality.

This leads to the second command: We are to "test the spirits" of teachers "to see whether they are from God" (4:1). I picture a well-trained guard dog, like a Doberman pinscher. The moment a Doberman hears a sound or catches a movement in its domain, its pointy ears pop up and its eyes fix on the source. And if there's a threat, that watchdog leaps into action to defend its territory. Christians need to be equally alert and equipped to discern between truth and error, particularly in relation to the fundamental doctrines of the Christian faith.

Test the spirits. Don't go by how large of a crowd the teacher is able to attract. Don't be impressed by titles, degrees, and letters after names. Don't be enamored by the beauty of the robe, the sheen of the suit, or the eloquence of the voice. Our standard is the Word of God, the gospel of the person and work of the Lord Jesus Christ, the essential truths of the historic Christian faith. Some today may call this narrow-minded. But the Bible calls the reception of these truths "noble-minded." Luke

The Erosion of the Modern Church

1 JOHN 4:1-6

I've lived long enough to watch an alarming erosion occur in modern Christianity. The church I entered back in the 1950s is not the same church as today. Large, influential churches are looking more and more like they got their genes crossed with Wall Street and Broadway. A strange mutation of techniques from corporate America and show business have replaced or at least watered down the sound and systematic teaching of the Word of God. There are notable exceptions, for which I'm grateful, but that's the tragedy: They are the exceptions, not the rule.

Instead of offering solid meat based on sound doctrine, our houses of worship have turned to the baby food of the world of entertainment. A consumer mentality is now an acceptable substitute for theological thinking and biblical literacy. Naive and impressionable infants in the faith gather to hear what they want to hear from preachers and teachers who are often not much better trained than their hearers!

When I consider these developments, I can't help but think of Eugene Peterson's paraphrase of 2 Timothy 4:3-4 in The Message—"You're going to find that there will be times when people will have no stomach for solid teaching, but will fill up on spiritual junk food—catchy opinions that tickle their fancy. They'll turn their backs on truth and chase mirages." It seems like pastors today will stop at nothing to entertain their audience—not congregation, but audience. And those audiences want nothing more than to hear things that "tickle their fancy."

I know this comes across to some people as the get-off-my-lawn rants of a grumpy old man. Or the desperate railings of a member of the "old guard" who can't bear to see an old-fashioned Churchianity replaced by something more "relevant." It's not that at all. I myself

(continued on next page)

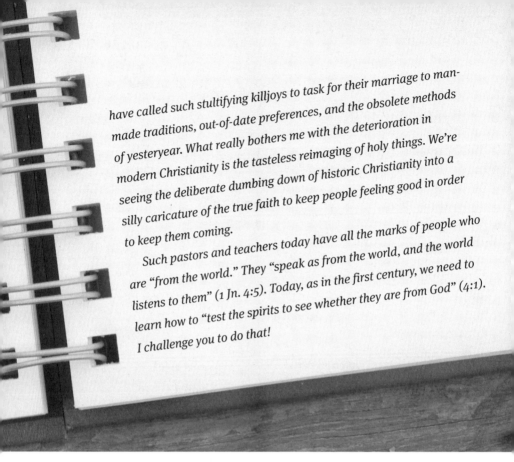

have called such stultifying killjoys to task for their marriage to man-made traditions, out-of-date preferences, and the obsolete methods of yesteryear. What really bothers me with the deterioration in modern Christianity is the tasteless reimaging of holy things. We're seeing the deliberate dumbing down of historic Christianity into a silly caricature of the true faith to keep people feeling good in order to keep them coming.

Such pastors and teachers today have all the marks of people who are "from the world." They "speak as from the world, and the world listens to them" (1 Jn. 4:5). Today, as in the first century, we need to learn how to "test the spirits to see whether they are from God" (4:1). I challenge you to do that!

describes those who heard the gospel in Berea in this way: "Now these were more noble-minded than those in Thessalonica, for they received the word with great eagerness, examining the Scriptures daily to see whether these things were so" (Acts 17:11).

John uses the term *dokimazō* [1381], "to test," in a way similar to Paul's use in 1 Thessalonians 5:21-22: "Examine [*dokimazō*] everything carefully; hold fast to that which is good; abstain from every form of evil." The word means "to make a critical examination of something to determine genuineness."[18] A gemologist can use her knowledge of diamonds to make a critical examination of a ring and determine whether it's genuine. A banker can usually discriminate between a genuine bill and a counterfeit by applying his thorough knowledge of the look, feel, and qualities of authentic currency. In the same way, believers must have a thorough understanding of the genuine Christian faith to be able to test competing truth claims.

John's warning isn't just theoretical. He doesn't follow up his statement with, "Don't worry, I'm only telling you these things in case of the possibility that maybe, someday, some false teacher just so happens to accidentally say something that might be a little questionable." No, John is addressing an immediate crisis in·his own day—and one that has only grown broader and deeper through the centuries.

He follows his commands with a purpose statement: "because many false prophets have gone out into the world" (1 Jn. 4:1). Notice, John doesn't say it's just one false prophet (e.g., Simon the Magician) . . . or just a few false prophets who all say the same thing. There are *many* false prophets. And note that he isn't saying that these false prophets *might* go out into the world . . . or will wait until the end times to start wreaking havoc on the church. They *have gone out* into the world! Already in John's day the prophecies of Christ had begun to be fulfilled—"Many false prophets will arise and will mislead many" (Matt. 24:11).

—4:2-3—

How do we exercise discernment between the true and the false? John addresses this question in 1 John 4:2-3. He says, "By this you know the Spirit of God." Listen up! By getting to know this one thing thoroughly, intimately, frontward, backward, and inside out—you'll be able to discern truth from error. Like the gemologist spotting the fake diamond through her magnifier or the banker identifying the fake $100 bill with a few simple tests, believers will be able to hear the voice of the spirit of truth in the authentic preachers and discern the spirit of error in the fakes.

What is this thing by which a person can know the Spirit of God? Actually, it's not a thing, but a *person*—the person of Jesus Christ. John says, "Every spirit that confesses that Jesus Christ has come in the flesh is from God; and every spirit that does not confess Jesus is not from God" (4:2-3). As we saw in our discussion of 2:20-21, the historic Christian faith that "was once for all handed down to the saints" (Jude 1:3) centers on the person and work of Jesus Christ. Genuine teachers must hold to the *right* Jesus, not a different Jesus. They must accept Him as the incarnate God-man, sent by God the Father in the power of God the Holy Spirit. They must believe in His virgin birth, His sinless life, His atoning death, and His glorious resurrection from the dead. This means accepting Him as the only Savior and Lord, and it means hoping for His future coming as King.

The right teaching concerning Jesus Christ is the litmus test. Does the person delivering the teaching confess Jesus as God incarnate? Do they believe Christ to be the eternal Son of God? Do they profess personal faith in Jesus as Savior and Lord . . . and point others to do the same? And does this preacher or teacher place Christ at the center of the teaching and at the head of the ministry, consistent with His right position as Savior and Lord? Or is the teacher putting himself or herself at the center of everything?

John couldn't have been clearer. Authentic teachers who are motivated by the spirit of truth confess faith in the true Jesus. The word translated "confess" (*homologeō* [3670]) implies a wholehearted, whole-life profession of personal faith in Jesus Christ. In its fullest sense, *homologeō* not only means "to concede that something is factual or true," but also conveys "a profession of allegiance."[19] Thus, Paul can warn about false teachers who "profess to know God, but [who] deny him by their works" (Titus 1:16, ESV). Both elements—words and deeds—mark a true confession.

Those who deny Christ—either in their twisted teaching or their lurid living—are motivated by "the spirit of the antichrist" (1 Jn. 4:3). The same anti-Christian disposition—empowered by the same spirits of wickedness—that will characterize the end-times Antichrist is already actively present in this world. What Satan will one day accomplish through one Antichrist and one false prophet (see Rev. 13), he is now trying to accomplish through many antichrists and many false prophets. Similarly, when Paul referred to the future Antichrist as the "man of lawlessness" (2 Thes. 2:3), he also warned that "the mystery of lawlessness is already at work," even as the ultimate lawless one is currently restrained by God until his unleashing in the end times (2 Thes. 2:6-7).

Present and Future Antichrists

Already in the world	Not yet in the world
"Many antichrists have appeared" (1 John 2:18; 4:3) "The mystery of lawlessness is already at work" (2 Thes. 2:7)	THE Antichrist (1 John 2:18; 4:3) THE Man of Lawlessness (2 Thes. 2:3)

Present antichrists and lawless ones foreshadow and anticipate the coming of the ultimate Antichrist.

Because the spirit of antichrist and the mystery of lawlessness are already at work in the world—and have been since the early days of the church—we must be ever-diligent to distinguish truth from error.

XCURSUS: ARE THERE APOSTLES AND PROPHETS TODAY?

1 JOHN 4:1

Sometimes I run across preachers or teachers today who claim to be "apostles" or "prophets." Often they're just using those titles in their most general senses. Missionaries may use the term "apostle" as "one who is sent" or preachers may use "prophet" as "one who proclaims a message." But occasionally, the self-styled "apostle" or "prophet" claims to be the same kind of apostle or prophet found in the New Testament, upon whom the church was built (Eph. 2:20). In fact, some today claim that the next great revival and reformation of the church will come through bona fide apostles and prophets . . . and only those Christians and churches who follow their lead will be part of the new wave of the Spirit.

Is this possible? Can there be real apostles and prophets with such authority today?

According to Scripture—and confirmed by the testimony of the early church—the authentic offices of the apostles and prophets were limited to the earliest church. Paul wrote, "God has appointed in the church, first apostles, second prophets" (1 Cor. 12:28), indicating that these are first in sequence as the foundational offices of the church. Paul also implied that one mark of an authentic apostle includes having "seen Jesus our Lord" (1 Cor. 9:1). In 1 Corinthians 15:5-8, when Paul lists the eyewitnesses of the resurrected Jesus, he indicates that Christ appeared to James and "then to all the apostles," he himself being "last of all." Another essential mark of "a true apostle" was the ability to perform authenticating "signs and wonders and miracles" (2 Cor. 12:12). This function of signs and wonders as confirming the original apostles' message is mentioned in Hebrews 2:3-4, when the author writes,

"After [the gospel] was at the first spoken through the Lord, it was confirmed to us by those who heard, God also testifying with them, both by signs and wonders and by various miracles and by gifts of the Holy Spirit according to His own will."

But someone might say, "Isn't it possible that God continued this foundational apostolic ministry beyond the first century? Wouldn't it make more sense if God continued to call apostles and prophets, confirm His message with signs and wonders, and broaden the foundation of the church in the future generations?"

When we turn to the earliest generation of Christians after the original apostles and prophets, we see that those original disciples of the apostles and prophets referred to those offices as foundational ministries of the church that had ceased.[20] This is especially important when we consider how the early church determined whether a Christian writing should be regarded as Scripture or not. The mid-second-century Muratorian Canon wisely rejected the inspiration of a book entitled *Shepherd of Hermas* based on the fact that it was written *after* the time of the apostles and prophets: "It cannot be read publicly to the people in church either among the Prophets *whose number is complete*, or among the Apostles, *for it is after their time*" (emphasis mine).[21]

So, both the Bible and the records of the earliest church immediately after the apostles demonstrate that the New Testament apostles and prophets were a fixed number in the first generation of the church. Their teachings concerning the crucified and risen Lord, as well as their writings, were foundational for the church.

(continued on next page)

When their lives on earth came to an end, so did their offices. Today their doctrines are preserved in Scripture and taught by their successors—the evangelists, pastors, and teachers throughout church history (Eph. 4:11). Nobody can legitimately claim to be an authoritative apostle or prophet in the church today.

—4:4-6—

John wraps up his urgent warning against false teachers and his timely exhortation on discernment by juxtaposing two contrasting groups. Note the opening words of these three verses: "You" (4:4) . . . "They" (4:5) . . . "We" (4:6). The first and the last refer to *those who are from God*; the middle refers to *those who are from the world*.

John first affirms his readers. He knows they are genuine believers and followers of Christ, who confess the true faith and live a life consistent with their confession. Because of this, they "have overcome them." That is, they were able to escape the deception, corruption, and darkness of the world and to arrive at a genuine saving faith in Jesus Christ. Later John will state this clearly: "Who is the one who overcomes the world, but he who believes that Jesus is the Son of God?" (1 Jn. 5:5).

When John says his readers have "overcome them," who is "them"? He's referring to the vast number of those who aren't from God, those who are "from the world" (4:5). John probably has in mind specifically those unbelievers who are antagonists, persecutors, and false teachers. How did true believers overcome them? Not by their own holiness, wisdom, or strength, but by the Spirit of God who lives within them.

They overcame "because greater is He who is in you than he who is in the world" (4:4). God's Spirit is the one who teaches us, leads us into truth, and strengthens us when we come toe-to-toe with deceivers (Luke 12:11-12; John 14:26; 16:13). The Spirit of God who is within us is mightier than any enemy of the truth—human or demonic.

He further describes "them" in 1 John 4:5: They are from the world, captivating others by their deception. Whether they're in worldly academics, worldly science, or worldly culture—false religion, politics, philosophy, or finance—these false teachers say things the rest of the world loves to hear, and their worldly hearers will eagerly swallow the lies without question. And when a Christian speaks out against the unsound doctrine and unholy living of these deceivers, the "world" rises up in unison to condemn the truth as foolish, ignorant, narrow-minded, bigoted, mean-spirited, or even hateful and dangerous. If this conflict were an us-against-them popularity contest, Christians would lose every time. But it's not. It's a them-against-God spiritual conflict, and greater is He who is in us than he who is in the world (4:4).

Finally, just as there is a connection between the word of the world and the worldly men and women who eagerly listen to its falsehood, there is an affinity between God's word and God's people. Jesus Himself said, "My sheep hear My voice, and I know them, and they follow Me" (John 10:27). True believers, enabled by the Spirit to understand and believe, embrace the true Jesus and therefore fellowship with His true followers. Furthermore, John says that "he who knows God listens to us; he who is not from God does not listen to us" (1 Jn. 4:6). The "us" here likely refers to the genuine apostles, John and his circle of truth tellers. Today, we "listen" to the apostles as we devote ourselves fully and unconditionally to their inspired words in God's Word.

These two tests—faithfulness in word and deed to the person of Jesus Christ and faithfulness and obedience to God's word—are sure, reliable guides for discerning between the spirit of truth and the spirit of error.

APPLICATION: 1 JOHN 4:1-6

There Really Is a Difference!

When you're trying to discern between the spirit of truth and the spirit of error, remember this two-pronged principle: (1) Listen carefully to the one who's teaching and (2) look closely at those who are following.

Regarding the first prong, you need to listen carefully not only to what is said but also to what's *not* said. What does the teacher conveniently leave out? Sometimes false teachers will go on and on without mentioning Jesus even once. Or they'll talk about how to make your life great without ever mentioning the problem of our sin and guilt solved by the work of Christ on the cross. Listen carefully to their wording. False teachers love to use classic Christian language with completely different definitions.

Regarding the second prong, you can tell a lot from the crowd those teachers attract and the principles that crowd puts into practice. Do they have their Bibles? Are they encouraged to read the Bible, study it, and live out its truths? Are they serious about their faith and about loving God and loving others? Or do they lead shallow lives? Do they share Christ far and wide? Or do they just recruit people to come to their church?

We must understand the need and value of discernment and take seriously our responsibility to apply this two-pronged principle to the teachers and churches we come across. Here are seven statements that will help us see the difference between the spirit of truth and the spirit of error.

1. *Never forget that we're living in treacherous times.* The Scriptures predicted it, so we shouldn't be surprised when we witness it. Discern that the days are evil; don't embrace the darkness, but work as lights to expose it.

2. *Doctrinal discernment plays a vital role in surviving . . . and thriving.* You and I don't have the luxury of shifting our brains into neutral if we hope to make a difference in our generation. We need to study (not just read) God's Word, growing in doctrinal knowledge and cultivating a meaningful life and ministry experience.

3. *Historical roots and doctrinal truth must continue to be valued and embraced.* Times and cultures change, and with that, worship styles and ministry methods will also change, which is understandable. But the classic Christian faith in the triune God and the person and work of Christ must remain the same. Never lose sight of the main focus of the church's ministry.

4. *Each generation of believers has a serious responsibility to keep the faith.* Just one weak link in the chain of receiving, believing, and passing down the faith can usher in an era of false doctrine and wickedness in the church. We want to be remembered as a generation of spiritual heroes, not spiritual drifters.

5. *The church's leaders are called to guide well the church's ministry.* Faithful leaders guide the church by making sure it's moving in the right direction, staying centered on Christ and staying true to the Scriptures, while equipping the saints for the work of ministry.

6. *The church's leaders are given the task of guarding the church's people.* Leaders are to watch over the church by equipping its members to discern between truth and falsehood and by standing up to those who seek to sabotage the ministry or prey on believers. Faithful shepherds guard their flocks.

7. *A strong and healthy church today is no guarantee of the same tomorrow.* Each and every day we must renew our commitment to discerning between truth and error, acknowledging Christ in doctrine and practice and passing the faith on to the next generation. Mentoring those who are young in the faith is crucially important if we hope to pass the baton to those who will run the race after we are gone.

A CONFIDENT LIFE
(1 JOHN 4:7-5:21)

So many people struggle with assurance of their salvation. They doubt whether they've believed the right quantity of truth, with the right quality of faith, maintained by the right quantity and quality of good works. Or their attention turns inward to their sinful thoughts and actions, impossible to completely eradicate in this life. They may then wrongly believe that there's just no way constantly dirty sinners like them could be accepted by a holy God. Or they pay too much attention to misguided preachers and teachers who pummel them with bad theology of uncertainty, much of which amounts to an old-fashioned, heretical works-righteousness no better than the false teachings of the Judaizers whom Paul dealt with.

What a tragedy! The greatness of the Christian message of salvation is that Jesus Christ has accomplished everything for us. He paid our debt in full and sent His Spirit to seal us for salvation. He did all this entirely by unearned grace. Not only did we not merit salvation; we *could* not merit it.

Those who lack assurance of salvation show it in their lack of confidence. The fear of losing salvation ironically doesn't produce faithful believers on fire for the Lord, but rather causes people to fizzle out by constantly fretting over whether they've done enough. Assurance of salvation through the completed work of Christ is needed if we're to walk in the light with confidence rather than sulk in the darkness of insecurity.

Because assurance is so important, John crowns his letter with the encouragement that fellowship produces a confident life (4:7–5:21). The key verse regarding assurance in this section is 5:13, a passage well worth memorizing: "These things I have written to you who believe in the name of the Son of God, so that you may know that you have eternal life." And the assurance of salvation by grace alone through faith alone in Christ alone won't lead us into laziness or complacency, as so many often teach. Instead, it will lead us into a deeper, more joyful, and more fruitful relationship with God and with one another.

KEY TERMS IN 1 JOHN 4:7–5:21

agapaō (ἀγαπάω) [25] "to love"
agapē (ἀγάπη) [26] "love," "benevolence"
Outside the New Testament, the Greek noun *agapē* is rare. Greek culture celebrated *erōs*, an intoxicating, impulsive love between men and women. The Greeks also honored *philia* [5373], the warm, noble affection of deep friendship. But *agapē* describes an unconditional, selfless love that expects nothing in return for its affections and benevolence. The related verb *agapaō* perfectly describes God's love toward people as well as Christians' responsibility to reflect that love toward others. For the apostle John, the Christian life was summed up by living out *agapē* for God and for fellow believers—perfectly modeled by Christ and empowered by the Holy Spirit.

nikaō (νικάω) [3528] "conquer," "overpower," "overcome"
The word *nikaō* has a range of meanings, from overpowering an enemy (Luke 11:22) to overcoming evil with good (Rom. 12:21). The meaning in John's writings relates to overcoming Satan and the world by faith in the finished work of Jesus Christ, who overcame the world on our behalf (John 16:33; 1 Jn. 4:4). The key to understanding what it means for believers to "overcome" is found in 1 John 5:4-5: "This is the victory that has overcome the world—our faith. Who is the one who overcomes the world, but he who believes that Jesus is the Son of God?"

The Supremacy of Love
1 JOHN 4:7-21

NASB

7 Beloved, let us love one another, for love is from God; and everyone who loves is ᵃborn of God and knows God. 8 The one who does not love does not know God, for God is love. 9 By this the love of God was manifested ᵃin us, that God has sent His ᵇonly begotten Son into the world so that we might live through Him. 10 In this is love, not that we loved God, but that He loved us and sent His Son *to be* the propitiation for our sins. 11 Beloved, if God so loved us, we also ought to love one another. 12 No one

NLT

7 Dear friends, let us continue to love one another, for love comes from God. Anyone who loves is a child of God and knows God. 8 But anyone who does not love does not know God, for God is love.

9 God showed how much he loved us by sending his one and only Son into the world so that we might have eternal life through him. 10 This is real love—not that we loved God, but that he loved us and sent his Son as a sacrifice to take away our sins. 11 Dear friends, since God loved us that much, we surely ought to love each other. 12 No one has ever seen

has seen God at any time; if we love one another, God abides in us, and His love is perfected in us. [13] By this we know that we abide in Him and He in us, because He has given us of His Spirit. [14] We have seen and testify that the Father has sent the Son *to be* the Savior of the world.

[15] Whoever confesses that Jesus is the Son of God, God abides in him, and he in God. [16] We have come to know and have believed the love which God has [a]for us. God is love, and the one who abides in love abides in God, and God abides in him. [17] By this, love is perfected with us, so that we may have confidence in the day of judgment; because as He is, so also are we in this world. [18] There is no fear in love; but perfect love casts out fear, because fear [a]involves punishment, and the one who fears is not perfected in love. [19] We love, because He first loved us. [20] If someone says, "I love God," and hates his brother, he is a liar; for the one who does not love his brother whom he has seen, cannot love God whom he has not seen. [21] And this commandment we have from Him, that the one who loves God should love his brother also.

4:7 [a]Or *begotten* 4:9 [a]Or *in our case* [b]Or *unique, only one of His kind* 4:16 [a]Lit *in* 4:18 [a]Lit *has*

God. But if we love each other, God lives in us, and his love is brought to full expression in us.

[13] And God has given us his Spirit as proof that we live in him and he in us. [14] Furthermore, we have seen with our own eyes and now testify that the Father sent his Son to be the Savior of the world. [15] All who declare that Jesus is the Son of God have God living in them, and they live in God. [16] We know how much God loves us, and we have put our trust in his love.

God is love, and all who live in love live in God, and God lives in them. [17] And as we live in God, our love grows more perfect. So we will not be afraid on the day of judgment, but we can face him with confidence because we live like Jesus here in this world.

[18] Such love has no fear, because perfect love expels all fear. If we are afraid, it is for fear of punishment, and this shows that we have not fully experienced his perfect love. [19] We love each other* because he loved us first.

[20] If someone says, "I love God," but hates a fellow believer,* that person is a liar; for if we don't love people we can see, how can we love God, whom we cannot see? [21] And he has given us this command: Those who love God must also love their fellow believers.*

4:19 Greek *We love.* Other manuscripts read *We love God;* still others read *We love him.* 4:20 Greek *hates his brother.* 4:21 Greek *The one who loves God must also love his brother.*

If I were to say, "Turn to the 'love chapter' in the New Testament," most people would probably flip straight to 1 Corinthians 13. That "ode to charity" has earned the honorific title "Love Chapter" for a reason. Its thirteen verses mention *agapē* eight times. And its poetic description of selfless love is fit for framing:

Love is patient, love is kind and is not jealous; love does not brag and is not arrogant, does not act unbecomingly; it does not seek its own, is not provoked, does not take into account a wrong suffered, does not rejoice in unrighteousness, but rejoices with the truth; bears all things, believes all things, hopes all things, endures all things. Love never fails. (1 Cor. 13:4-8)

However, without detracting from the beauty and power of Paul's words in 1 Corinthians, let me suggest that a far stronger case can be made for a different passage of Scripture earning the title "Love Chapter"—the fourth chapter of 1 John. The noun "love" (*agapē*) and the verb "to love" (*agapaō*) appear a combined twenty-seven times in 1 John 4:7-21 alone. No other chapter in the Bible comes close to such a direct and sustained emphasis on love.

This Christlike, self-sacrificial, others-focused love transformed the apostle John's life. In the Gospel of John, he referred to himself as "the disciple whom Jesus loved" (John 13:23; 19:26; 21:7, 20). This self-identification wasn't a way of pointing out how great he was to earn Christ's love—not with this kind of love. Rather, I think John couldn't stop marveling that Jesus would express such unconditional, selfless love to anyone, particularly him. John viewed himself as the disciple whom Jesus loved in spite of who he was, not because of it.

This jaw-dropping wonder at the love of God fuels John's "love chapter" in 1 John 4:7-21. This is the third time in this letter that John touches on the subject of loving one another (2:7-10; 3:11-18). But in this passage, he builds his strongest case for the central place of love in the Christian life.

—4:7-12—

As a congregation grows in size and significance and its leadership passes from the passionate founders to the next generation, one of the first things to suffer is not sound doctrine, solid preaching, or the priority of evangelism. One of the first things to wane is love (see Rev. 2:4). Already in John's day, only a generation after the gospel of Jesus Christ went forth from Jerusalem and churches were established throughout the Roman world, the love of the brethren had begun to cool.

Apparently, the problem of a weakening love for one another had become so acute that John saw fit to repeat his appeal to love several times in his letter and to highlight, underscore, and circle it in chapter 4. He begins this section with a straightforward but gentle command, one he's written before: "Beloved, let us love one another" (1 Jn. 4:7; see 2:10; 3:11, 23). In the next handful of verses, he'll say it two more times (4:11, 12). This wasn't the mindless repetition of an old man teetering at the brink of senility. He said it over and over again because his readers needed to hear it over and over again. Clearly, their lackluster love broke John's heart.

To urge his readers to take seriously the command to "love one another," John provides three reasons for his imperative: a theological reason (4:7-10), a reciprocal reason (4:11), and a practical reason (4:12).

A theological reason for loving one another (4:7-10). John begins his persuasive apologetic for loving one another by pointing to the nature of God and the implications of that nature for our intimate union with Him. "Love is from God" (4:7), and "God is love" (4:8). Self-giving, other-centered *agapē* love is God's very nature. It's the essence of His person. When we know Him personally through the new birth and are indwelled by the Spirit, we are in union with Him. Since this is true—we are in God and He is in us—then the same loving character of God should flow through us.

John touches on the negative aspect of this truth in 4:8. The person who doesn't love "does not know God" because love is of the very essence of God's character—"God is love." If a hose is connected to a water supply, water will flow through the hose. If a wire is connected to an electrical source, power will flow through the wire. If a branch of a tree is connected to the root and trunk system, the sap of the tree will flow through the branch. And if a man or woman is truly connected to the loving Father, through the Son, by the indwelling Spirit, the love of God will flow through his or her life toward others.

John takes the theological reason deeper in 4:9-10, focusing his attention on the ultimate expression of God's *agapē* love: Jesus Christ. God's love was made clear, visible, and observable among us when God sent His only Son to be the propitiation for our sins. Through Him we have complete forgiveness and eternal life.[1] God didn't *have* to do this. After all, we hadn't earned it, and He didn't owe it to us as a reward. Rather, the act of sending His Son as our Savior was purely by grace—selfless, sacrificial, other-centered love. Jesus Himself said, "Greater love has no one than this, that one lay down his life for his friends" (John 15:13). Jesus did exactly that, according to the plan and purpose of God the Father.

The theological reason for loving one another is that other-focused love is of the very essence of God, which He demonstrated clearly by sending Jesus Christ to earth to die for the sins of undeserving sinners (John 3:16).

A reciprocal reason for loving one another (1 Jn. 4:11). To "reciprocate" means to return a favor—if somebody scratches your back, you should scratch theirs; if somebody treats you to a meal, you should treat them back. But in the divine economy, reciprocation for God's loving, gracious actions toward us can't be paid back to God. He doesn't need anything from us, and we couldn't think, feel, say, or do anything that would benefit Him in any way. When it comes to personally responding to God's love shown to us through Christ, God desires not that we "pay it back," but that we "pay it forward."

What a clear picture of the absolute other-centeredness of God's love! He shows unconditional love toward us and, in return, expects us to direct unconditional love toward others. How contrary to typical human nature, driven by a karmic approach to life in which "one good turn deserves another." God's will that we reciprocate His love by loving others isn't karma—it's grace! It topples the whole basis of spiritual manipulation, pagan magic, and religious rituals in which we must do something for God to get something from Him. The reciprocal reason for loving one another turns around the worldly quid-pro-quo approach to the spiritual life and makes God's recipients of love a conduit for His grace.

A practical reason for loving one another (4:12). This isn't the first time John has asserted that "no one has seen God at any time." He affirmed the same thing in his Gospel: "No one has seen God at any time; the only begotten God who is in the bosom of the Father, He has explained Him" (John 1:18). John's point in the Gospel is this: Had Jesus not manifested God to people, God the Father's character would have remained hidden in abstraction. The coming of Christ revealed the invisible things of God, even though the divine nature itself cannot be observed by physical eyes.

But in 1 John 4:12, John adds another way—besides the coming of Christ—that God reveals His character to the world: "If we love one another, God abides in us, and His love is perfected in us." The term translated "perfected" in 4:12 (and later in 4:17) is *teleioō* [5048], which means "complete, bring to an end, finish, accomplish."[2] The love of God is brought to fruition in us and is brought to its intended purpose when we love one another. And this "perfected" love reveals God to the world.

The apostle John was one of those few people who actually got to see, hear, and even touch the incarnate God-man, Jesus (1:1). From the second century onward, nobody alive has directly encountered Jesus like that. We read the accounts of those who had, and we believe in of the mystic—to ascend into the heights of the love of God personally, privately, and profoundly; to be lost, as it were, in an indescribable experience of loving God and being loved by Him. In that kind of vertical pursuit, the horizontal things of this world—even the people of this world—are a distraction from loving God.

The apostle John completely rules out this kind of mystical, personal, private love of God that ignores, neglects, rejects, or hates a brother or sister in Christ (1 Jn. 4:20). Such a person who "hates his brother" while claiming to love God "is a liar." The reason? The brother or sister in Christ right before our eyes should be the first, natural object of our mercy, grace, charity, affection, and unconditional love. God is invisible, intangible, and unreachable. No amount of meditation or mantras will be able to bridge the gap between our physical world and the heights of heaven. If we can't love the ones whom God has placed in front of us, how can we seriously claim to have a genuine love for the invisible God?

Our love for God must be visible in our love for others; otherwise, it is inauthentic. And as we love one another, we reflect God who first loved us.

APPLICATION: 1 JOHN 4:7-21
Loving One Another

We're to love one another—those brothers and sisters in Christ beside whom we worship during our Sunday services, among whom we sit in Sunday school, with whom we minister in the nursery, and whom we pass by silently in the hallways. And that's just the brothers and sisters in our own churches! We're to love them unconditionally, selflessly, and sacrificially.

But how? What's that supposed to look like? Isn't it enough that we drop a few bucks in the offering plate on Sunday morning so the church has enough money to turn on the air conditioning and my brother in Christ doesn't overheat? Or does the Lord Jesus expect something more tangible . . . more real?

To help get a clearer picture of what's involved in genuinely loving our brothers and sisters in Christ, take some time to reflect on some verses that flesh out the concept of loving one another. For each of the six passages below, jot down a few words that summarize what specific *actions* would be expected in light of this kind of love. Then note a specific person (or persons) in your life for whom you can exercise this love. When you've completed the chart, prayerfully consider how you can start living in light of Christ's command to love, by the power of the abiding Spirit.

PASSAGE	ACTION(S)	PERSON(S)
John 15:12-13		
Romans 12:9-13		
Romans 13:8-10		
Galatians 5:13-15		
Ephesians 4:1-3		
Hebrews 10:24-25		

Believers, Overcomers, Witnesses
1 JOHN 5:1-12

NASB

¹Whoever believes that Jesus is the ªChrist is ᵇborn of God, and whoever loves the ᶜFather loves the *child* ᵇborn of Him. ²By this we know that we love the children of God, when we love God and ªobserve His commandments. ³For this is the love of God, that we keep His commandments; and His commandments are not burdensome. ⁴For whatever is

NLT

¹Everyone who believes that Jesus is the Christ* has become a child of God. And everyone who loves the Father loves his children, too. ²We know we love God's children if we love God and obey his commandments. ³Loving God means keeping his commandments, and his commandments are not burdensome. ⁴For every child of God defeats this

[a]born of God overcomes the world; and this is the victory that has overcome the world—our faith. [5]Who is the one who overcomes the world, but he who believes that Jesus is the Son of God? [6]This is the One who came by water and blood, Jesus Christ; not [a]with the water only, but [a]with the water and [a]with the blood. It is the Spirit who testifies, because the Spirit is the truth. [7]For there are three that testify: [8a]the Spirit and the water and the blood; and the three are [b]in agreement. [9]If we receive the testimony of men, the testimony of God is greater; for the testimony of God is this, that He has testified concerning His Son. [10]The one who believes in the Son of God has the testimony in himself; the one who does not believe God has made Him a liar, because he has not believed in the testimony that God has given concerning His Son. [11]And the testimony is this, that God has given us eternal life, and this life is in His Son. [12]He who has the Son has the life; he who does not have the Son of God does not have the life.

5:1 [a]I.e. Messiah [b]Or begotten [c]Lit one who begets 5:2 [a]Lit do 5:4 [a]Or begotten 5:6 [a]Lit in 5:8 [a]A few late mss add ...in heaven, the Father, the Word, and the Holy Spirit, and these three are one. And there are three that testify on earth, the Spirit [b]Lit for the one thing

evil world, and we achieve this victory through our faith. [5]And who can win this battle against the world? Only those who believe that Jesus is the Son of God.

[6]And Jesus Christ was revealed as God's Son by his baptism in water and by shedding his blood on the cross*—not by water only, but by water and blood. And the Spirit, who is truth, confirms it with his testimony. [7]So we have these three witnesses*—[8]the Spirit, the water, and the blood—and all three agree. [9]Since we believe human testimony, surely we can believe the greater testimony that comes from God. And God has testified about his Son. [10]All who believe in the Son of God know in their hearts that this testimony is true. Those who don't believe this are actually calling God a liar because they don't believe what God has testified about his Son.

[11]And this is what God has testified: He has given us eternal life, and this life is in his Son. [12]Whoever has the Son has life; whoever does not have God's Son does not have life.

5:1 Or the Messiah.   5:6 Greek This is he who came by water and blood.   5:7 A few very late manuscripts add in heaven—the Father, the Word, and the Holy Spirit, and these three are one. And we have three witnesses on earth.

Believers are identified by various titles throughout Scripture. We're called Christians, disciples, followers, saints, sheep, salt, light, ambassadors for Christ, members of the body of Christ, royal priests, aliens, strangers, servants of Christ, and the people of God, among other titles. Like a jeweler turning a diamond under a bright light, each designation reveals another facet of our character, role, position, or privilege.

Near the end of his letter, John introduces two more titles for believers, and he also makes us aware in this section of the three witnesses that testify in full agreement regarding God's Son. All of this will prove helpful as we deepen our understanding of what it means to be a part of God's forever family. As we arrive at the last two verses in this section, we come to one of the clearest statements of the gospel found in the entire Word of God.

—5:1-3—

The great Bible teacher of yesteryear Merrill Tenney summed up the purpose of the Gospel of John this way:

> The entire book is an attempt to swing the reader to the side of acceptance, as embodied in the word *believe*. The underlying Greek word, *pisteuo*, is used no less than ninety-eight times in the Gospel and is customarily translated *believe*, though in a few instances it is rendered *trust* or *commit*. Never does it mean a mere assent to a proposition. It usually means acknowledgement of some personal claim, or even a complete personal commitment to some ideal or person. John sought to lead his readers to a settled faith.[4]

Approaching the end of his life of ministry, the apostle John penned the fourth Gospel with an evangelistic purpose: that his readers would believe, commit to, trust in, and rely upon the person and work of Jesus Christ as their sole means of salvation. When that same apostle, about that same time, wrote 1 John, the assumption was that his readers had already embraced Christ with genuine faith. They believed that Jesus is the God-man, the promised Messiah, who died for their sins and rose from the dead. This faith in Jesus as the Christ (5:1) became the epicenter for a blast wave of spiritual blessings that radiated outward.

First, the believer is "born of God" (5:1). To understand this expression, we need to look at the third chapter of John's Gospel, when Jesus told Nicodemus, "Truly, truly, I say to you, unless one is born again he cannot see the kingdom of God" (John 3:3). Being "born again" means to be "born of the Spirit" (John 3:5-6, 8). Peter reflected on Jesus' teaching regarding this spiritual new birth when he wrote, in his first letter, "Blessed be the God and Father of our Lord Jesus Christ, who according to His great mercy has caused us to be born again to a living hope through the resurrection of Jesus Christ from the dead" (1 Pet. 1:3). Peter went on to say, "You have been born again not of seed which is perishable but imperishable, that is, through the living and enduring word of God" (1 Pet. 1:23).

Second, the born-again believer enters into a loving relationship with the Father (1 Jn. 5:1). As those born again by the Holy Spirit through faith in Christ, we are spiritual children of God, adopted into

His forever family. As such, the Spirit within us leads us to love God the Father. In Galatians 4:6, Paul wrote, "Because you are sons, God has sent forth the Spirit of His Son into our hearts, crying, 'Abba! Father!'" The Aramaic word *Abba* is a term of familiar affection for the head of the household. Thus, its use by Paul emphasizes that we have become God's children and that we enjoy an intimate relationship with Him.

Our new relationship as children of God is more than positional; it's also experiential. Not only did God declare us righteous and, as it were, sign the legal documents to call us His children, He also gave us His Spirit to seal our sonship. By virtue of our being in union with Christ and by participating—through adoption—in Christ's relationship of sonship with the Father, we, too, can call God "Abba" and have a personal, family relationship with God through the Holy Spirit (Rom. 8:15).

Third, our loving family relationship with the Father leads to a loving family relationship with fellow children of God (1 Jn. 5:1-2a). John says that whoever loves the Father will also love their spiritual siblings (5:1), the fellow "children of God" (5:2). To John it's inconceivable that one would abide in a loving family relationship with God the Father as an adopted child and despise their brothers and sisters in Christ, especially since God commanded that we love one another.

Fourth, our loving family relationship with God and one another leads us to obey His commands joyfully (5:2b-3). These commands are nothing more or less than the commands upon which the whole Law hangs, as Jesus said,

> "YOU SHALL LOVE THE LORD YOUR GOD WITH ALL YOUR HEART, AND WITH ALL YOUR SOUL, AND WITH ALL YOUR MIND." This is the great and foremost commandment. The second is like it, "YOU SHALL LOVE YOUR NEIGHBOR AS YOURSELF." On these two commandments depend the whole Law and the Prophets. (Matt. 22:37-40)

These two commands go together like two sides of a sheet of paper; without the one, it's impossible to have the other. They are inseparable.

Note that the commands of God are "not burdensome." The Greek word translated as "burdensome" here is *barys* [926]. This term is used when Jesus said of the Pharisees, "They tie up heavy burdens [*barys*] and lay them on men's shoulders, but they themselves are unwilling to move them with so much as a finger" (Matt. 23:4). When motivated by a love enabled by the Spirit, the commands of God are not a burden but a joy. They flow from a heart filled with love for the Father and love for His spiritual children.

—5:4-5—

John begins 5:4 with a connective "for," meaning "because." He explains *why* obedience to God's commands to love Him and love others is not burdensome or irksome: because the man or woman who is born again "overcomes the world" (5:4). The verb translated as "overcomes" is *nikaō* [3528], which can also mean "to conquer." Here John uses it to refer to those who overcome Satan and the world—including its debilitating deceptions and damaging temptations—through the inner work of the Holy Spirit by faith in Christ. He makes this clear in 5:4: "This is the victory that has overcome the world—our faith."

Notice it isn't any good work or personal perseverance that overcomes the world, but it's our faith. Faith in what? In the finished work of Jesus Christ and the power of the Holy Spirit. John makes this abundantly clear, leaving no room for a misunderstanding that we overcome the world by even one ounce of our own exerted strength: "Who is the one who overcomes the world, but he who believes that Jesus is the Son of God?" (5:5).

The new birth—by grace alone through faith alone in Christ alone—removes us from the ranks of the world and places us into God's family. In that new relationship, which comes solely by grace through faith, we have been given the possibility of keeping the commands of God to love. We've been equipped with an inner enablement. God not only gives us the commands, but He also works in us to observe them by the power of the Holy Spirit. No wonder Paul can exclaim, "Who will separate us from the love of Christ? Will tribulation, or distress, or persecution, or famine, or nakedness, or peril, or sword? . . . But in all these things we overwhelmingly conquer through Him who loved us" (Rom. 8:35, 37).

—5:6-12—

We believe in Christ and have been united with Him. We've become children of the same heavenly Father that Jesus Himself called "Abba"! We're empowered by the same Spirit who empowered Christ throughout His earthly ministry. Yet as John has already made clear in this book, there were false teachers in the first century—as there are in the twenty-first century—who believe blasphemous things about the Father, Son, and Holy Spirit. They doubt the holiness of God. They deny the deity of Christ. They scoff at the idea that Jesus' death could pay the penalty for our sins. They call the resurrection of Jesus a myth. And they reduce the Holy Spirit to the best of human nature, an inner voice that inspires all of us.

Knowing that God's children will be facing detractors and deceivers, John turns his attention to Jesus and mentions three proofs that verify Christ's divine role. These are three things John himself witnessed decades earlier. He says that Jesus Christ came "by water and blood" (1 Jn. 5:6). Along with the water and blood, the Spirit Himself testifies, making three things that stand in complete agreement with one another regarding the person and work of Christ—"the Spirit and the water and the blood" (5:7-8).

At this point you may be scratching your head, wondering what he is talking about. Though different people have interpreted "the Spirit and the water and the blood" in various ways, let me suggest what I think are the most likely meanings of John's language here, and why. Let me start with the easy one, because that will actually help us interpret the others. We know that "Spirit" refers to the Holy Spirit. When did the Holy Spirit testify or bear witness regarding Christ?

Actually, the Spirit's testimony concerning Christ began in the Old Testament when He moved the prophets to write about the coming Messiah (see Luke 24:27, 44; 2 Pet. 1:21). But the apostle John had something more direct in mind. He was, after all, an eyewitness of John the Baptist's ministry. In fact, I'm convinced that the apostle John was one of the two disciples of John the Baptist mentioned in John 1:35-37, the other being Andrew: "Again the next day John was standing with two of his disciples, and he looked at Jesus as He walked, and said, 'Behold, the Lamb of God!' The two disciples heard him speak, and they followed Jesus."

As an original disciple of John the Baptist, the apostle John would have likely been present at Jesus' baptism just the day before. In any case, he certainly would have heard John the Baptist's testimony concerning the baptism of Jesus: "I have seen the Spirit descending as a dove out of heaven, and He remained upon Him. I did not recognize Him, but He who sent me to baptize in water said to me, 'He upon whom you see the Spirit descending and remaining upon Him, this is the One who baptizes in the Holy Spirit.' I myself have seen, and have testified that this is the Son of God" (John 1:32-34). Not only did the Spirit alight upon Jesus at His baptism in a visible form, but the Spirit also continued to work astonishing miracles during Jesus' ministry. The apostle John, of course, was present for most of these proofs of Jesus' divine sonship.

So, the apostle John had ample opportunity to witness the testimony of the Spirit. But he also witnessed what he calls the testimony of "the water" (1 Jn. 5:6-8). Here again, I believe, is a reference to the event of Jesus' baptism. But this time, John focuses on a different aspect of that event, which has been recorded for us in the Gospel of Matthew. When the Spirit descended upon Jesus while He was in the water, a voice from heaven declared, "This is My beloved Son, in whom I am well-pleased" (Matt. 3:17). This powerful testimony from heaven—an audible voice from God the Father—would have left a lifelong impact on the apostle John. It's intriguing to recall that the apostle John was also one of the three handpicked disciples to witness the transfiguration of Jesus some time later, during which a voice from a cloud declared, "This is My beloved Son, with whom I am well-pleased; listen to Him!" (Matt. 17:5). John would have associated the heavenly voice—at the water of baptism and in the cloud on the Mount of Transfiguration—as the unimpeachable testimony of God the Father regarding the divine sonship of Jesus.

This then brings us to the testimony of the "blood" (1 Jn. 5:6-8). I think "blood" here clearly points to Jesus' death on the cross, where His blood was "poured out for many for forgiveness of sins" (Matt. 26:28). John was there when Jesus uttered those prophetic words at the Last Supper. He was there, at the cross, when Jesus was crucified (John 19:25-27). And in his Gospel he emphasized the point that when one of the soldiers pierced Jesus' side with a spear, "immediately blood and water came out" (John 19:34-35).

What's significant about John's eyewitness testimony concerning the blood and water pouring from Jesus' side? Remember that at the time of the writing of 1 John, the false teachers known as Docetists had been asserting that Jesus was really just a phantom, that He didn't really have a body; or, if He did have a body of some sort, He didn't really die. Death would have been unbecoming of deity. However, the atoning death of Christ is so central to the whole Christian faith that the apostle John underscored the fact that Jesus did, in fact, die a real, physical death: "And he who has seen has testified, and his testimony is true; and he knows that he is telling the truth, so that you also may believe" (John 19:35).

Even here, John appeals also to the testimony of the Holy Spirit by referring to Spirit-inspired Scripture fulfilled at the cross: "For these things came to pass to fulfill the Scripture, 'Not a bone of Him shall be broken.' And again another Scripture says, 'They shall look on Him whom they pierced'" (John 19:36-37). Thus, the testimony of Jesus Himself through His bloody suffering and death proved that He was the long-awaited Messiah who would die for sins.

THREE WHO BEAR WITNESS IN HEAVEN?

1 JOHN 5:7

In most modern translations of the Bible, 1 John 5:7-8 states, "For there are three that testify: the Spirit and the water and the blood; and the three are in agreement." However, some older translations—most notably the original King James Version of 1611—included an additional clause in verse 7 (shown in italics below) that makes a clear reference to the Trinity: "For there are three that bear record *in heaven, the Father, the Word, and the Holy Ghost: and these three are one. And there are three that bear witness in earth,* the Spirit, and the water, and the blood: and these three agree in one."

Why would modern translations remove a reference to the unity of the Father, the Word, and the Spirit? Were they motivated by anti-Trinitarian heresy? Or just guilty of editorial incompetence? Were they impious translators? Or did they just make an innocent mistake nobody has bothered to fix for centuries?

The truth is, these additional words, called by scholars the *Comma Johanneum* (Latin for "the Johannine comma"), is left out of modern translations because, after the King James Version was translated, Christians discovered clear and convincing evidence that those words had been added to John's original letter. They were not penned by the apostle John himself. New Testament scholar Bruce Metzger notes, "That these words are spurious and have no right to stand in the New Testament is certain."[5] A number of facts point to this conclusion.

First, out of hundreds of Greek manuscripts available to us for discovering the original text of 1 John, only eight manuscripts contain the *Comma Johanneum*. Of these eight manuscripts, two are from the sixteenth century, and one is from the eighteenth century. In all of the remaining five texts, the *Comma Johanneum* was added later to manuscripts that originally didn't contain the verse! In short, the earliest hand-copied manuscript in which the verse appears as the originally written text by the copyist comes from the time of the Reformation![6]

Second, besides lacking reliable Greek manuscript support, the *Comma Johanneum* also lacks historical support. It appears in none of the ancient translations of the Greek Bible such as the Syriac, Coptic, Armenian, Ethiopic, Arabic, Slavonic, and earliest Latin translations.[7] It first appears in Latin manuscripts in later editions of the Roman Catholic Church's Vulgate (a Latin translation of the Bible) around the sixth century. Furthermore, the first person in history to clearly show knowledge of the passage was a Spanish heretic in the fourth century. Some Latin-speaking church Fathers began referring to the phrase in the fifth century, but none of the Greek Fathers seem to have been aware of its existence.[8]

With such skimpy evidence for its authenticity, how did these words get into the Roman Catholic Vulgate by the Middle Ages and ultimately into the King James Version after the Reformation? Metzger explains that the *Comma Johanneum* "arose when the original passage was understood to symbolize the Trinity . . . , an interpretation that may have been written first as a marginal note that afterwards found its way into the text."[9]

Around the time of the Reformation, the Roman Catholic scholar Erasmus originally left out the *Comma Johanneum* when he published his first edition of the Greek New Testament in 1516. Why did he exclude this clause? Because he couldn't find the words in any of the Greek manuscripts available to him when he began to typeset and print the Greek Bible. However, because the Roman Catholic Church's official translation, the Vulgate, contained the additional words, Church leaders pressured Erasmus to add the *Comma Johanneum*. He did so, with strong reservations, in his 1521 edition.[10] Once the words were added, later editors of the Greek New Testament based on Erasmus's work were reluctant to remove the words for fear that they might be the Word of God. Thus, the translators of the King James Version of 1611 included the *Comma Johanneum* in their translation.

Modern translations, however, have corrected the error of the Roman Catholic Church's Latin Vulgate and the politically motivated Greek New Testament of Erasmus. They have restored the shorter reading of 1 John 5:7-8 originally penned by the apostle John.

Not only this, but when Jesus died, the surrounding region also experienced wondrous signs that this was no mere mortal who succumbed to death. A deep darkness fell over the land, a great earthquake shook the region, and the veil of the temple was torn (Matt. 27:45, 51). So alarming were the signs accompanying Christ's death that they drove a centurion to declare, "Truly this man was the Son of God!" (Mark 15:39).

This is what John means by the threefold testimony of "the Spirit and the water and the blood" (1 Jn. 5:6-8). Note that these pieces of evidence all point to the fact that Jesus was no mere mortal man; nor was He merely some ghostly heavenly being. He was the God-man whose identity as the long-anticipated Messiah was verified from the beginning to the end of His life by numerous miraculous testimonies of the Father, Son, and Holy Spirit. This testimony of God concerning the Son is greater than any testimony of men (5:9). To reject God's own witness concerning the identity and work of His Son is to call God a liar (5:10). What could such a person expect from God but eternal punishment?

However, the one who has believed the testimony concerning the

Son has fully embraced the truth that "God has given [past tense] us eternal life, and this life is in His Son" (5:11). Let me reemphasize the past-tense nature of this gift. Eternal life isn't something we're growing into. It's not a prize we win or a reward for hard work. It isn't the earned result of an achievement. It's something that has been given by grace alone through faith alone in Christ alone, just as Paul says in Ephesians 2:8-9, "For by grace you have been saved [past tense] through faith; and that not of yourselves, it is the gift of God; not as a result of works, so that no one may boast."

In 1 John 5:12, John drives this fundamental truth deeper with a present tense verb: "He who has the Son has [present tense] the life; he who does not have the Son of God does not have the life." John doesn't say those who have the Son simply have access to eternal life . . . or that they have hope of eternal life. They have, as a present reality, eternal life. This life can never be taken away or lost, or John couldn't call it "eternal." John couldn't be clearer: If you have the Son—trusting in Him alone for salvation—you have life.

APPLICATION: 1 JOHN 5:1-12
Being True to the Titles

In these twelve verses, the apostle John covers some important ground. Our identity as Christians has been founded firmly on solid ground and has been driven deeply with three stakes. We are *believers born of God* (5:1-3). We are *overcomers through Christ* (5:4-5). And we are *witnesses bearing the testimony of the Spirit* (5:6-12). Let's consider our personal responses to each of these pivotal truths.

We're believers born of God. Because we are born of God through faith in Christ, we are all children of one heavenly Father. But if you look at the way some believers treat each other in their churches, you'd think they were part of a bad reality TV show with plotting, backbiting, conspiring, and outright conflict! If we live up to the title "child of God," we'll treat our brothers and sisters in Christ with self-sacrificial love and respect.

We're overcomers through Christ. Brothers and sisters in Christ, when you realize your position as overcomers and take hold of the Spirit's power to overcome as children of God, it changes everything. You no longer need to live in constant defeat by temptations or failures. You no longer run scared when facing apparently insurmountable odds and extreme crises. You no longer feel intimidated by persecutors or overwhelmed by adversaries. Why? Because, as John wrote earlier, "You are from God, little children, and have overcome them; because greater is He who is in you than he who is in the world" (4:4).

We're witnesses bearing the testimony of the Spirit. John says that the one who believes in the Son of God "has the testimony in himself"—the testimony of the Spirit and the water and the blood (5:10). What are we to do with this testimony? Jesus answers this question for us directly: "You are the light of the world. A city set on a hill cannot be hidden; nor does anyone light a lamp and put it under a basket, but on the lampstand, and it gives light to all who are in the house. Let your light shine before men in such a way that they may see your good works, and glorify your Father who is in heaven" (Matt. 5:14-16). As bearers of the testimony, *testify!* Bear witness with your words and your works! Don't hold back. Let your light shine!

Absolute Assurance
1 JOHN 5:13-21

NASB

[13] These things I have written to you who believe in the name of the Son of God, so that you may know that you have eternal life. [14] This is the confidence which we have [a]before Him, that, if we ask anything according to His will, He hears us. [15] And if we know that He hears us *in* whatever we ask, we know that we have the requests which we have asked from Him.

[16] If anyone sees his brother [a]committing a sin not *leading* to death, he shall ask and [b]*God* will for him give life to those who commit sin not *leading* to death. There is a sin *leading* to death; I do not say that he should make request for this. [17] All unrighteousness is sin, and there is a sin not *leading* to death.

[18] We know that no one who is

NLT

[13] I have written this to you who believe in the name of the Son of God, so that you may know you have eternal life. [14] And we are confident that he hears us whenever we ask for anything that pleases him. [15] And since we know he hears us when we make our requests, we also know that he will give us what we ask for.

[16] If you see a fellow believer* sinning in a way that does not lead to death, you should pray, and God will give that person life. But there is a sin that leads to death, and I am not saying you should pray for those who commit it. [17] All wicked actions are sin, but not every sin leads to death.

[18] We know that God's children do not make a practice of sinning, for God's Son holds them securely,

ᵃborn of God sins; but He who was ᵃborn of God keeps him, and the evil one does not touch him. ¹⁹We know that we are of God, and that the whole world lies in *the power of* the evil one. ²⁰And we know that the Son of God has come, and has given us understanding so that we may know Him who is true; and we are in Him who is true, in His Son Jesus Christ. This is the true God and eternal life. ²¹Little children, guard yourselves from idols.

5:14 ᵃLit *toward* **5:16** ᵃLit *sinning* ᵇOr *God will give him life,* that is, *to those who...* **5:18** ᵃOr *begotten*

and the evil one cannot touch them. ¹⁹We know that we are children of God and that the world around us is under the control of the evil one. ²⁰And we know that the Son of God has come, and he has given us understanding so that we can know the true God.* And now we live in fellowship with the true God because we live in fellowship with his Son, Jesus Christ. He is the only true God, and he is eternal life. ²¹Dear children, keep away from anything that might take God's place in your hearts.*

5:16 Greek *a brother.* **5:20** Greek *the one who is true.* **5:21** Greek *keep yourselves from idols.*

I know two young men who grew up in the Northwest. Whenever they reach critical moments in their lives, they read letters written by their mother—letters in her familiar handwriting, sent to encourage and exhort her boys as they grow from childhood to manhood. Letters written for birthdays, for Christmas, for graduation from high school. To these boys, those letters from Mom are expressions of her endearing and enduring love. They are frameable.

Why do these sons hold these letters from Mom so dear? Because their mother died of cancer years earlier, when they were very young. The disease was taking its toll on her day after day, but instead of lying there wasting away, she spent her time writing letters to her two boys to be delivered to them at specific times in their lives. And on these occasions, the boys' father would deliver the letters. They would hear from their mother in her own words, words of endearing and enduring love.

Similarly, the apostle John has left all of God's spiritual children a frameable letter—a letter of endearing and enduring love. A letter of encouragement and exhortation. A letter of warning and instruction. A letter of absolute assurance. This letter, 1 John, has been preserved for us through the centuries. It's a simple, straightforward, but profound and practical, letter of love.

—5:13—

John ended the previous section with great words of assurance: "God has given us eternal life, and this life is in His Son. He who has the

129

Son has the life" (1 Jn. 5:11-12). In 5:13, he begins wrapping up his letter with another pointed statement of assurance that is definitely worth remembering. John presents in clear terms the purpose of writing this endearing and enduring letter to his readers. He wrote "these things"— everything in the book of 1 John—so that they would know they have eternal life (5:13). This assurance of the present possession of eternal life is limited, though, to those "who believe in the name of the Son of God." Those who have placed their faith in Christ's person and work alone can *know* that they have eternal life. Assurance of salvation is not only possible; it's part of the gift of salvation by grace alone through faith alone in Christ alone.

The verb translated "know" (*oida* [1492]) is found in 1 John a total of fifteen times. Almost half of these occurrences are concentrated in this final section. It's evident that as John wraps up this letter, he wants to impart stable knowledge to his readers to give them a basis for confident assurance. What are the things he wants them to *know*? (Emphasis below is mine.)

"These things I have written . . . that you may *know* that you have eternal life." (5:13)

"If we *know* that He hears us in whatever we ask, we *know* that we have the requests which we have asked from Him." (5:15)

"We *know* that no one who is born of God sins." (5:18)

"We *know* that we are of God." (5:19)

"We *know* that the Son of God has come, and has given us understanding so that we may *know* Him who is true." (5:20)

Note that many of these things touch on themes John has already visited—and revisited—previously in his letter. But John wants to leave his readers with a powerful reminder of assurance so we can have a growing sense of confidence in matters concerning our relationship with Christ. We maintain this confidence through constant reminders. As we walk through 5:14-21, let's take a closer look at the things—in addition to eternal life—that John wants us to know.

—5:14-17—

John wants us to know that we can receive what we ask of God through prayer. We need to be careful here because John frames this statement in a certain theological and biblical context. Prayer is not wishful thinking, hoping against hope, dreaming big, or desiring to fulfill the longing of the flesh. God's not a heavenly genie who operates at our beck and call, and prayer isn't the Christian method of rubbing the lamp to get God's attention. We must never fall into the unspiritual and dangerous trap of regarding prayer as a convenient method for imposing our will on God or bending His will to our wants. Rather, prayer is a means of submitting our will to His. So, every true prayer is a variation of the theme, "Not my will, but Yours be done" (see Luke 22:42).

In all cases, God holds the outcome of the prayer in His hands and answers it according to His plan and purpose—always for His glory and our good. Remember Hebrews 4:16: "Let us draw near with confidence to the throne of grace." We don't come groveling, pleading, begging, or bargaining. Entering His presence boldly, but with proper humility, we acknowledge that He has the power to give us what we ask . . . but also the right to answer however He pleases. And we know that however He answers—"Yes," "No," "Wait," or "Here's something better"—He's going to work everything out for our good, not for our harm (Rom. 8:28).

So, we approach Him with confidence according to His will. Not our will, *His will*. Of course, this means we need to be saturated by His Word in order to know His will. I'm convinced that this is why mature believers who have experienced a lifetime of learning and submitting to God's will can be such powerful prayer warriors. They know what to ask for. They know how to ask for it. They know—with the confidence that comes from knowing God's will—that He hears them (1 Jn. 5:15). And if He hears them, they know they will receive what they ask from Him.

Because we can't always know what God's will might be or what answer He has in store for us in His own time, we need to be careful about expecting God to do things just because we ask Him. God never promised to make us rich. Or to move in our boss's heart to give us a promotion. Or to heal us of our bodily infirmities. Or to take away this or that particular trial or tribulation. Because God has not explicitly revealed His will in these matters, we would overstep our bounds to "claim" them as answered according to our own will. Never promise somebody else that their prayers or your prayers will bring about something God has not specifically promised.

John underscores this fact in 5:16-17, in which he refers to two kinds of sins—"a sin not leading to death" and "a sin leading to death." For the former kind of sin, prayer on a person's behalf is completely appropriate and will result in God's healing and forgiveness. For the second kind of sin, prayer on a person's behalf will be ineffectual. This much is clear from the text: For some things, prayer is according to God's will, but for other things, it's not.

But what, exactly, does John mean by "a sin leading to death" and "a sin not leading to death"? To what sin, specifically, is he referring? Is it a single sin? Or a category of sins? And what kind of "death" is this? Physical death? Spiritual death?

Having racked my brain for years over these two verses, I have to commend Kenneth Wuest for his honesty when faced with this puzzling passage: "The present writer confesses his utter inability to understand this verse . . . and he will not attempt to offer even a suggestion as to its possible interpretation."[11] I'm tempted to follow in that great man's footsteps and do the same. However, even though I may not be able to completely untie this knot of a passage, let me offer a few comments that at least might help loosen it a bit.

First, we need to determine whether John was referring to a specific sin . . . or to a type of sin . . . or to a certain duration of sin. If this is a specific sin, it could be a reference to what Jesus calls the "blasphemy against the Holy Spirit" (see Mark 3:29).[12] On the seriousness of the blasphemy against the Holy Spirit, William Hendriksen writes, "When a man has become hardened, so that he has made up his mind not to pay any attention to the promptings of the Spirit, not even to listen to his pleading and warning voice, he has placed himself on the road that leads to perdition. He has sinned the sin 'unto death.'"[13] If this is the kind of sin "unto death" John meant in 1 John 5:16-17, then the kind of "death" John meant was eternal damnation—the death of the unsaved.[14]

However, it is equally plausible that John was referring not to a specific kind or quality of sin, but to a situation in which a person's persistent sin ultimately results in their being punished by *physical* death as judgment from the Lord.[15] We see examples of this in the New Testament, as in the cases of Ananias and Sapphira (Acts 5:1-11) and those in Corinth who were judged with physical death because of their sin against the corporate body of Christ in mistreating the Lord's Supper (1 Cor. 11:27-30). James may also allude to this kind of scenario in James 5:14-16:

> Is anyone among you sick? Then he must call for the elders of the church and they are to pray over him, anointing him with

oil in the name of the Lord; and the prayer offered in faith will restore the one who is sick, and the Lord will raise him up, and if he has committed sins, they will be forgiven him. Therefore, confess your sins to one another, and pray for one another so that you may be healed.

If John had in mind a similar situation in 1 John 5:16-17, in which a person presumed to be a believer is not just sick but is actually judged with physical death for their sin, then John is simply saying that after a person has died, there is no place for praying for that person. This would call into question the Roman Catholic doctrine of prayers on behalf of the dead or any sort of opportunity for repentance or forgiveness after death.[16] A person may be prayed for all the way up to their death, but "it is appointed for men to die once and after this comes judgment" (Heb. 9:27).

This discussion has only scratched the surface. I agree with commentators who suggest the key to unlocking this riddle was likely lost in the first century with John and his original readers, who may have had a clearer understanding of what John was writing about. However, let's not lose sight of the big picture: Praying according to God's revealed will is effective. We can have absolute confidence that He hears us.

—5:18-19—

John returns to his assertion that those who are truly born again do not live lives of perpetual sinfulness (1 Jn. 5:18). I understand the present tense of the verb "to sin" as a reference to continuous action, emphasizing the person's lifestyle. It doesn't mean that we never slip into acts of sin (see 1:8-10). It means that we don't permanently persist in sin. Thus, John is simply reiterating the teaching from 3:9: "No one who is born of God practices sin."

As harsh as it may sound, the implication of John's teaching here is that we can know with a fair amount of assurance that if a person's lifestyle—start to finish, dawn to dusk, day in and day out, month after month—is characterized by stubborn wickedness, that person is not truly born again. Habitual, unrepentant sin and the new birth are incompatible.

John explains why a truly saved person cannot continuously sin: because "He who was born of God keeps him, and the evil one does not touch him" (5:18). Those who are "of God" are freed from the domain of death, the devil, and the darkness of the world, which "lies in the power of the evil one" (5:19). If a person is truly born of God, Satan has no power over them. Jesus—"He who was born of God"—is ultimately able to keep the saved child of God out of the grip of the devil. How? As John has said before, "Greater is He who is in you than he who is in the world" (4:4).

—5:20-21—

The last thing John says "we know" is that the Son of God has come, has given us a saving knowledge of God, and has united us to Him by the Spirit, so that we are "in Him who is true" (5:20). This line sums up so much of what John has been teaching throughout the letter—our union with God through an intimate knowledge of Him, and Jesus' true identity as the God-man who has come to earth as our Savior. John then says, "This [referring to the Son Jesus Christ] is the true God and eternal life" (5:20).

Anything else we might be tempted to rely upon for our salvation is an idol. It may be a different "Jesus" other than the God-man. It may be a different "gospel" other than the atoning death and resurrection of Christ. It may be a different means of salvation other than by grace alone through faith alone in Christ alone. Anything we might conjure up ourselves that replaces "the true God and eternal life" is an idol.

Thus, John leaves his readers with this final warning: "Little children, guard yourselves from idols" (5:21). Idols can be anything in our hearts, minds, or lives that we elevate above the living God:

- any object of devotion that distracts us from Christ
- any sin that separates us from reconciliation and intimacy with Him
- any good work that we perform to try to gain His favor, which is received only by grace through faith
- any person we adore more than Him
- any truth claim we prefer to God's inspired Word

For those of us who have absolute assurance of our salvation, Christ and Christ alone should be the object of our priorities, passions, and pursuits. All other things must take second place to an intimate, obedient, and loving communion with Him. Such fellowship with the Father, through the Son and by the Holy Spirit, will result in a confident life.

APPLICATION: 1 JOHN 5:13-21

Living Right in a Wrong World

Before we turn the page on 1 John, let's pause, step back, and take one last look at the book as a whole to reflect on the journey we've taken. In so doing, we'll glean some final practical applications. Remember that John wrote this letter to remind his readers that Spirit-enabled fellowship with the Father and Son produces a joyful life (1:1-10), a clean life (2:1-17), a discerning life (2:18–4:6), and a confident life (4:7–5:21). Let's retrace the steps of that outline and reflect on its implications for living right in a wrong world.

First, *in an angry, dark world, the joyful Christian is a bright light.* If you let the joy of the Lord shine through your life, and people learn that the source of this joy is your relationship with Christ, that does something to people—to believers and to unbelievers. Your joy will bring encouragement to believers who may have lost their own joy. And even if unbelievers can't yet make heads or tails of your faith, many will be drawn to your joy. At first, you may just arouse curiosity in them. But then, many of them will be drawn to the light. Such joy can be infectious. It will lead others to escape the darkness.

Second, *in a lawless society, the clean Christian is a contagious witness.* Back in my days in the Corps, my fellow Marines couldn't figure out why I refused to get drunk with them. Many couldn't understand why I held my marriage vows so sacred when I was thousands of miles from home and nobody would know if I had been unfaithful. Those who were under the influence of the "lust of the flesh" and the "lust of the eyes" couldn't relate. So they ridiculed me, calling me "Friar," "Deacon," and "Preacher." Then they'd get themselves neck-deep in trouble from drinking or they'd catch a dreadful disease . . . and who'd they come to for help? Not their fellow inebriates or philanderers. They'd come to the "friar" who stayed clean in a dirty world. Without flaunting your purity, when you stand your ground on doing what's right in a wrong world, people may find it strange at first; but when they begin to reap the rotten fruit of their sin, you'll be the lifeguard ready to pull them to recovery and turn them to Christ.

Third, *in a deceptive culture, the discerning Christian is a convicting presence.* When you size things up and draw clear lines between right and wrong, righteous and wicked, true and false, your presence will be convicting. Our world is declining into a hazy twilight of relativism—a drab gray cultural "morality" that refuses to judge things as black or white. In this misty background, our stand on biblical standards will stick out. People will take notice. Some will be angry or offended. But the Spirit of truth can use your discerning presence to provoke the consciences of others to see their need for forgiveness and reconciliation with the holy God.

Finally, *in a confused age, the confident Christian is a strong magnet.* In a world flooded with anxiety, uncertainty, and fear, the calm assurance of a Christian who rests on the promises of God will be attractive. People will shake their heads at your confidence in things unseen. They'll marvel that you aren't swept away with every piece of bad news. And they'll want to know what you have that they don't. Some will think you're crazy. You can't help that. But others will begin to see you as the sanest person they know.

Our intimate, personal relationship with God through Jesus Christ by the power of the Spirit gives us joy, holiness, discernment, and assurance. When we display these virtues to outsiders, some will ponder anew what the Lord Jesus might be able to do for them. Of course, not all those who see our light of joy, purity, truth, and confidence will respond positively. Some will pit themselves against us and everything we stand for. But in the end, we'll be able to stand before our Lord and Savior in confidence, knowing that we overcame the world and maintained our walk in the light.

Balancing Love and Truth
2 JOHN 1:1-13

NASB

[1] The elder to the chosen lady and her children, whom I love in truth; and not only I, but also all who know the truth, [2] for the sake of the truth which abides in us and will be with us forever: [3] Grace, mercy *and* peace will be with us, from God the Father and from Jesus Christ, the Son of the Father, in truth and love.

[4] I was very glad to find *some* of your children walking in truth, just as we have received commandment *to do* from the Father. [5] Now I ask you, lady, not as though *I were* writing to you a new commandment, but the one which we have had from the beginning, that we love one another. [6] And this is love, that we walk according to His commandments. This is the commandment, just as you have heard from the beginning, that you should walk in it.

[7] For many deceivers have gone out into the world, those who do not acknowledge Jesus Christ *as* coming in the flesh. This is the deceiver and the antichrist. [8] Watch yourselves, that you do not lose what we have accomplished, but that you may receive a full reward. [9a] Anyone who [b]goes too far and does not abide in the teaching of Christ, does not have God; the one who abides in the teaching, he has both the Father and the Son. [10] If anyone comes to you and does not bring this teaching, do not receive him into *your* house, and do not give him a greeting; [11] for the one who gives him a greeting participates in his evil deeds.

[12] Though I have many things to

NLT

[1] This letter is from John, the elder.*

I am writing to the chosen lady and to her children,* whom I love in the truth—as does everyone else who knows the truth—[2] because the truth lives in us and will be with us forever.

[3] Grace, mercy, and peace, which come from God the Father and from Jesus Christ—the Son of the Father—will continue to be with us who live in truth and love.

[4] How happy I was to meet some of your children and find them living according to the truth, just as the Father commanded.

[5] I am writing to remind you, dear friends,* that we should love one another. This is not a new commandment, but one we have had from the beginning. [6] Love means doing what God has commanded us, and he has commanded us to love one another, just as you heard from the beginning.

[7] I say this because many deceivers have gone out into the world. They deny that Jesus Christ came* in a real body. Such a person is a deceiver and an antichrist. [8] Watch out that you do not lose what we* have worked so hard to achieve. Be diligent so that you receive your full reward. [9] Anyone who wanders away from this teaching has no relationship with God. But anyone who remains in the teaching of Christ has a relationship with both the Father and the Son.

[10] If anyone comes to your meeting and does not teach the truth about Christ, don't invite that person into your home or give any kind of encouragement. [11] Anyone who encourages such people becomes a partner in their evil work.

[12] I have much more to say to you,

137

NASB

write to you, I do not want to *do so* with paper and ink; but I hope to come to you and speak face to face, so that [a]your joy may be made full.

[13]The children of your chosen sister greet you.

1:9 [a]Lit *Everyone* [b]Lit *goes on ahead* 1:12 [a]One early ms reads *our*

NLT

but I don't want to do it with paper and ink. For I hope to visit you soon and talk with you face to face. Then our joy will be complete.

[13]Greetings from the children of your sister,* chosen by God.

1a Greek *From the elder.* 1b Or *the church God has chosen and its members.* 5 Greek *I urge you, lady.* 7 Or *will come.* 8 Some manuscripts read *you.* 13 Or *from the members of your sister church.*

From its shallow headwaters on Lake Itasca in northern Minnesota, the Mississippi River meanders southward to the Gulf of Mexico, spawning and sustaining life along its nearly 2,400-mile journey. To many, the river is a gentle giant, an untiring benefactor of good gifts. The mighty Mississippi is a bountiful, self-replenishing storehouse of nutrients for farmland, a habitat for wildlife, and a busy highway for barges. However, if it escapes its well-defined boundaries, that gentle giant becomes an unwieldy monster.

More than forty dams and about sixteen hundred miles of levees attempt to control the mighty tide, but there are frightening times when Old Man River puffs up his chest and pushes over these meager defenses. Disastrous floods turn prime riverside property into lakes, whole towns are erased from the map, and levees in multiple states are wiped out. Without its boundaries, the river brings destruction, not blessing.

In many ways, love is like the Mississippi River. Love flows with life-giving power, but without boundaries, it can do great harm. This may sound strange at first, but it's true: In the name of loving sinners, we can go too far, to the point that we tolerate, accept, justify, and—in recent years—even applaud sin. This kind of love calmly sets others adrift in dangerous waters rather than moving them from death to life.

The little letter of 2 John shows us how to keep love within safe boundaries by building into our lives two solid riverbanks—truth and discernment.

KEY TERMS IN 2 JOHN 1:1-13

alētheia (ἀλήθεια) [225] "truth," "reality," "faithfulness"
This term is based on the ancient Greek concept of presenting things as
they really are, not hidden or falsified.[1] Whereas philosophers used the
word to denote the true nature of something as opposed to its mere appearance, John employs the term to exalt Jesus Christ, His teachings, and
His way of life as that which should serve as the standard of reality, righteousness, and faithfulness (John 1:17; 3:21; 2 Jn. 1:2, 4).

teknon (τέκνον) [5043] "child," literally or figuratively
The term *teknon*, meaning "child," can refer literally to those who have
not yet reached adolescence developmentally (Matt. 2:18). However, it is
used frequently in the New Testament for "a spiritual child in relation to
master, apostle, or teacher," as in 1 Timothy 1:2.[2] The apostle John most
often uses the term to refer to members of the church who belong to God's
family and whom John sees as his spiritual descendants (John 1:12; 11:52;
1 Jn. 3:1, 2, 10; 5:2; 3 Jn. 1:4). In 2 John, the apostle addresses not only the
"chosen lady" but also her "children," which may refer to members of her
literal family or to those in her church family, or both.

didachē (διδαχή) [1322] "teaching," "body of teaching,"
   "doctrine"
The term *didachē*, used three times in 2 John, refers in this context to
the right teaching or doctrine concerning Jesus Christ. In this case, it is
shorthand for the person and work of Christ as the God-man who came in
the flesh, died, and rose again; it may also refer to the lifestyle expected
of believers that Jesus taught. It stands in contrast to the teachings of the
deceivers and antichrists mentioned in 1:7. Believers are to "abide in the
teaching of Christ," and those who do not abide in the teaching are to be
rejected (1:9-10).

—1:1-3—

In the introduction, we already showed that the "elder" is the apostle
John's reference to himself. It's quite clear by the personal tone of
the letter as a whole that the recipient knew the author personally
and would have identified him immediately. So why call himself the
"elder"? Why not "the apostle"? Or simply "John"?

By using the title "elder," John actually lent more intimacy and
warmth to his letter. It would be similar to a modern-day minister
writing a note to their congregation while away on a mission trip and
signing the personal letter simply with "Your pastor." John wasn't

giving himself a demotion, as if he had resigned from his position as apostle. Even the apostle Peter referred to himself as a "fellow elder" of the church leaders he addressed in one of his letters
(1 Pet. 5:1).

The recipients of the letter are "the chosen lady and her children"
(2 Jn. 1:1). As I mentioned in the introduction above, I take the position that the "chosen lady" is a literal individual, not a figurative
personification of the church as a whole. If this is the case, then the
reference to her "children" (Greek *teknon*) could be addressing literal
children or even spiritual children for whom she was responsible.
Was the chosen lady a widow with a large family? A single woman
devoted to caring for orphans? A diligent worker in the church who la-
bored at ministering to younger members of the body—her "spiritual
children"? We don't know the details. Whatever the case, it remains
true that much of what John writes is intended for a larger group ("her
children"), even though the letter draws attention to this individual
("the chosen lady").

Some commentators have understood the Greek word translated
"chosen" (*eklektos* [1588]) as a proper name, thus "Lady Electa."[3] Likewise, the word translated "lady" (*kyria* [2959]) could be a proper name.
In fact, the Aramaic equivalent of "Kyria" is "Martha," the name of a
well-known figure in the New Testament (see John 11:1).[4] Could it be
that John was writing a letter to the same Martha, the sister of Mary
and Lazarus, mentioned in the book of John? Could the "chosen sister"
mentioned in 2 John 1:13 be a reference to Martha's sister, Mary (see
Luke 10:38-42)? As intriguing as these speculations are, they are just
that. We have no way of knowing who the "elect lady" was. Nor does it
matter for our understanding the message of this letter.

John's love for the chosen lady and her children is grounded "in
truth." And he's not alone—all who know the truth have a love for
them (2 Jn. 1:1). Yet John is writing "for the sake of the truth which
abides in us and will be with us forever" (1:2). Notice that in 1:3, John
inseparably links "truth and love" to the grace, mercy, and peace that
come from God the Father and God the Son. Firm conviction in a saving
knowledge of the truth should always be accompanied by love, just as
unconditional love for others should be extended within the bounds of
doctrinal truth. How these two should be kept in balance requires discernment. Commentator John R. W. Stott puts it well: "Our love grows
soft if it is not strengthened by truth, and our truth grows hard if it is
not softened by love."[5]

—1:4-6—

It's always encouraging when you see children walking in the faith in which they were raised. I've always appreciated hearing the good news about someone's son, daughter, or grandchild I hadn't heard about for years—that he or she has maintained a Christian walk, or is serving as a camp counselor, or is involved in church ministry or missions, or is passing the faith on to their own children. It doesn't always work that way, and there's no guarantee that all of our children will faithfully walk in the truth.

The apostle John puts it a little more realistically. He says to the chosen lady that "some" of her children were walking in the truth. The way the Greek reads, the "some" who were faithful to their spiritual roots could refer to a majority or to a minority. The fact that John is overjoyed at what he had learned, though, suggests that the faithfulness of the lady's children was the rule rather than the exception. Still, not all of them were faithful.

This highlights an important principle of spiritual nurturing and discipleship. Both our physical families and our spiritual families will have members who deviate from the teaching of parents or mentors. I've experienced this firsthand and have seen it in countless families throughout my ministry. It breaks our hearts when it happens. It drives us to prayer in the hopes that those children will one day return. However, when some go astray, we shouldn't lose sight of those who remain on the "truth walk." John didn't dwell on those who had taken a spiritual detour but on those who had received the commandment to walk in the truth (1:4).

What does this "walking in truth" look like? To define this, John refers to Christ's original command that we "love one another" (1:5; see John 13:34). This isn't a new command, but one that had characterized the Christian life from the beginning. Loving one another and walking in truth were not meant to be an either-or prospect. If we love someone unconditionally, but they are distracting us from the truth, then we may need to infuse more truth into the relationship. John goes on to say, "This is love, that we walk according to His commandments" (2 Jn. 1:6).

It doesn't have to be one or the other—either standing strong in the truth or showing love toward others. In actuality, the test of true love is whether it leads us closer to Christ. It never compromises Christ's standards for the sake of a loosely defined unity. It never consents to sin in the name of grace and tolerance. This point bears repeating: Unconditional love must be balanced by discerning truth.

A FIRST-CENTURY HANDBOOK ON DISCERNMENT

2 JOHN 1:7-11
In the latter half of the first century, the problem of wandering false prophets leeching off of loving communities of Christians became a widespread threat. In response, the church of Antioch had to establish some rules for smaller, remote churches with less experienced leadership to be able to discern between true and false prophets. The first-century church ministry manual known as *The Didache* (or "The Teaching") gives us a glimpse of these precautions established for the churches' protection:

> Every apostle coming to you, let him be welcomed as the Lord. He will not stay more than one day and, if it is necessary, another. But if he stays three days he is a false prophet. When going out, the apostle is to receive nothing except bread until his lodging is located. And if he asks for money, he is a false prophet. . . . But not everyone who speaks in the Spirit is a prophet, only if he has the manner of the Lord. Therefore, from his manner you shall distinguish between the false prophet and the prophet. . . . But any prophet teaching the truth, if he does not do what he teaches, he is a false prophet.
>
> But everyone who comes in the name of the Lord, let him be welcomed. And then, having tested him you will know him. . . . And if he desires to stay with you, being an artisan, let him work and let him earn his keep. And if he has no craft, take this into consideration according to your understanding how he shall live among you as a Christian without being idle. And if he does not want to act in this way, he is a Christmonger. Beware of such as these.[6]

—1:7-11—

Love is like a hinge on which the door of generous hospitality turns. But doors also have locks and peepholes . . . and some even have alarms. So it is with authentic Christian love. Think about your own home. An open-door policy of hospitality toward friends and neighbors doesn't mean you leave the front door unlocked at night. Nor does a generally welcoming attitude toward strangers mean you'll fling open the door to a home invader bent on harming your family. True love never opens the door to a predator. This is the thrust of John's instruction in 1:7-11.

If the "chosen lady" was prone to err on the side of openhearted hospitality in showing love to all who passed her way, the potential was great for allowing dangerous spiritual pathogens to get through her wide filter. Cautiousness was especially necessary when poison-ous heretics were on the prowl, eager to infect well-meaning but un-suspecting believers wherever they could. John knew for a fact—both by experience and by word of mouth—that "many deceivers have gone out into the world" (1:7). They were guilty of denying the Incarnation. Jesus Christ, the true "Son of the Father" (1:3), had come in the flesh (1:7). This is an essential foundation of Christian faith. Though the false teachers may have talked about "Jesus Christ" in order to get their feet in the door, in reality they were deceivers—in fact, anti-christs (1:7).

Most likely, John had in mind a heretical movement that was still in its incubation stages in the first century but would break out in full infection by the second century. This heresy, often called Gnosticism, based its teachings on the Greek dualistic notion that spirit was good and matter was evil. The Gnostics believed that Christ could not have actually come in the flesh, otherwise He would have been tainted with evil. Instead, they argued that Christ only appeared to take on human form. (For more information, see "The First Heretics' Fleshless Christ," page 25.)

In light of the presence of deceivers in the world, the practice of hospitality could potentially put the lady and her family at spiritual risk. This is why John urges his readers—this time both the lady and her children—to "watch [them]selves" (1:8). The consequences for being led astray into wrong teaching and wrong practice would be dire: not a loss of genuine salvation, which can never be forfeited (see 1 Jn. 5:11-13), but a loss of "full reward." This is probably a reference to what many call "the judgment seat of Christ," when each true child of God will "give an account of himself to God" (Rom. 14:12).

When we stand before our Savior and Lord, Christ will not judge be-lievers to determine innocence or guilt—heaven or hell. That judgment of "not guilty" was already rendered when God declared us righteous at our conversion based on the saving death of Christ (2 Cor. 5:21). Because of the finished work of Christ, received as our own by faith in Him, our resurrection is guaranteed and our place in the kingdom of heaven is permanently assured (2 Cor. 1:21-22; 5:5; Eph. 1:13-14). However, at the judgment seat of Christ, our future reward in the kingdom of God will be determined by the quality of our deeds and the motives behind them (see 1 Cor. 3:10-15; 4:4-5). Thus, John says, we must take seriously how we balance unconditional love with discerning truth in this life. If we allow the truth to be compromised (even in the name of love), then we

143

[handwritten margin note: extraviado]

open ourselves up to being led astray, which can have serious consequences (1 Cor. 3:12-15).

Of course, there are those who go "too far" and fail to "abide in the teaching of Christ" (2 Jn. 1:9). That is, they are not guilty simply of being deceived or falling into sin; rather, they have completely abandoned the faith they once professed. They have demonstrated by their actions a total disregard for God's truth and love. In such acute cases, John says, such people do "not have God" (1:9). They are among the deceivers, not the deceived. They are themselves antichrists (1:7).

John treats this kind of apostasy in more detail in 1 John 2:19, where he asserts that such false teachers never truly experienced the saving grace of Jesus Christ. Those who so radically depart from the core teachings of the true Christian faith demonstrate that "they were not really of us" (1 Jn. 2:19). Had those antichrists been truly united to Christ by the regenerating work of the Holy Spirit, they "would have remained" with the true church. Their departure makes it clear, however, that "they all are not of us" (1 Jn. 2:19).

Again, this isn't talking about Christians who entertain doubts, backslide into sin, or even temporarily stray from the right path. John's definition of "antichrists" in 1 John and 2 John speaks to something more serious than the normal struggles of faith we all experience. "Antichrists" are guilty of outright heresies that deny the core doctrines of the faith and fully embrace a lifestyle of sin contrary to God's commands.

The world is full of deceivers—people who would lure us away from the truth and our eternal reward. Most false teachers use the very same Bible we use. But they twist it, adding to or taking away from its true meaning. John refers to "the teaching of Christ," "the teaching," and "this teaching" (2 Jn.1:9-10). We are to abide in the teaching. Those who do not bring this same teaching should be shown the door—or better yet, not invited into our homes (1:10).

What is the content of this basic Christian "teaching" to which John refers? Though this list is not exhaustive, the following fundamentals of our faith form a good checklist by which we can test the teachers who knock on our doors or come into our homes through TV, radio, print, or the Internet:

- the inspiration and inerrancy of Scripture (2 Tim. 3:16; 2 Pet. 1:21)
- the Triunity of God—Father, Son, and Holy Spirit—Creator of all things (Gen. 1–2; Matt. 28:19)

- the fallen condition of humanity and the need for God's grace (Gen. 3; Rom. 3:23)
- the Virgin Birth, the full deity and the full humanity of Christ, and His sinless life (Isa. 7:14; Matt. 1:18-25; Luke 1:26-38; John 1:1, 14; 8:53-58; Col. 1:15-20; Heb. 1:3, 8; 4:15)
- the substitutionary death of Christ for our sins, and his miraculous, bodily resurrection (Rom. 5:6-8; 1 Cor. 15:1-11; 2 Cor. 5:21; Heb. 9:22, 26; 1 Jn. 1:7, 9)
- the ascension of Christ and His present ministry to the believer through the Holy Spirit (John 14:12-21; Acts 1:6-9; Rom. 8:34; Eph. 4:7-10)
- the literal, future return of Christ to the earth (John 14:1-3; 1 Thes. 4:13-18)

False teachers will never stand up and openly declare, "We twist the Scriptures." No cultist knocking on your door will say, "We use 'Jesus' in our literature, but truth be told, we actually preach a different Jesus." No flashy TV preacher will look straight into the camera and shout, "I'm a heretic, but send me your money anyway!" In light of the fact that deceivers are masters at cloaking their own beliefs and practices, we need discernment. And as soon as we catch a whiff of their putrid doctrine, we need to keep them at arm's length. John puts it even more bluntly: "If anyone comes to you and does not bring this teaching, do not receive him into your house, and do not give him a greeting; for the one who gives him a greeting participates in his evil deeds" (2 Jn. 1:10-11).

That may seem harsh, but think about it. John is using the second-person plural, indicating that he is now speaking to the chosen lady and her children who are walking in the truth. If the lady had a problem with overemphasizing love and downplaying truth, the children would have also had an undeveloped understanding of the truth, thus lacking discernment. When a person is a novice in the faith, it's always best to shield them from false teaching, to protect them from antichrists aimed at confusing people and leading them astray. I'm not saying evangelists, apologists, and trained teachers should shy away from confronting the errors of heretics; but effectively engaging false teachers requires a great amount of training and experience, which most young believers don't have.

Until we learn how to properly balance love and truth, the best policy is to simply close the door on those conversations that could poison believers who have not yet developed the spiritual strength to resist infection.

—1:12-13—

John ends this tiny letter with some personal greetings. The warmth of his affection comes through as he expresses his earnest desire to see the chosen lady and her children "face to face." He had so much more to say, but paper and ink weren't the proper medium. What a great endorsement of the need for personal, in-the-flesh, life-on-life interaction! Even in his old age, John wanted to make the trip to be present with his brothers and sisters in Christ. This is a lesson all of us could learn in our impersonal world of texting, e-mail, and social media. Personal presence matters. Only through face-to-face interaction would John be able to make their joy full and complete (1:12).

Finally, John extends warm greetings from "the children of your chosen sister" (1:13). This might imply that the sister herself was no longer living, and that her children, dwelling in the city of Ephesus with John, wanted their aunt to know of their love for her. However, without more definite details we can't be sure. In any case, this letter that began with words of tender love concludes with the same warmth of affection.

APPLICATION: 2 JOHN 1:1-13
Principles for Balancing Truth and Love

Although only thirteen verses long, 2 John contains three principles we can spend the rest of our lives putting into practice. These aren't complicated, but they are difficult, because navigating between unconditional love and discerning truth will always be a challenge for believers striving to live a balanced Christian life.

First, *loving others is a fundamental expression of authentic Christianity*. The chosen lady and her children were excellent examples of this kind of loving hospitality and welcoming spirit. Nowhere does John seek to downplay or dismiss the need for this kind of open-armed love. One of the greatest witnesses we can have in a world of hate is to show love and charity toward both the family of God and those outside the church. Therefore, let's walk in love.

Second, *embracing the truth is equally essential*. The one who loves

BALANCING LOVE AND TRUTH | **2 JOHN 1:1-13**

you the most is the one who tells you the truth. If I'm engaged in destructive behavior, I would hope somebody loves me enough to tell me. It isn't loving to let a person go to hell because we don't want to offend them. This means we need to know the truth, grow in the truth, and study Scripture and sound theology for the rest of our lives. If you don't know what you believe and why, you won't know where to stand on any doctrinal or moral issue—at least not with any solid conviction. Therefore, take time to study and be strengthened in the truth.

Third, *when error is discerned, love must be kept within its bounds.* The challenge today is to know the truth and to take a stand for it without backtracking, compromising, or downplaying. At the same time, we need to be gracious and winsome in our witness. We must always be ready "to make a defense to everyone" regarding the hope that we embrace, but we do this "with gentleness and reverence" (1 Pet. 3:15). We must stand for the truth, but at the same time, we must extend love and walk in grace. We must love within the banks of truth and discernment . . . and learn to live in the dynamic tension between grace and truth. Therefore, learn the language of "speaking the truth in love" (Eph. 4:15) to both believers and unbelievers.

Balancing Truth and Love
3 JOHN 1:1-15

NASB

¹The elder to the beloved Gaius, whom I love in truth.

²Beloved, I pray that in all respects you may prosper and be in good health, just as your soul prospers. ³For I was very glad when brethren came and testified to your truth, *that is,* how you are walking in truth. ⁴I have no greater joy than ªthis, to hear of my children walking in the truth.

⁵Beloved, you are acting faithfully in whatever you accomplish for the brethren, and ªespecially *when they are* strangers; ⁶and they have testified to your love before the church. You will do well to send them on their way in a manner worthy of God. ⁷For they went out for the sake of the Name, accepting nothing from the Gentiles. ⁸Therefore we ought to ªsupport such men, so that we may ᵇbe fellow workers ᶜwith the truth.

⁹I wrote something to the church; but Diotrephes, who loves to be first among them, does not accept ªwhat we say. ¹⁰For this reason, if I come, I will call attention to his deeds which he does, unjustly accusing us with wicked words; and not satisfied with this, he himself does not receive the brethren, either, and he forbids those who desire *to do so* and puts *them* out of the church.

¹¹Beloved, do not imitate what is evil, but what is good. The one who does good is of God; the one who does evil has not seen God. ¹²Demetrius has received a *good* testimony

NLT

¹This letter is from John, the elder.*

I am writing to Gaius, my dear friend, whom I love in the truth.

²Dear friend, I hope all is well with you and that you are as healthy in body as you are strong in spirit. ³Some of the traveling teachers* recently returned and made me very happy by telling me about your faithfulness and that you are living according to the truth. ⁴I could have no greater joy than to hear that my children are following the truth.

⁵Dear friend, you are being faithful to God when you care for the traveling teachers who pass through, even though they are strangers to you. ⁶They have told the church here of your loving friendship. Please continue providing for such teachers in a manner that pleases God. ⁷For they are traveling for the Lord,* and they accept nothing from people who are not believers.* ⁸So we ourselves should support them so that we can be their partners as they teach the truth.

⁹I wrote to the church about this, but Diotrephes, who loves to be the leader, refuses to have anything to do with us. ¹⁰When I come, I will report some of the things he is doing and the evil accusations he is making against us. Not only does he refuse to welcome the traveling teachers, he also tells others not to help them. And when they do help, he puts them out of the church.

¹¹Dear friend, don't let this bad example influence you. Follow only what is good. Remember that those who do good prove that they are God's children, and those who do evil prove that they do not know God.*

¹²Everyone speaks highly of Demetrius, as does the truth itself. We

from everyone, and from the truth itself; and we add our testimony, and you know that our testimony is true. ¹³I had many things to write to you, but I am not willing to write *them* to you with pen and ink; ¹⁴but I hope to see you shortly, and we will speak face to face.

¹⁵Peace *be* to you. The friends greet you. Greet the friends by name.

ourselves can say the same for him, and you know we speak the truth. ¹³I have much more to say to you, but I don't want to write it with pen and ink. ¹⁴For I hope to see you soon, and then we will talk face to face.

¹⁵*Peace be with you.

Your friends here send you their greetings. Please give my personal greetings to each of our friends there.

1:4 ᵃLit *these things, that I hear* 1:5 ᵃLit *this* 1:8 ᵃOr *receive such men as guests* ᵇOr *prove ourselves to be* ᶜOr *for* 1:9 ᵃLit *us*

1 Greek *From the elder.* 3 Greek *the brothers;* also in verses 5 and 10. 7a Greek *They went out on behalf of the Name.* 7b Greek *from Gentiles.* 11 Greek *they have not seen God.* 15 Some English translations combine verses 14 and 15 into verse 14.

Sometimes I hear Christians talk about going back to the simplicity, the innocence, and the purity of the early church. Before doctrinal decline. Before moral corruption. Before power-hungry leaders started wrangling over position. Before the sun set on the golden age of the apostles. The idea seems to be that the first generation of Christians could simply focus their attention on preaching the gospel without constantly dealing with problems in the churches.

Not true. Not even close. It only takes a few page flips through the New Testament to see that such a period never existed. A simple glance reveals that the church in Corinth was fraught with conflict, the churches in Colossae and Galatia wrestled with doctrinal error, the Jerusalem church teetered on the brink of financial collapse, and the church at Laodicea was almost ruined by tepid obedience. From the very beginning the apostles themselves had to contend against false teachers (2 Pet. 2:1), exhort believers to live holy lives (Eph. 4:1), and, yes, even confront leaders in the midst of a power grab (3 Jn. 1:9). Problems from the outside, problems on the inside, problems from below, and problems at the top . . . the church has always faced challenges that threaten to undo the work of proclaiming the gospel and building up the church.

The fifteen verses that comprise 3 John testify to and typify a conflict that has been faced by genuine Christian churches throughout history. It may be the best snapshot evidencing the fact that we don't want to go back to the days of the first-century church. Rather, we need to look back to the examples preserved for us in Scripture to help the twenty-first-century church handle its own church conflicts.

KEY TERMS IN 3 JOHN 1:1-15

agapētos (ἀγαπητός) [27] "beloved," "dear," "prized"
The word *agapētos*, "beloved," is used frequently in the New Testament as a term of great affection (Matt. 3:17; Acts 15:25; Rom. 1:7; Phil. 2:12; Jas. 1:16; 1 Pet. 2:11). The apostle John did not use it in his Gospel but used it six times in the five chapters of 1 John (2:7; 3:2, 21; 4:1, 7, 11). This makes it all the more striking that in the fifteen verses of 3 John, the apostle refers to Gaius as "beloved" four times. Two of these are in the first two verses, and the others in verses 5 and 11. It refers to "one who is dearly loved, dear, beloved, prized, valued."[1] Here, it communicates a very close, personal relationship between John and Gaius.

peripateō (περιπατέω) [4043] "to walk," "to behave," "to conduct oneself"
Though, literally, *peripateō* means "to walk around" (see Matt. 4:18), it has a common idiomatic usage referring to one's lifestyle or pattern of behavior (Rom. 6:4; 1 Jn. 1:6). In 3 John, the apostle rejoices that the beloved Gaius was "walking in truth" (3 Jn. 1:3-4). In Colossians 1:10, Paul describes what this Christian walk looks like when he says, "You will walk in a manner worthy of the Lord, to please Him in all respects, bearing fruit in every good work and increasing in the knowledge of God."

—1:1-8—

After introducing himself as "the elder" (see 2 Jn. 1:1), the apostle John directly addresses his recipient as "the beloved Gaius." His genuine declaration of "love in truth" (3 Jn. 1:1) leads immediately into a prayer for Gaius's welfare—physically and spiritually, in body and soul (1:2). Knowing what we do about the challenges facing the churches in the late first century, this prayer for Gaius's physical health is significant. Many false teachers at the time looked down on material things, viewing them as at least irrelevant and trivial, if not actually evil. The body itself was regarded merely as a disposable shell for the real spiritual being inside—a distraction to spiritual progress. But John's concern for Gaius's physical well-being reveals a superior theology: God is not merely a God of the soul; He's God of the body as well.

Perhaps John's prayer was in response to reports that Gaius was in poor health, either from a physical ailment, stress over church conflicts, or both. Maybe Gaius, like Paul, had been burdened by a "thorn in the flesh" that constantly drove him to find his sufficiency in Christ

(2 Cor. 12:7-10). In spite of these possible afflictions, or perhaps because of them (Ps. 119:71), Gaius's devotion to Christ had flourished.

One day God will vanquish sickness and suffering when our bodies are resurrected and glorified (1 Cor. 15:53-54; Rev. 21:4). In the meantime, it isn't God's will that every believer always be healthy. That lie of prosperity theology seems to have infected almost every corner of the church today. Though it's right and proper to pray for the health and healing of those who are suffering and to lend aid where we are able, sometimes it's God's will that his children grow spiritually in and through their physical suffering. However, it's always God's will that our souls prosper. And this kind of prosperity was true of Gaius. Regardless of the state of his physical strength and health, which apparently needed some prayer support, Gaius was spiritually "walking in the truth," which filled John's heart with joy (3 Jn. 1:3-4).

How did John know of Gaius's condition? Apparently, that aged apostle had a steady stream of visitors who brought word about the conditions of the churches and believers. With this information, John knew when and how to pray for others, when he needed to send a letter, and when he needed to make a personal, in-the-flesh visit (see 2 Jn. 1:12; 3 Jn. 1:13-14). This reveals the depth of John's constant care and concern for the churches and for his own converts. Up to the end of his life, John exerted all his energy to pray for and care for others.

In 1:5-8, the apostle gives us a glimpse into the inner workings of ministry during the first century as the church was transitioning from the foundational, temporary era of the apostles to the permanent era of pastors and teachers. In the New Testament church, there were basically two kinds of ministers. We might categorize them as "pioneers" and "settlers." (For more historical background on this, see "From Pioneers to Settlers," page 153.) The pioneers included traveling apostles, prophets, and missionaries, along with their envoys and associates. These individuals proclaimed the gospel in new territories and established new churches. Often these pioneers continued to travel to various churches, training and ordaining leaders (Acts 14:23) until the congregation was self-sustaining. Paul refers to these types of ministers in Ephesians 4:11 as apostles, prophets, and evangelists.

The settlers, on the other hand, were those ministers who were responsible for the continuing care and growth of the local churches. These were the elders and deacons, the pastors and teachers, who ministered to a particular flock, traveled very little, and nurtured the faith of believers for years. Paul refers to these types of ministers in

Ephesians 4:11 as pastors and teachers, who are the elders of the local churches assisted by deacons (Phil. 1:1). These established churches then became the primary bases of support for the itinerant pioneer ministers (see 1 Cor. 9:1-14).

At first, the baby churches eagerly welcomed the wise teaching of the pioneers, as they, like infants, required constant care. But as the local churches grew from infancy to the toddler stage, their wobbly legs grew stronger, and the churches entered an awkward period of transition from dependence to independence. Like adolescents today who need Mom and Dad for food, shelter, and clothing but don't want them around for anything else, some of the young church-plants in the first century still needed guidance from the apostles and their associates but sometimes resisted outside authority. In time, a rift between the pioneers and the settlers might form, and the local church might even refuse to accommodate the traveling leadership, failing to show basic hospitality.

Gaius, one of the "settler" leaders of the church, understood the continuing need for doctrinal and practical guidance from the apostles and their messengers. He kept his doors open to the dedicated pioneer ministers. He was "acting faithfully" even to apostolic messengers he had never met (3 Jn. 1:5). He treated them with the honor, respect, and even financial support they deserved, knowing that they had no other source of sustenance (1:6-7). By supporting these itinerants and showing generous hospitality, Gaius became a partner in the work they were doing (1:8). This welcoming attitude reached the ears of the apostle John. Even John's church, probably in Ephesus, had heard of Gaius's love for the traveling ministry team (1:6).

Not everyone was as hospitable as Gaius, however.

— 1:9-10 —

We know next to nothing about the hostile figure known as Diotrephes except the few pieces of information given to us in this passage. But it's enough of a snapshot to serve as a warning against this kind of jostling for position and scrapping over turf. Like Gaius, Diotrephes was probably one of the appointed "settler" ministers in the church. However, unlike Gaius, Diotrephes rejected John's messengers, John's letter, and even the authority of the apostle himself!

It's possible that the letter John says he wrote "to the church" (1:9) is 1 John, but it's much more likely that it's a letter lost to us.[2] How did it get lost? John's language in 1:9 implies that instead of reading it to the

FROM PIONEERS TO SETTLERS

3 JOHN 1:5-8

One ancient historical account gives us a clearer picture of the transition from pioneer to settler ministries in the first century. Around AD 95—about the same time as the writing of 3 John—the leader of the church in Rome, Clement, wrote an account of the apostles' pioneer activities during that formative period. This account wasn't merely the fading echoes of oral tradition; Clement lived at a time and place in which he would have been a direct disciple of one or more of the original generation of pioneer ministers. So his words preserve a firsthand recollection of what actually happened. He wrote:

> Having received commands and being fully convinced by the resurrection of our Lord Jesus Christ, and full of faith in the word of God, they [the original apostles] went forth with the full assurance of the Holy Spirit, proclaiming the gospel, that the kingdom of God was about to come. Therefore, preaching among regions and cities, they appointed their first fruits, testing them by the Spirit to be bishops [literally "overseers"] and deacons of the future believers. . . .
>
> And our apostles knew through our Lord Jesus Christ that there would be strife concerning the title of bishop [literally "overseer"]. Because of this reason, therefore, having received complete foreknowledge, they appointed those previously mentioned and afterwards they gave a rule that if they should die, other approved men should succeed their ministry. [3]

In this passage, Clement of Rome reports that the pioneer ministers (the apostles) established the settler ministers (overseers and deacons) to provide stability and prevent wrangling over the office. This permanent ministry was intended to endure beyond the age of the apostles—even to our present day.

church as a form of continued instruction from their apostolic leader, Diotrephes intercepted the letter. Because he did not accept what the apostle and his messengers said, Diotrephes likely destroyed the letter. Beyond this, he refused to show hospitality to any of the apostle's delegates, made up lies about them, and even forbade other members and leaders of the church to show any hospitality toward them. In his self-promoting rage, Diotrephes even put out of the church anybody who tried to restore contact with the apostle's line of communication (1:10-11).

Why would he do all of this? Because he loved "to be first" in the church. The apostles originally established a plurality of leaders in each church (Acts 14:23; 20:17; Titus 1:5; Jas. 5:14; 1 Pet. 5:1-5). Even if one of these leaders served as a chairman, presiding elder, or something like what we would call a senior pastor, they would still be regarded as a "prime among equals" and probably not as a boss over the council of elders. Diotrephes, however, had completely lost sight of this apostolic ideal, wanting instead to call the shots like a dictator. This was utterly in conflict with the clear instructions from both Jesus and Peter that leaders should not "lord it over" those placed in their charge (Matt. 20:25-26; 1 Pet. 5:1-3)!

I'd love to be able to say the days of Diotrephes are over, that they died in the first century, and that his spirit never made it out of those two verses in 3 John. Sadly, the spirit of Diotrephes outlived that era and continues into our own day. One author of yesteryear described the type well:

> Seeking great things for themselves, making their personal advancement the one thing in life, scheming and plotting, blustering and sneaking, trampling on others, and bloating themselves with vain ambition, and creating their own false and poisonous inspirations by their subtle self-appreciation—all to secure some advantage for themselves.[4]

In my life of ministry, I can attest to the fact that an acute case of "Diotrephes Disease," with those kinds of symptoms, can bring an otherwise healthy church to its deathbed. As strong-minded but spiritually immature people weasel their way into positions of influence, they begin intimidating others to get their way. The problem usually isn't a matter of bad theology, but pride; not false teaching, but faulty leading. If left untreated, "Diotrephes Disease" can infect a whole congregation, leading to conflict, schism, and the death of a local church.

The apostle John also knew exactly where that original outbreak of "Diotrephes Disease" would end if it didn't get isolated and removed. This is why he mentions in 1:10, "If I come, I will call attention to his deeds." In fact, by the time he gets to 1:13, John seems to have settled it in his mind. He determined to set down the pen and pick up the staff for the physical journey to "speak face to face" (1:14). I can imagine that if Diotrephes got hold of the letter delivered to Gaius, the prospect of the apostle John himself showing up at his doorstep would have given him cause to reconsider his stand. Or maybe he had so deeply succumbed to the disease of conceit that he would have given the cold shoulder even to the "disciple whom Jesus loved" (John 20:2).

A Case of Feline Diotrephes Disease

3 JOHN 1:9

Back in 1961, Cynthia and I moved to Palo Alto, California, to serve in a pastoral apprenticeship under Ray Stedman. We lived in a home owned by a lunar scientist out of Cal Tech whose specialty was planetary terrain. This was the early 1960s, before anyone had set foot on the moon. As part of his research on the lunar terrain, he and his family relocated temporarily to West Texas, where the rocky land was thought to be similar to the moon's. So, Cynthia and I were blessed to have a house to live in while they were gone.

Or so we thought.

You see, they left one member of the household behind: a Siamese cat named Sinbad. He was the most intelligent, orneriest cat you could imagine. And Sinbad wanted to have the first place in everything. He had gotten used to top treatment over the years. The two most irksome accommodations to his feline Diotrephes Disease, though, crossed the line. Sinbad was used to sleeping on—not beside, not under—the master bed . . . and eating at—not near, not under—the dining room table with the rest of the family.

"No way!" I said. "No way is that cat sitting at my table or sleeping in my bed!"

Now, this may sound crazy, but I'm convinced that cat understood English and had the calculating mind of a psychopath. So that first night after I locked up the house and closed the bedroom door, Sinbad began to live up to his name. He began screaming and scratching and clawing at the door. When I refused to open the door to let his majesty have the master bed, Sinbad began charging the door over and over again. He would run down the hall, turn around, pick up speed, and hurl himself at the door, trying to break it down.

(continued on next page)

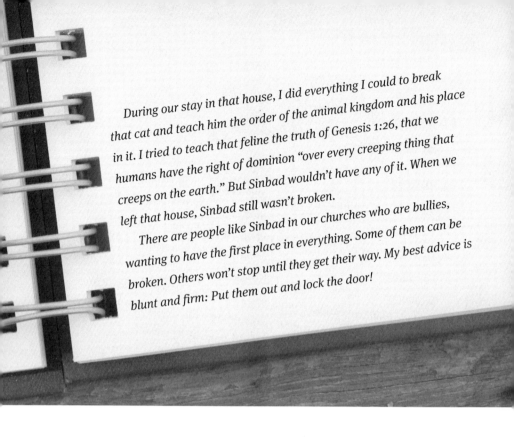

During our stay in that house, I did everything I could to break that cat and teach him the order of the animal kingdom and his place in it. I tried to teach that feline the truth of Genesis 1:26, that we humans have the right of dominion "over every creeping thing that creeps on the earth." But Sinbad wouldn't have any of it. When we left that house, Sinbad still wasn't broken.

There are people like Sinbad in our churches who are bullies, wanting to have the first place in everything. Some of them can be broken. Others won't stop until they get their way. My best advice is blunt and firm: Put them out and lock the door!

—1:11-12—

The apostle John was clearly taking steps to resolve the Diotrephes problem either by curing the man of his "me first" syndrome or by surgically removing him from the church body. In the meantime, though, John urges Gaius "not [to] imitate what is evil, but what is good" (3 Jn. 1:11). The "evil" thing in the immediate context is the example of wicked Diotrephes. Though the pressure to capitulate to his bullying would have been great, Gaius is instructed to stand strong. John then employs language reminiscent of his first epistle to add gravity to the circumstance: "The one who does good is of God; the one who does evil has not seen God" (1:11; cf. 1 Jn. 2:4-5).

Besides this, John instructs Gaius to imitate and align himself with a positive example, specifically a man named Demetrius (3 Jn. 1:12). Perhaps Gaius felt alone in the midst of the Diotrephes conflict—like a tiny lamplight barely flickering in an oppressive darkness. John's comment about Demetrius in 1:12 gave Gaius the fuel he needed to keep his flame burning until dawn broke. Even though Demetrius received only a one-verse commendation, that tiny verse is a bright beacon of light in an otherwise dark passage.

Was Demetrius a fellow elder with Gaius—another who hadn't given in to Diotrephes Disease? Possibly. But a better explanation is that Demetrius was the person carrying John's letter to deliver to Gaius. Thus, Demetrius may have been one of the messengers of the apostle John whom Diotrephes had already rejected (1:9). Smalley writes, "It is reasonable, however, to suppose that Demetrius was . . . on his way to the congregation addressed in 3 John to stand with the elder in his confrontation of Diotrephes."[5] I like to imagine that the apostle John was sending Gaius air support in the form of Demetrius.

Demetrius was certainly fit for the task. John provided three impressive references for Demetrius, marking him as one worthy of imitation (1:11). First, everyone who knew Demetrius vouched for him. Not a soul lacked confidence in his character and integrity. Second, he lived his life in a way that lined up with "the truth itself" (1:12). Unlike Diotrephes, who was not living in accordance with truth and love, Demetrius lived an exemplary life in terms of doctrine and practice. Third, John gave Demetrius a personal stamp of approval from his own circle of apostolic leadership.

—1:13-15—

By the time Gaius was reading 1:13-15, Demetrius was probably standing with him, having likely delivered the letter. I can almost picture Gaius letting out a sigh of relief as he looked up from John's endorsement of Demetrius in 1:12 to see the man before him, ready to lend aid against the tyrant Diotrephes. But then his tear-filled eyes would fall back down to the letter, and he would read the words that would lift his weary soul and send it soaring: "I had many things to write to you," John said, "but I am not willing to write them to you with pen and ink; but I hope to see you shortly, and we will speak face to face" (1:13-14).

John was on his way!

What joy Gaius must have felt as he read the final words of this encouraging epistle: "Peace be to you. The friends greet you. Greet the friends by name." Gaius and the faithful remnant were not alone in the dark. The friendship and brotherly love expressed across distances would strengthen them, and the distance would soon be bridged by the apostle's physical presence.

Then Diotrephes's unloving ire would be doused by a balance of truth and love.

APPLICATION: 3 JOHN 1:1-15
Treating Diotrephes Disease

I'm convinced that almost every church has its own Diotrephes—someone who will try to cast a gray shadow across the ministry by unjustly accusing leaders, shutting out people in need, and intimidating church members. Sometimes the Diotrephes Disease spreads to infect a whole group in the church, who strive for dominance and absolute lordship over everyone—members and leaders alike. They may be sound in propositional truth, able to cross their theological t's and dot their doctrinal i's, but they lack love for their fellow members within the church and for their brothers and sisters in other churches.

At the same time, I'm encouraged that every church has its own Gaius or Demetrius—those with character and fortitude, who display body-building virtues of love, hospitality, generosity, integrity, and purity. They're willing to take a stand for truth balanced by love, even if it means getting crosswise with the bullies. They speak out against injustice, confront the lack of grace and mercy, and protect those too intimidated to defend themselves. May their tribe increase!

Are we going to succumb to Diotrephes Disease, allowing pride to turn us into domineering, me-centered bullies? Or will we cave to such people's threats, siding with "what is evil" rather than embracing "what is good"? Will we resist the duly ordained leadership of the church over petty differences? Will we believe gossip and criticism about them and their supporters, receiving and spreading lies and innuendos of wrongdoing that can't be substantiated? Or will we show our leaders the respect they deserve (1 Tim. 5:19; Heb. 13:17)?

On the flip side, to whom can we look as an example of "what is good"? Who is a Demetrius in your life—somebody who has a good testimony from all people, who is commended by church leadership, and who lives a life that balances love and truth? Often these people will be the seasoned members of the church who have maintained a consistent walk for decades. Quiet, not loud. Servant-minded, not self-seeking. Walking epitomes of the fruit of the Spirit in Galatians 5:22-23 and the "love chapter" of 1 Corinthians 13. Find these healthy and wholesome people, spend time with them, and imitate them. They will inoculate you from contracting Diotrephes Disease.

INSIGHTS ON JUDE

If we were first-century believers immersed in the theological and moral crisis of Jude's day, his words would strike like a hammerblow on the anvil of our hearts, fashioning our attitudes and sharpening our actions. The book was profoundly relevant and practical . . . and it can be just as relevant and practical for us when we understand its vibrant language and imagery.

	AD 30	AD 35	AD 40	AD 45	AD 50	AD 55

● Simon Peter called AD 27

● Peter's denial and restoration AD 30

● Paul's conversion AD 38

● Conversion of Cornelius AD 40

● Silvanus sent to Antioch AD 49

● Jerusalem council AD 49

Marcellus AD 36–37

Cuspius Fadus AD 44–46

Tiberius Julius Alexander AD 46–47

Ventidius Cumanus AD 48–52

Herod Agrippa I AD 37–44

Pontius Pilate AD 26–36

Marullus AD 37–41

Antonius Felix

Tiberius AD 14–37

Caligula AD 37–41

Claudius AD 41–54

The Roman Empire spanned the entire Mediterranean world, from Syria to Spain and from Egypt to Macedonia. Jude doesn't state his location nor that of his readers, but most commentators think he was writing to Syrian Christians in Antioch or Egyptian Christians near Alexandria.

┌Jude

| AD 65 | AD 70 | AD 75 | AD 80 | AD 85 | AD 90 |

Fire in Rome —•   •— Peter martyred? AD 67
ero's persecution —•
ʌish revolt in Jerusalem —•   •— Temple destroyed

Festus   Lucceius Albinus AD 62–64   Marcus Antonius Julianus AD 66–70
9–62   Gessius Florus AD 64–66

Herod Agrippa II AD 50–93

Roman Legate Rule

AD 54–68   Vespasian AD 69–79   Titus   Domitian AD 81-96

JUDE

INTRODUCTION

Except for the resounding, magnificent doxology with which it ends, the short letter of Jude is a little-known piece of the New Testament. Those few who attempt to read and understand it struggle under its bewildering, even mysterious language and imagery. Jude constantly reaches back into the Old Testament—and into some extrabiblical traditions—to make his case. Besides this, he draws parallels from trees, clouds, and stars to illustrate his points. Admittedly, Jude's sometimes obscure references and strange word pictures fall on our ears like a foreign language.

But if we were first-century believers immersed in the theological and moral crisis of Jude's day, his words would strike like a hammerblow on the anvil of our hearts, fashioning our attitudes and sharpening our actions. The book was profoundly relevant and practical . . . and it can be just as relevant and practical for us when we understand its vibrant language and imagery.

AUTHOR, DATE, AND OCCASION

If you were to stand in the center of a crowded market in first-century Jerusalem and shout, "Hey, Jude!" chances are dozens of faces would turn your way. The name Jude—a Greek translation of "Judah" or "Judas"—was very common among first-century Jews.[1] Had the author of the letter of Jude left us only this name, we would be at a loss as to his specific identity. All we would be able to say for sure is he was Jewish.

However, this Jude calls himself the "brother of James" (1:1). This identification strongly suggests that the author was the half brother of Jesus. As the "brother of James," he was probably not the original disciple named Jude, son of James (Luke 6:16), who was also called

161

THE BOOK OF JUDE AT A GLANCE

SECTION	THE ACTS OF THE APOSTATES	
PASSAGE	1:1-4	1:5-16
THEMES	Greeting Purpose: Contend for the faith because false teachers have "crept in unnoticed."	Exposure of False Teacher • Fallen angels • Cain and Abel • Rebellious Israelites
KEY TERMS	Contend . . . Destroy	

of David, and they confessed that they were. Then he asked them how much property they had, or how much money they owned. And both of them answered that they had only nine thousand denarii, half of which belonged to each of them; and this property did not consist of silver, but of a piece of land which contained only thirty-nine acres, and from which they raised their taxes and supported themselves by their own labor. Then they showed their hands, exhibiting the hardness of their bodies and the callousness produced upon their hands by continuous toil as evidence of their own labor. And when they were asked concerning Christ and his kingdom, of what sort it was and where and when it was to appear, they answered that it was not a temporal nor an earthly kingdom, but a heavenly and angelic one, which would appear at the end of the world, when he should come in glory to judge the quick and the dead, and to give unto every one according to his works. Upon hearing this, Domitian did not pass judgment against them, but, despising them as of no account, he let them go, and by a decree put a stop to the persecution of the Church. But when they were released they ruled the churches, because they were witnesses and were also relatives of the Lord.[2]

From this portrait, we begin to picture Jude as a man who at first lived in skepticism about his half brother. But he eventually came to faith in Jesus. As a result, he had an impact not only on his own generation through missions but also on subsequent generations through his children and grandchildren. As he traveled on behalf of the gospel—with his believing wife and children—he moved from city to city declaring Jesus to be the Messiah, Son of God, and Savior of the world.

But when did Jude, the half brother of Jesus, write this book? Because Jude is listed last among the brothers of Jesus in Matthew 13:55, it's likely that he was the youngest son of Joseph and Mary. He was therefore probably in his teens or early twenties during Jesus's ministry. Jude could have lived into his eighties, possibly as long as the apostle John. Therefore, any date within the first century—even as late as the nineties—is plausible.

One clue to dating the letter is its relationship to 2 Peter. There is little doubt, as we will see in the commentary sections below, that either Peter knew of Jude's letter when he wrote . . . or Jude knew of Peter's letter. There are certain verbal similarities and common images used in both letters. I take the view that Peter wrote first, sometime around

QUICK FACTS ON JUDE

When was it written? Probably sometime between AD 67 and 90

Where was it written? Uncertain

Who wrote it? Jude, the brother of James and the half brother of Jesus

Why was it written? To expose false teachers and to encourage believers to stand firm in the faith

AD 66. In that letter, Peter referred prophetically to the coming of false teachers: "Know this first of all, that in the last days mockers will come with their mocking, following after their own lusts" (2 Pet. 3:3). Jude refers to this prediction in his letter, informing his readers that what Peter said had come to pass: "But you, beloved, ought to remember the words that were spoken beforehand by the apostles of our Lord Jesus Christ, that they were saying to you, 'In the last time there will be mockers, following after their own ungodly lusts'" (Jude 1:17-18).

It seems to me that the best explanation for this relationship is that Jude was reminding his readers of the words in 2 Peter; therefore, Jude was written sometime after AD 66. Because we can't be sure of exactly when, I'll place the probable time of the writing of Jude sometime between AD 67 and 90, though a date closer to 80 is probably preferred.

Finally, what was the occasion of this brief letter? What prompted Jude to write it? The occasion is clearly stated in the opening of the book: "Beloved, while I was making every effort to write you about our common salvation, I felt the necessity to write to you appealing that you contend earnestly for the faith which was once for all handed down to the saints" (1:3). The rest of the letter develops this theme as Jude labors to expose false teachers and to encourage the believers to stand firm in the faith.

Jude's brevity shouldn't be confused with lack of concern. Instead of dancing around the issues, Jude wasted no pen strokes getting to his point. So obvious and egregious were the errors of the false teachers that Jude instantly called out their wicked deeds and passed judgment on them, even from afar.

OVERVIEW OF JUDE

Jude's purpose in writing his letter was twofold: He needed to expose the false teachers that had infiltrated the Christian community, and he had to encourage the believers to stand firm in the faith and fight for it. The book breaks down nicely into two primary sections (1:1-16 and 1:17-25) each containing two subsections. After an abrupt, cut-to-the-chase greeting and statement of his purpose (1:1-4), Jude barrels headlong into an exposure of false teachers (1:5-16). From there he engages his readers directly with urgent warnings and commands (1:17-23), closing the short but powerful message with an encouraging benediction (1:24-25).

Greeting and Purpose (1:1-4). Like an action film that opens in the middle of a high-speed chase, Jude focuses the readers' attention on his main concern within a couple of verses. After a fairly standard greeting (1:1-2), he establishes an urgent tone in 1:3-4, blowing the whistle on "certain persons" who "have crept in unnoticed"—false teachers bent on destroying the church.

Exposure of False Teachers (1:5-16). To emphasize his point, Jude brings forth a series of biblical images and meaningful metaphors that paralleled the crisis of false teachers in the church. From fallen angels to falling stars, from Cain killing Abel to Israelites rebelling in the wilderness, Jude unleashes an all-out assault on the spiritual pirates bent on mutiny in the church, casting them in the most unfavorable light.

Warnings and Commands (1:17-23). Jude's purpose went beyond just castigating the apostates. His purpose was also to protect the faithful. So, in this third section, Jude works to sharpen the discernment of his readers by issuing commands to remember former warnings (1:17-19), to keep themselves in the love of God (1:20-21), to have mercy on those who had been deceived by false teachers (1:22-23), and to save those who were being threatened by the apostates (1:23).

Benediction (1:24-25). Finally, Jude prays for the supernatural strength of the Holy Spirit, without whom nobody would be able to stand in the face of such spiritual attacks (1:24). He concludes with a soaring doxology of praise to the Father, through the Son, whose power and dominion will never end (1:25).

KEY TERMS IN JUDE

epagōnizomai (ἐπαγωνίζομαι) [1864] "contend,"
"struggle for"

The word for "contend" in Jude 1:3 means "to exert intense effort on behalf of something."[3] It was used to describe athletes striving for victory over their opponents in competitions and tournaments.[4] The meaning can be illustrated by two wrestlers contending for the prize of victory or two armies waging war over a city. If you look carefully, you'll see the root from which we get our English word "agonize." Jude uses the term for the theological and moral conflict between true believers and false teachers (1:3).

apollymi (ἀπόλλυμι) [622] "destroy," "perish," "lose"

The cost of rebellion and false teaching is dire. Jude uses this vivid term that communicates utter destruction and ruin.[5] Paul used the word for those who are perishing because they refuse to embrace the truth and be saved (2 Thes. 2:10), and Peter used the term for the destruction of the world during the Flood (2 Pet. 3:6). The gospel, Paul said, is veiled "to those who are perishing [*apollymi*]" (2 Cor. 4:3). The clear implication is that this kind of destruction is for those who have not been saved. In particular, Jude uses the term to describe the destruction of Israelites who didn't truly believe (Jude 1:5) and the perishing of the rebels of Korah who had turned against Moses (1:11). This is the kind of judgment and destruction that the false teachers in the church will experience.

A MANUAL FOR SURVIVAL
(JUDE 1:1-25)

Like a one-room chapel built beside a massive cathedral, the little book of Jude is often lost in the shadow of its towering next-door neighbor, the book of Revelation. While most believers could rattle off a dozen images from John's Apocalypse, few could recall even one or two of Jude's numerous vivid metaphors. In fact, I have a hunch that if Philemon and Jude were to run a race for "most neglected book of the New Testament," it would be a photo finish.

However, this tiny book contains powerful images and passionate language that constitute a vital manual for survival in a world of spiritual confusion and contention. In our modern world where people emphasize love without truth and tolerance without limits, the letter of Jude stands as a timely call for believers to "contend earnestly for the faith" (1:3). As such, Jude isn't what I would call "easy reading." Though brief, it's dense. But wading through its warnings and pondering its principles will help prepare us to survive—and thrive—in a world of spiritual conflict.

The Acts of the Apostates
JUDE 1:1-16

NASB

¹ᵃJude, a bond-servant of Jesus Christ, and brother of ᵇJames,
To those who are the called, beloved in God the Father, and kept for Jesus Christ: ²May mercy and peace and love be multiplied to you.
³Beloved, while I was making every effort to write you about our common salvation, I felt the necessity to write to you appealing that

NLT

¹This letter is from Jude, a slave of Jesus Christ and a brother of James.
I am writing to all who have been called by God the Father, who loves you and keeps you safe in the care of Jesus Christ.*
²May God give you more and more mercy, peace, and love.
³Dear friends, I had been eagerly planning to write to you about the salvation we all share. But now I find that I must write about something

you contend earnestly for the faith which was once for all handed down to the ªsaints. ⁴For certain persons have crept in unnoticed, those who were long beforehand ªmarked out for this condemnation, ungodly persons who turn the grace of our God into licentiousness and deny our only Master and Lord, Jesus Christ.

⁵Now I desire to remind you, though you know all things once for all, that ªthe Lord, after saving a people out of the land of Egypt, ᵇsubsequently destroyed those who did not believe. ⁶And angels who did not keep their own domain, but abandoned their proper abode, He has kept in eternal bonds under darkness for the judgment of the great day, ⁷just as Sodom and Gomorrah and the cities around them, since they in the same way as these indulged in gross immorality and went after ªstrange flesh, are exhibited as an ᵇexample in undergoing the punishment of eternal fire.

⁸Yet in the same way these men, also by dreaming, defile the flesh, and reject authority, and revile ªangelic majesties. ⁹But Michael the archangel, when he disputed with the devil and argued about the body of Moses, did not dare pronounce against him a railing judgment, but said, "The Lord rebuke you!" ¹⁰But these men revile the things which they do not understand; and the things which they know by instinct, like unreasoning animals, by these things they are ªdestroyed. ¹¹Woe to them! For they have gone the way of Cain, and for pay ªthey have rushed

else, urging you to defend the faith that God has entrusted once for all time to his holy people. ⁴I say this because some ungodly people have wormed their way into your churches, saying that God's marvelous grace allows us to live immoral lives. The condemnation of such people was recorded long ago, for they have denied our only Master and Lord, Jesus Christ.

⁵So I want to remind you, though you already know these things, that Jesus* first rescued the nation of Israel from Egypt, but later he destroyed those who did not remain faithful. ⁶And I remind you of the angels who did not stay within the limits of authority God gave them but left the place where they belonged. God has kept them securely chained in prisons of darkness, waiting for the great day of judgment. ⁷And don't forget Sodom and Gomorrah and their neighboring towns, which were filled with immorality and every kind of sexual perversion. Those cities were destroyed by fire and serve as a warning of the eternal fire of God's judgment.

⁸In the same way, these people—who claim authority from their dreams—live immoral lives, defy authority, and scoff at supernatural beings.* ⁹But even Michael, one of the mightiest of the angels,* did not dare accuse the devil of blasphemy, but simply said, "The Lord rebuke you!" (This took place when Michael was arguing with the devil about Moses' body.) ¹⁰But these people scoff at things they do not understand. Like unthinking animals, they do whatever their instincts tell them, and so they bring about their own destruction. ¹¹What sorrow awaits them! For they follow in the footsteps of Cain, who killed his brother. Like Balaam, they deceive people for money.

headlong into the error of Balaam, and perished in the rebellion of Korah. ¹²These are the men who are ᵃhidden reefs in your love feasts when they feast with you without fear, caring for themselves; clouds without water, carried along by winds; autumn trees without fruit, ᵇdoubly dead, uprooted; ¹³wild waves of the sea, casting up their own ᵃshame like foam; wandering stars, for whom the ᵇblack darkness has been reserved forever.

¹⁴*It was* also about these men *that* Enoch, *in* the seventh *generation* from Adam, prophesied, saying, "Behold, the Lord came with ᵃmany thousands of His holy ones, ¹⁵to execute judgment upon all, and to convict all the ungodly of all their ungodly deeds which they have done in an ungodly way, and of all the harsh things which ungodly sinners have spoken against Him." ¹⁶These are grumblers, finding fault, following after their *own* lusts; ᵃthey speak arrogantly, flattering people for the sake of *gaining an* advantage.

1:1 ᵃGr *Judas* ᵇOr *Jacob* 1:3 ᵃOr *holy ones* 1:4 ᵃOr *written about...long ago* 1:5 ᵃTwo early mss read *Jesus* ᵇLit *the second time* 1:7 ᵃLit *different* or *other flesh* ᵇOr *example of eternal fire, in undergoing punishment* 1:8 ᵃLit *glories* 1:10 ᵃLit *corrupted* 1:11 ᵃLit *they have poured themselves out* 1:12 ᵃOr *stains* ᵇLit *twice* 1:13 ᵃOr *shameless deeds* ᵇLit *blackness of darkness;* or *netherworld gloom* 1:14 ᵃLit *His holy ten thousands* 1:16 ᵃLit *their mouth speaks*

And like Korah, they perish in their rebellion.

¹²When these people eat with you in your fellowship meals commemorating the Lord's love, they are like dangerous reefs that can shipwreck you.* They are like shameless shepherds who care only for themselves. They are like clouds blowing over the land without giving any rain. They are like trees in autumn that are doubly dead, for they bear no fruit and have been pulled up by the roots. ¹³They are like wild waves of the sea, churning up the foam of their shameful deeds. They are like wandering stars, doomed forever to blackest darkness.

¹⁴Enoch, who lived in the seventh generation after Adam, prophesied about these people. He said, "Listen! The Lord is coming with countless thousands of his holy ones ¹⁵to execute judgment on the people of the world. He will convict every person of all the ungodly things they have done and for all the insults that ungodly sinners have spoken against him."*

¹⁶These people are grumblers and complainers, living only to satisfy their desires. They brag loudly about themselves, and they flatter others to get what they want.

1 Or *keeps you for Jesus Christ.* 5 Other manuscripts read *[the] Lord,* or *God,* or *God Christ.* 8 Greek *at glorious ones,* which are probably evil angels. 9 Greek *Michael, the archangel.* 12 Or *they are contaminants among you;* or *they are stains.* 14-15 The quotation comes from intertestamental literature: 1 Enoch 1:9.

In Jude's day, the latter part of the first century, a battle was raging—not open warfare with weapons and violence, but a real and dangerous one nonetheless. It started at the time of Jesus with the traitorous disciple Judas Iscariot (Matt. 26:47), continued with turncoats like Simon the Magician (Acts 8:9-24), and swelled with the defectors who, the apostle John said, "went out from us, but . . . were not really of us" (1 Jn. 2:19).

The battle was against apostasy. And it wasn't just a problem in the first century. In fact, that spiritual conflict against those who depart from the truth in doctrine or practice has been intensifying through the centuries. It has resulted in numerous cults, sects, false religions, aberrant denominations, and countless twisted teachers all claiming to be true Christians. No book of the Bible concentrates more attention on this ancient and ongoing battle than the little letter of Jude, written to expose false teachers and to encourage believers to stand firm in the faith.

In the first half of the book, Jude makes his intention clear: to urge his readers to contend for the faith against an onslaught of false teachers (Jude 1:3-4). In doing so, Jude exposes them for what they are—deceptive, immoral, blasphemous, rebellious, ignorant, selfish, ungodly sinners (1:4-16). Though such false teachers have taken numerous forms throughout the history of the church, their basic ingredients remain the same. In order for us to contend for the faith today, we need to understand Jude's description better and be equipped to counter the acts of the apostates.

—1:1-4—

Jude was the half brother of Jesus. His father was Joseph and his mother, Mary. He was the brother of James, who wrote the book of James. Jude, who was presumably among the group that at one time thought Jesus had lost His mind (Mark 3:21), quickly came to realize that what sounded like the claims of a madman were actually the claims of the God-man! His own half brother was the long-awaited Messiah who died for the sins of the world and rose again from the dead. Jude had been hanging out with the God of the universe!

Yet Jude doesn't flaunt this relationship or pull rank because of his close kinship to the Savior. Instead, he calls himself His "bond-servant" (Jude 1:1). Jude had no desire to advance himself, his reputation, or his own personal agenda. His singular goal was to serve the Lord Jesus Christ as a faithful servant. So, instead of opening his letter as "Jude, brother of Jesus according to the flesh," he identified himself as "brother of James" and placed himself spiritually on the same level as his readers.

Jude names his readers as "called," "beloved," and "kept." Here we catch a casual, almost unnoticeable, glimpse of the work of the Trinity in the life of believers. One commentator notes: "The calling is the active work of the Holy Spirit; the love emanates from the Father (cf. 2 Cor. 13:14); and the keeping work is the ministry of the Son. Thus the entire

Godhead is included in Jude's salutation. The knowledge of God's calling, loving, and keeping brings believers assurance and peace during times of apostasy."[1] To this triad of divine Persons, Jude adds a triad of blessing, praying that his readers would be blessed with "mercy and peace and love" (Jude 1:2). These, too, come from the Father, through the Son, by the Spirit.

In connection with this uplifting greeting, Jude originally wanted to write concerning the glories of the salvation shared in common with his readers (1:3). He had desired to unpack the richness of the calling of the Spirit, the love of the Father, and the saving and preserving work of Christ and to explore the profound and practical aspects of mercy, peace, and love shared by all true believers in the triune faith. However, a massive threat appeared in Jude's path that caused him to slam on the brakes, shift into low gear, and abruptly turn down a darker path through a more urgent subject: the threat of apostates.

Jude said it was a "necessity" that he write with a new purpose, which was to "contend earnestly for the faith which was once for all handed down to the saints" (1:3). Though the word translated "contend earnestly" (*epagōnizomai* [1864]) appears only here in the New Testament, it is an intensification of a more common word, *agōnizomai* [75]. Paul used this common term when he urged Timothy to "*fight* the good fight of faith" (1 Tim. 6:12 [emphasis mine]). It's a term used to describe the striving of an athlete competing for a prize (1 Cor. 9:25). The intensified form found in Jude 1:3 underscores, italicizes, and highlights the greatness of the conflict and the need for spiritual strength to "contend earnestly." Where does this power to strive for the faith come from? Paul makes this clear: "I labor, striving [*agōnizomai*] according to His power, which mightily works within me" (Col. 1:29).

What did Jude mean when he wrote about "the faith" for which his readers were to contend? "The faith" doesn't refer to the personal faith of individual believers, but to the Christian faith taught by the apostles, contained in the Scriptures, and repeated in hymns, confessions, and creeds throughout history—the central doctrines of the faith (see, "Excursus: Apostates—Defectors from What?" page 179). This "faith" in Jude 1:3 was "once for all" delivered from God through Jesus Christ. Though it may be better understood and explained throughout history, the Christian faith cannot be added to, taken from, or molded to suit each generation's worldview. Finally, "the faith" was delivered "to the saints"—to all believers. It wasn't given for the world to criticize, for historians to evaluate, for philosophers to deconstruct, or for entertainers to lampoon. God intended every believer to understand the faith, to study it, and to live it—not only the theologian and the pastor but also the little child who places simple trust in Christ.

Having urged his readers to fight for the Christian faith, Jude then explains why this admonition was so pressing. Certain ungodly people had crept into the churches, bringing with them moral depravity and doctrinal deviation (1:4). These people had been "long beforehand marked out for this condemnation," so the presence of defectors from the faith shouldn't have surprised anyone. In fact, Jesus predicted, "Many will fall away and. . . many false prophets will arise and will mislead many" (Matt. 24:10-11). The apostle Paul warned, "The Spirit explicitly says that in later times some will fall away from the faith, paying attention to deceitful spirits and doctrines of demons" (1 Tim. 4:1). And the author of Hebrews sternly warns, "Take care, brethren, that there not be in any one of you an evil, unbelieving heart that falls away from the living God" (Heb. 3:12). An unbelieving heart, drawn away by the deceptive teachings of demons, leads to apostasy—the falling away from the true doctrines of the Christian faith.

Jude says the apostates "crept in unnoticed" (1:4). The Greek word *pareisdyō* [3921] implies a sinister and secret infiltration. In his commentary on Jude, William Barclay illustrates the term:

> It is used of the plausible and seductive words of someone who pleads their case cleverly, seeping gradually into the minds of a judge and jury; it is used of an outlaw slipping secretly back into the country from which he has been expelled; it is used of the slow and subtle entry of innovations into the life of society, which in the end undermine and break down the ancestral laws. It always indicates a stealthy insinuation of something evil into a society or situation.[2]

These impostors were as insidious and dangerous as foreign spies disguising themselves as red-white-and-blue-blooded Americans in order to destroy the nation from within. The apostates quietly penetrated the church, feigning faith. Once established and trusted, they sprang their subtle attack on the core of Christian truth in two ways.

First, the apostates turned the grace of God into "licentiousness" (1:4). Instead of receiving grace as God's forgiveness from guilt and as freedom to live the Christian life of holiness, they reinterpreted the grace of God as freedom to indulge in all sorts of immoral behavior (see Rom. 6:15-23). The word translated "licentiousness" is *aselgeia* [766]. It

Crept in Unaware

JUDE 1:4

When I was a kid, my parents would take the family on vacation every year to a small bay cottage. We'd spend most of our time at the saltwater bay a couple miles inland from the Gulf of Mexico. But sometimes my brother, my sister, and I would walk a little farther to swim in an irrigation reservoir. It was a nice change to get out of the murky, lukewarm saltwater of the bay and splash in a freshwater pond fed by a well. I remember the water was always pretty cool, clean, and clear.

But one day something crept in unaware. I dove in, and my two siblings and a friend dove in after me. The four of us were having a great time until I opened my eyes under the water and caught movement out of the corner of my eye. A tree branch? Too flaccid. Seaweed? No, not attached to anything. Then I realized what it was: a huge water moccasin, about as long as my dad was tall!

I didn't have to think about what to do next. As soon as I got my head up out of the water and air in my lungs, I sounded the alarm: "There's a snake in the water!"

Boom. Boom. Boom. Boom.

It was like four reverse cannonballs as we each leapt out of the reservoir faster than you could say "venomous snake."

That snake had just crept in . . . and we were completely unaware.

refers to "lack of self-constraint which involves one in conduct that violates all bounds of what is socially acceptable."[3] They engaged in calloused, guilt-free, sensual indulgence—all in the name of God's grace. In other words, they brought in moral depravity of the worst kind.

Second, the apostates denied Jesus Christ, the "only Master and Lord" (Jude 1:4). A rejection of moral standards always affects fidelity to doctrinal truth, and departure from doctrinal standards always leads to lax morality. In the minds of the apostates, Jesus was no more than a free public defender who got them out of jail and back on the streets to continue with business as usual. They rejected His true status as Master and Lord—terms appropriate for deity but also of lordship. Doctrinal and practical deviancy was the result.

—1:5-11—

The invaders who roused Jude's ire were twisting grace into a license to sin and were also denying the person and work of Christ. This description matches a particular category of heresies that eventually became known as Gnosticism. The various groups of Gnostics blended Christianity with Greek philosophy and added a measure of Middle Eastern religions and a dash of mysticism. In essence, they taught that our physical bodies, as part of this physical world, are evil, but our spirits are good. According to theologian Millard Erickson, this teaching led to two extremes:

> Whereas some Gnostics drew the conclusion that, the body being evil, a strict asceticism should be practiced, others concluded that what is done with the body is spiritually irrelevant, and hence engaged in licentious behavior.[4]

Apparently, teachers like the second type of Gnostics—the blatantly immoral—had infiltrated the church and claimed that the grace of Christ freed their spirits from their bodies, rendering their spiritual parts "holy" and making their physical deeds irrelevant. One commentator notes, "Those who fussed about sexual purity seemed to them astonishingly naïve."[5] (For more information, see "Gnostic Hedonism," page 84).

In keeping with this dualistic worldview that separated physical from spiritual and exalted the latter, these false teachers also denied the incarnation of Christ. At best, they taught that the divine "Christ" temporarily inhabited the body of the human "Jesus" to carry out his mission. At worst, they believed Christ to have been a ghostlike

176

(Gen. 6:1-4). The effect of this was widespread: rampant, worldwide wickedness (Gen. 6:5). The warning is again clear to the heinously immoral false teachers in Jude's day: Those who engage in such acts will be severely judged.

The third example takes us to the horrific events in Sodom and Gomorrah, recorded in Genesis 19. According to Genesis 13:13, "The men of Sodom were wicked exceedingly and sinners against the LORD." And Genesis 18:20 says, "The outcry of Sodom and Gomorrah is indeed great, and their sin is exceedingly grave." God didn't wink at their sexual immorality, and He condemned them to destruction. As such, the judgment of Sodom and Gomorrah became an archetype and foreshadowed the judgment of "eternal fire" that awaited unsaved apostates who also engaged in such wickedness. The immoral false teachers of Jude's day were indulging in this kind of "gross immorality" and were thus in line for similar punishment.

Because such apostasy brings certain doom, believers must strive against these false doctrines and wicked lifestyles. And unbelievers who are led astray by such false teachers will lose the opportunity to hear the truth and to be genuinely saved both from the disastrous lifestyle of wickedness and from eternal judgment.

Another reason believers must contend for the faith is because *the tongues of apostates are blasphemous* (Jude 1:8-10). Apostates can do great damage to new believers as well as unbelievers by their sneering cynicism and irreverence toward things that are sacred. They get their ideas not from God's revelation but from their own "dreaming" imaginations, by which they become their own authority over what's true and right. The result is a reviling or blaspheming of spiritual things (1:8, 10).

In 1:9, Jude illustrates the extreme folly of the apostates' blasphemies through an episode reported in an apocryphal book that would have been familiar to his audience. This book was known as the *Assumption of Moses* or the *Testament of Moses*.[6] By citing this literature from outside the Bible, Jude was leaving these false teachers nowhere to turn. If they appealed to Scripture, they were condemned (1:5-7). If they tried to find support from other writings, they were still condemned (1:8-9). According to the *Assumption of Moses*, the archangel Michael had been sent to bury Moses' body, but Lucifer intercepted him, claiming the body was his. Instead of showing disrespect toward Lucifer, Michael left the matter with the Judge of all creatures, saying, "The Lord rebuke you!" Jude's point was this: If Michael weighed his words carefully when addressing Lucifer, how presumptuous it was for the apostates to rail against angelic beings!

Those blaspheming apostates "revile the things which they do not understand"—that is, spiritual things. But what they are familiar with— natural things of the flesh—they indulge to the point of self-destruction (1:10). In other words, they live by sight, not by faith. As they recklessly ride the downward spiral of humanism, apostates consider themselves masters of their own bodies, to do with them as they please. They neglected the truth Paul underscored: "Do you not know that your body is a temple of the Holy Spirit who is in you, whom you have from God, and that you are not your own? For you have been bought with a price: therefore glorify God in your body" (1 Cor. 6:19-20). Instead of glorifying God with their bodies, they had become like animals, gratifying their every bodily craving.

A third reason believers should contend for the faith is because *the religion of apostates is empty* (Jude 1:11-13). It's not as though they were a valid alternative, wrong on a few minor points, but close enough. Instead, they had *nothing* to offer their followers. The errors of the apostates were manifold, as shown by further comparisons with negative figures from the past. Cain offered a sacrifice that went against God's requirements for the kind of offering He desired. By doing things his own way and presenting an offering from the fruit of his labors (rather than an animal sacrifice), Cain's offering did not meet God's approval (Gen. 4:1-7; Heb. 11:4). What Cain offered had the outside appearance of piety, but it lacked the substance of sincere faith and obedience.

Motivated by greed, the apostates also rushed into "the error of Balaam," who set out to sell his prophecies against Israel to the Moabites until the Lord stopped him (Num. 22; Deut. 23:3-4; Neh. 13:1-2; 2 Pet. 2:15-16). Balaam also lured the men of Israel into sexual immorality and the worship of idols (Num. 25:1-3; 31:15-16). So, Balaam served as an Old Testament parallel of the apostates, who not only twisted doctrine until it broke but also deceived people into sin.

Finally, Jude summons the testimony of the rebels of Korah, a Levite who led a mutiny against the legitimate leadership of Moses and Aaron. In his arrogance, Korah presumed that he could approach God on his own terms. Because of his presumptuous defiance, God caused the earth to open up and swallow him and his followers (Num. 16:1-33). In the same way, the apostates in Jude's day defied the authority of Christ and the apostles, choosing instead to cobble together a religion that filled up their own egos but provided no saving power to its adherents.

XCURSUS: ANGELIC APOSTATES

JUDE 1:6

Who were the angels "who did not keep their own domain," mentioned in Jude 1:6? We have three options. First, Jude could be referring to an original fall of angelic beings that coincided with the fall of Satan (Ezek. 28:11-19). However, Jude says these angels are being kept "in eternal bonds under darkness for the judgment of the great day" (Jude 1:6), whereas Satan and his angels are free and active in the world today (Eph. 6:11-12; 1 Pet. 5:8).

A second option is that Jude could be referring to a subsequent fall among the righteous angels that took place sometime after the earlier fall of Satan and his demons. However, the Bible records no such second wave of apostasy among the angels. In fact, it seems likely that those angels who did not fall with Satan were immediately sealed in their state of righteousness, unable to succumb to future temptations. The apostle Paul refers to "chosen angels" (1 Tim. 5:21), which has often been understood to refer to angels who passed the test of Satan's fall and were thus sealed in their state of tested perfection. If this is so, then the idea that Jude refers to a second apostasy among righteous angels can't be true.

The third and most likely option is that the wicked angels in Jude 1:6 were among the angels who fell with Satan, but who then committed a subsequent heinous sin that necessitated a more severe judgment than what had already befallen them. In a parallel passage in 2 Peter 2, Peter says that God "cast them into hell and committed them to pits of darkness," reserving them for future judgment (2 Pet. 2:4).

The language of Jude 1:6, as well as 2 Peter 2:4, reflects a popular book among Jews and Christians in the first century called *1 Enoch*. The writers of that book creatively recast the biblical account of the Flood (Gen. 6), describing the sins of the angelic beings who cohabited with human women. For this heinous and unnatural crime, they were cast into the place of deepest darkness and reserved for the Day of Judgment. On that day, the spirits of wickedness would be cast into fire (*1 Enoch* 10.6-9).[7]

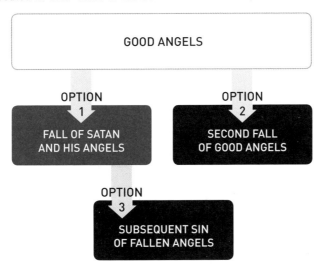

GOOD ANGELS

OPTION 1
FALL OF SATAN AND HIS ANGELS

OPTION 2
SECOND FALL OF GOOD ANGELS

OPTION 3
SUBSEQUENT SIN OF FALLEN ANGELS

—1:12-16—

In 1:5-11, Jude summoned a long roster of Old Testament and even extra-biblical witnesses to testify against the wickedness of the apostates. In 1:12-13, he unleashes a tirade of vivid images from nature itself to illustrate his argument. The false teachers showed up for the church's "love feasts" as if they were genuine members of the community of the faithful, but in reality, they were like "hidden reefs" that lurked just under the surface, ready to shipwreck others' faith (1:12). They were eager to fill their bellies from the pantries of the church, but they were

WHAT WAS THE "LOVE FEAST"?

JUDE 1:12

The expression "love feast" occurs only once in the New Testament (Jude 1:12). It has often been identified as the Lord's Supper . . . or at least a larger fellowship meal that preceded or followed the observance of the Lord's Supper. The "love feast" was likely held to create fellowship among the diverse members of the church by encouraging them to share with and care for one another, especially in terms of wealthy members expressing Christian charity (other-centered love) toward the poor and needy in the church. In other words, it was a clear, tangible expression of a church's concern for the physical needs of the poor, such as widows, orphans, the homeless, and the hungry.

While the commemorative observance of the Lord's Supper (with bread and wine) may have been held in conjunction with such meals, these two "meals" were clearly distinguished in the early church. One scholar writes,

> The Lord's supper and the love feast were two distinct activities—the one a remembrance and proclamation of the death and resurrection of Jesus and the other an act of benevolence and fellowship. It took some time before a distinct and fixed terminology prevailed, even as some time passed before the functions were separated in time, but the activities themselves had discreet meanings from the beginning.[8]

One expert on the history of Christian worship describes how these charity meals probably began: "The community meals were at once a realization and an expression of charity and mutual support, another aspect of communion in one single body. In times of want and famine . . . the demands of mutual help led in all likelihood to the organization of daily meals for the benefit of the needy."[9]

The fact that the heretics and apostates showed up at these meals (1:12) indicated that they were willing to partake of the material benefits of the church without subscribing to its spiritual truths.

unwilling to fulfill their obligations to the people of the church! They cared nothing about others, only themselves.

Their emptiness is underscored when Jude says the apostates were like "clouds without water," having nothing real to offer a thirsting soul (1:12). Along these same lines, the heretics were like fruitless and rootless trees—bearing no marks of holiness in their lives and, in fact, removed from the life-nourishing ministry of the church. In this sense, they were "doubly dead" (1:12). Jude illustrates their destructive nature by comparing them to foaming waves of the sea, washing up their flotsam and jetsam of impurity onto the otherwise pleasant beaches of the church (1:13). Finally, their lives are like "wandering stars," which appear for a time but fail at providing guidance. Instead, they lead into the darkness of destruction any who count on them for direction.

Jude uses a number of illustrations for the depravity of the apostates. Among these are the images of a waterless cloud carried about by winds and a rootless tree totally barren of fruit during harvest season.

After these illustrations from nature, Jude caps off his description of the apostates' judgment with a quote from the popular apocryphal book, *1 Enoch*. The strong language used in *1 Enoch* 1.9 applied well to the condemnation of these false teachers. Did this mean that Jude believed the whole book of *1 Enoch* should be included in the Old Testament canon? Richard Bauckham clarifies that even though Jude regarded the words of *1 Enoch* 1.9 as prophecy, "it need not imply that he regarded the book as canonical Scripture. At Qumran, for example, the Enoch literature and other apocryphal works were evidently valued without being included in the canon of Scripture."[10] The apostle Paul used truth from a non-inspired Cretan poet Epimenides in a similar way when he wrote in Titus 1:12-13, "One of themselves, a prophet of their own, said, 'Cretans are always liars, evil beasts, lazy gluttons.' This testimony is true."[11] To illustrate truth, Jude likewise drew from a variety of uninspired sources that nevertheless contained truth, like the *Assumption of Moses* in Jude 1:8-9 and *1 Enoch* in Jude 1:14-15.

What was the content of *1 Enoch* that caught Jude's attention and led him to apply it to the acts of the apostates? The passage quoted emphasizes the absolute certainty of the judgment of the ungodly. This quote serves to cap off and sum up the preceding discussion. Think of it as Jude's "closing argument" as he presents his final case to his readers that they must contend earnestly for the faith in the face of the false teachers: "Behold, the Lord came with many thousands of His holy ones, to execute judgment upon all, and to convict all the ungodly of all their ungodly deeds which they have done in an ungodly way, and of all the harsh things which ungodly sinners have spoken against Him" (1:14-15).

Did you notice the repeated word "ungodly"? It's the same term used in Romans 1:18, where Paul says "The wrath of God is revealed from heaven against all ungodliness and unrighteousness of men." One day, Christ will come with an entourage of angelic warriors and a parade of glorified saints to make war against the ungodly and to vanquish them. None will escape the judgment. They will be judged both for their ungodly deeds and for the words of blasphemy they spoke when they rejected their only Master and Lord, Jesus Christ (1:15).

Finally, Jude lays into the apostates with a litany of vices that clothe the false teachers from head to toe. Grumbling, faultfinding, lusting, boasting, and flattering, they were the exact opposite of what they were supposed to be. And because of their conscious, willing, stubborn rebellion, God will punish them one day.

APPLICATION: JUDE 1:1-16
A Balanced Response to Apostates

Jude's purpose in detailing the depravity and predicting the destruction of the ungodly apostates was to instill in his readers a deep sense of righteous anger against their wicked deeds and deceptions. Has it worked with you? Are you ready to take on these types of apostates? Before you do, beware. If you're not careful, righteous indignation could boil over and become uncontrolled hostility. Too quickly, calm confrontation can explode into name-calling and shouting matches. Then nobody wins.

How can you contend earnestly for the faith without losing your head? The key is to be thoroughly prepared. The most persuasive argument in any debate is the truth, so use it. Know where you stand doctrinally on vital issues of the Christian faith. Know where false teachers stand too. Find out what they're teaching; listen to their words and discern the meaning behind them. Most of the time they will sound like normal evangelical Christians with the same Scriptures and the same gospel as us . . . but if you listen closely, you'll discover that they define terms differently than we do. Don't be afraid to take a stand. You may be the only flickering flame in the darkness, the only dissenting voice in a crowd carried away by deception.

Admittedly, engaging false teachers isn't an easy task. A believer must be prepared not only mentally (with accurate answers) but also spiritually (with the right attitude). Some who are prepared mentally have the wrong heart. Some who are prepared spiritually have the wrong answers. We need both! Mental preparation requires study and knowledge. Spiritual preparation requires maturity and wisdom. Both of these come from the Spirit (Isa. 11:2), are epitomized in Christ (Col. 2:1-3), and are received through prayer from God the Father (Eph. 1:17). Diligent, prayerful study and loving, intentional engagement work hand in hand as we seek to contend earnestly for the faith once for all delivered.

Get Your Act Together!
JUDE 1:17-25

NASB

[17]But you, beloved, ought to remember the words that were spoken beforehand by the apostles of our Lord Jesus Christ, [18]that they were saying to you, "In the last time there will be mockers, following after their own ungodly lusts." [19]These are the ones who cause divisions, [a]worldly-minded, [b]devoid of the Spirit. [20]But you, beloved, building yourselves up on your most holy faith, praying in the Holy Spirit, [21]keep yourselves

NLT

[17]But you, my dear friends, must remember what the apostles of our Lord Jesus Christ predicted. [18]They told you that in the last times there would be scoffers whose purpose in life is to satisfy their ungodly desires. [19]These people are the ones who are creating divisions among you. They follow their natural instincts because they do not have God's Spirit in them.

[20]But you, dear friends, must build each other up in your most holy faith, pray in the power of the Holy Spirit,* [21]and await the mercy of our

NASB

in the love of God, waiting anxiously for the mercy of our Lord Jesus Christ to eternal life. [22]And have mercy on some, who are doubting; [23]save others, snatching them out of the fire; and on some have mercy with fear, hating even the garment polluted by the flesh.

[24]Now to Him who is able to keep you from stumbling, and to make you stand in the presence of His glory blameless with great joy, [25]to the only God our Savior, through Jesus Christ our Lord, *be* glory, majesty, dominion and authority, before all time and now and [a]forever. Amen.

1:19 [a]Or *merely natural* [b]Lit *not having*   1:25 [a]Lit *to all the ages*

NLT

Lord Jesus Christ, who will bring you eternal life. In this way, you will keep yourselves safe in God's love. [22]And you must show mercy to* those whose faith is wavering. [23]Rescue others by snatching them from the flames of judgment. Show mercy to still others,* but do so with great caution, hating the sins that contaminate their lives.*

[24]Now all glory to God, who is able to keep you from falling away and will bring you with great joy into his glorious presence without a single fault. [25]All glory to him who alone is God, our Savior through Jesus Christ our Lord. All glory, majesty, power, and authority are his before all time, and in the present, and beyond all time! Amen.

20 Greek *pray in the Holy Spirit.*   **22** Some manuscripts read *must reprove.*   **22-23a** Some manuscripts have only two categories of people: (1) those whose faith is wavering and therefore need to be snatched from the flames of judgment, and (2) those who need to be shown mercy. **23b** Greek *with fear, hating even the clothing stained by the flesh.*

In 1940, as the war against Hitler raged in Europe, British ships rescued more than three hundred thousand Allied troops who had been surrounded by the Germans at Dunkirk, France. Thirty thousand French and British soldiers were killed or taken prisoner, but Winston Churchill, the prime minister of Great Britain, stood his ground. In a speech to the House of Commons on June 4, 1940, he said these famous words:

We shall go on to the end. We shall fight in France, we shall fight on the seas and oceans, we shall fight with growing confidence and growing strength in the air, we shall defend our island, whatever the cost may be, we shall fight on the beaches, we shall fight on the landing grounds, we shall fight in the fields and in the streets, we shall fight in the hills; we shall never surrender![12]

This, and many other stirring speeches by Churchill, helped to strengthen the resolve of a war-torn nation and its beleaguered military. It also instilled hope in the midst of despair, confidence in the midst of doubt, and renewed vigor in the midst of waning determination.

With similar resolve and determination, Jude exhorted his readers to "contend earnestly for the faith" (Jude 1:3) Today, heresy storms our own beaches. The preservation of truth and morality hangs in the balance. At the end of Jude's letter, he makes a final appeal to the soldiers of the faith who are in the midst of a raging battle against the onslaught of false teachers. Concerned that his readers might become spiritual casualties, he urges them to pick up their spiritual weapons and fight back. To accomplish this, Jude fortifies his readers with five commands in the closing verses of the letter: Remember (1:17-19), keep (1:20-21), convince (1:22), save (1:23), and have mercy (1:23)!

Although the circumstances have clearly changed since the first century, the broader issue remains the same. Many enemies of Christ lurk outside and inside the church, waiting to assault our faith. That's why, once we've girded ourselves with a protective armor of truth, we need to take action on behalf of those around us.

—1:17-19—

Toward the end of his life, around the year AD 66, the apostle Peter wrote a letter from Rome to Christians in Asia Minor warning them that "in the last days mockers will come" (2 Pet. 3:3) From his perspective, this statement was prophetic. Yes, false prophets had already begun to pop up, challenging the apostles and offering their own counterfeit doctrines. Many believers had already abandoned the faith, being led astray by heresy, lust, or greed. But Peter's words suggested that these were just harbingers of even greater threats to come. Just as distant lightning flashes and thunderclaps warn us that a storm is rolling in, the false teachers in Peter's day were a precursor of a flash flood of false prophets that would soon threaten to wipe away the weak in faith.

Though Peter cast this warning about mockers as a prophecy, within a decade or so the first wave of these mockers had already begun to arrive on the scene. In fact, it seems likely that the words in Jude 1:17-19 refer directly to Peter's prophecy (and indirectly to similar warnings from Jesus and other apostles). Jude tells his readers to "remember the words that were spoken beforehand by the apostles of our Lord Jesus Christ" (1:17)—the first of five imperatives to his readers. As recorded in the New Testament, the apostles had warned against false teachers, whose presence would be a certainty in the last days (Acts 20:28-30; 1 Tim. 4:1-2; 2 Pet. 3:3-4). By bracing ourselves for the flood, we're less likely to be swept away when the waves of wickedness flow into our churches. In 1:18-19, Jude proceeds to give five identifying marks of the apostates.

 First, they are mockers, spouting cynical jabs and serving up contrarian opinions. They tease, poke fun, roll their eyes, and ridicule the classic faith and morality of Christianity. By dodging the truth of Scripture, they thus free themselves to believe whatever they want and to live however they please.

This leads to the second mark of the apostates: They are immoral, "following after their own ungodly lusts" (1:18). Corrupt theology almost always erodes into corrupt morality. Once apostates break free from the safety harness of God's Word, they plummet in a freefall of depravity, descending toward destruction.

Such mocking and immorality never affect only the individual; they also impact the church. The third mark of the apostates is that they are divisive. They cause division by rejecting the teaching authority of legitimate leadership in the church (see 1:8, 11) and by sowing seeds of discord in the community (1:12).

Fourth, they are "worldly-minded" (1:19), not setting their minds "on the things above" (Col. 3:2). The term translated "worldly-minded," *psychikos* [5591], is the same word Paul uses to describe the "natural man" who "does not accept the things of the Spirit of God, for they are foolishness to him" (1 Cor. 2:14). And James, the brother of Jude, refers to the worldliness that causes jealousy, selfish ambition, and arrogance, labeling it "earthly, natural [*psychikos*], demonic" (Jas. 3:14-15). So, the fourth mark of the apostates is that they are ruled by their worldly, natural desires.

Finally, the fifth mark of the apostates is that they are "devoid of the Spirit" (Jude 1:19). A true believer cannot be devoid of the Spirit, as Paul clearly teaches: "If anyone does not have the Spirit of Christ, he does not belong to Him" (Rom. 8:9). The evidence of their lack of the Holy Spirit's indwelling is seen in the first four marks. But even a false believer can fake it for a while. The sustained and unrepentant heresy and immorality of these apostates provide proof of their spiritual emptiness.

—1:20-21—

In the second imperative, Jude instructs his readers to keep themselves in the love of God (Jude 1:20-21). There are three means by which they are to do this, indicated by three present participles: building up, praying, and waiting.

JUDE'S LOGIC IN 1:20-21	
WHAT TO DO	**HOW TO DO IT**
Keep yourselves in the love of God (1:21)	Building yourselves up on your most holy faith (1:20)
	Praying in the Holy Spirit (1:20)
	Waiting anxiously for the mercy of our Lord Jesus Christ to eternal life (1:21)

The imperative itself brings to mind Jesus' command recorded in John 15:9: "Just as the Father has loved Me, I have also loved you; abide in My love." To keep ourselves in God's love is to abide in Christ, so that His love flows through us. Apart from Him, we can do nothing (John 15:5). Jude doesn't advocate a theology of the Christian life in which we are wholly responsible for maintaining our salvation by our own strength. Earlier, he reminded his readers that they "know all things once for all" (Jude 1:5), and he will conclude with an affirmation that it is God "who is able to keep" them from stumbling (1:24). So in 1:21, when Jude commands them to "keep [them]selves in the love of God," we are to understand that this is done only as we lean on God's grace and depend wholly on His enabling power.

How then do we cultivate His love in our lives as we depend on Him and walk in faith? First, by *building ourselves up on the faith* (1:20). Just as in 1:3, Jude has in mind not the subjective element of faith (our believing) but the objective content of faith ("the faith which was once for all handed down to the saints"). This requires that we study the Scriptures and doctrines of the faith, submit to trained, proven, and trustworthy teachers for instruction, and hold firmly to the doctrines that have been handed down through the centuries. As we learn about the faith, feeding on it for nourishment and strength, we will grow in our love for Him and for one another.

Second, we keep ourselves in the love of God by *praying in the Holy Spirit* (1:20). What does this mean? One commentator defines it as praying "in His communion and power, not in reliance on [our] own wisdom and strength."[13] That is, we are to pray in absolute dependence on the Spirit, with an admission of our weakness and an acknowledgment that "the Spirit Himself intercedes for us . . . according to the will of God" (Rom. 8:26-27). When we pray, we start in our weakness, but we end in God's strength. We begin with nothing, but He gives us everything. We come empty, but He fills us. Praying by the power of the Spirit is a key component of keeping ourselves in the love of God.

Third, we keep ourselves in the love of God by *waiting for the second coming of Christ with eager anticipation* (Jude 1:21). Though the storms of doctrinal error and the floods of rampant immorality may saturate the world around us, we keep our heads up in hope for the return of Christ, who will set all things right. By His great mercy, He will descend from heaven one day, raise the dead, and transform the living into a glorified state fit for eternal life (1 Thes. 4:16-17). With this hope kept close at hand, we will be delivered from fears and prepared to face whatever challenges may come. And this hope will firm up our faith and enable us to keep ourselves in the love of God until that glorious day.

—1:22-23—

Jude's third, fourth, and fifth imperatives relate to how believers are to treat those who have been wounded by the apostates—perhaps dragged partway into their deceptive doctrines and destructive practices. Are those casualties of spiritual warfare to be written off, cut off, or laid to rest? In 1:22-23, Jude refers to three groups of people who are to be treated in three different ways: those who doubt, those who need snatching from the fire, and those who have polluted their flesh.

With regard to the first category—the doubters—there is a question about the original text written by Jude in the first century.[14] Some ancient manuscripts have the verb "convince" in 1:22 rather than the verb "have mercy." Though one could make arguments in favor of the originality of either reading, I believe it fits Jude's style of distinct triplets better if he originally wrote three distinct commands in 1:22-23 ("convince . . . save . . . have mercy") rather than two of the same command with a different one in the middle ("have mercy . . . save . . . have mercy"). If that's correct, the passage would read: "And convince some, who doubt; save some, by snatching them out of the fire; on some have mercy with fear, hating even the garment spotted by the flesh" (1:22-23, RSV). This would make three categories and three distinct commands.

The third imperative for believers, then, is: "Convince some, who doubt" (1:22, RSV). Some believers are caught between those who proclaim the truth and those who twist it. With such people wavering in the faith because of deception, contending for the faith means persuading the doubters of the right way and refuting the wrong. This may mean long hours of patient instruction, prayerful interaction, and lengthy dialogue to show them the biblical, theological, and historical facts

by deception. To wrap up our careful reading of Jude, let's focus on coming to the aid of the fellow believer who has been wounded in spiritual combat, paralyzed by fear and doubt, or dazed by the trauma of the battle. How can we minister to those who have been disillusioned by seeds of doubt or weakened by the claims of false teachers? Several practical steps will help us as we seek to rescue a wayward brother or sister in Christ.

First, *listen to the person*. Don't shun or avoid them. Find out exactly what's causing the doubts. They may have experienced more than just a seed of untruth planted by a deceptive source. In fact, sometimes these seeds are able to take root only because deeper problems have fertilized the soil. Has the person been through a faith-challenging struggle with suffering or loss? Have they been wounded in the context of the church, perhaps through observing the moral fall of a spiritual authority or through experiencing a lack of acceptance or care in the midst of a spiritual, emotional, or physical crisis? Be sensitive and watch for deeper issues.

Second, *keep in contact and meet with them regularly*. A very wise person once said, "They won't care how much you know until they know how much you care." Don't browbeat or condescend. Take time to build your relationship on a foundation of honesty and transparency. You're far more likely to make a difference in that person's life if you treat them with love and respect, taking the time to understand their deep struggle with these issues and sharing the weight of their burden.

Third, *approach the problem with outside help from experts*. If it's an emotional or moral problem, locate resources that address these issues, such as pastoral counselors or qualified Christian counselors. Ask your pastor or another church leader for suggestions. Sometimes merely demonstrating your concern about the person at this level will go a long way toward helping them. If the problem is more of an intellectual one, find resources that address the specific need. Get two copies—one for the person you're trying to help and another for yourself—then, if the person is willing, agree to meet together to discuss the issue. Come alongside them and model grace rather than talking down to them.

Finally, after several meetings, you may notice that the person's heart does not change. Or maybe they further harden against the truth. In that case, *you may have to confront the individual with a strong warning and appeal for repentance* (Jas. 5:19-20). You may even want to involve other caring friends. If your friend remains hardened or rejects your intervention, you must "have mercy with fear" (Jude 1:23). In other words, keep showing love and continue to pray, turning them over to the Lord's care and discipline.

Yes, you are your brother's or sister's keeper—not in the ultimate sense, which is the role of God alone (1:24), but in the mediate sense because God uses His children to hold one another accountable. Each one of us is responsible for the spiritual safety of our Christian brothers and sisters. And we are also accountable to intervene when they're in danger of deception. Have you been motivated to help others who may have been led astray by Satan's sweet-sounding propaganda? Has God placed somebody in your path today? If so, don't delay. Step up and get involved now!

ENDNOTES

1, 2 & 3 JOHN

INTRODUCTION

1 One scholar notes, "If the criteria of vocabulary and style are ever adequate for pronouncing judgment on authorship, these three short letters [1, 2, and 3 John] must be attributed to one author who is also the author of the Fourth Gospel" (Merrill C. Tenney, *New Testament Survey*, rev. ed., ed. Walter M. Dunnett [Grand Rapids: Eerdmans, 1961], 374).

2 H. D. M. Spence-Jones, *1 John*, The Pulpit Commentary (New York: Funk & Wagnalls, 1909), i.

3 Quoted from a translation of the Muratorian Canon fragment in Henry Melvill Gwatkin, *Selections from Early Writers Illustrative of Church History to the Time of Constantine* (London: Macmillan, 1897), 83–89.

4 Polycarp, *Epistle to the Philippians*, 7.1. Translation from Rick Brannan, trans., *The Apostolic Fathers in English* (Bellingham, WA: Lexham Press, 2012).

5 Irenaeus of Lyons, *Against Heresies* 3.16.5, in Alexander Roberts and James Donaldson, eds., *Ante-Nicene Fathers: The Writings of the Fathers Down to A.D. 325*, vol. 1, *The Apostolic Fathers with Justin Martyr and Irenaeus*, repr. ed. (Grand Rapids: Eerdmans, 2001), 442.

6 Tertullian, *Prescription Against the Heretics* 36.

7 See an early account in Eusebius of Caesarea, *Ecclesiastical History* 3.17–20.

8 Stephen S. Smalley, *1, 2, 3 John*, Word Biblical Commentary, vol. 51, ed. David A. Hubbard and Glenn W. Barker (Waco, TX: Word Books, 1984), 314.

9 Walter Bauer et al., *A Greek-English Lexicon of the New Testament and Other Early Christian Literature* (Chicago: University of Chicago Press, 2000), 862.

10 Ibid.

11 See the more detailed discussion on the authorship of the Gospel of John and 1–3 John earlier in this volume, pages 6–9.

12 See J. R. W. Stott, *The Epistles of John* (1964; repr., Grand Rapids: Eerdmans, 1969), 200–202.

13 William Barclay, *The Letters of John and Jude*, rev. ed., The Daily Study Bible (Philadelphia: Westminster, 1976), 133–134.

14 See the more detailed discussion on the authorship of the Gospel of John and 1–3 John earlier in this volume, pages 6–9.

1 JOHN

A JOYFUL LIFE (1 JOHN 1:1-10)

[1] Walter Bauer et al., *A Greek-English Lexicon of the New Testament and Other Early Christian Literature* (Chicago: University of Chicago Press, 2000), 552.

[2] See the analysis in John R. W. Stott, *The Letters of John: An Introduction and Commentary*, rev. ed. Tyndale New Testament Commentaries (Grand Rapids: Eerdmans, 1988), 62.

[3] Anthony Preus, *Historical Dictionary of Ancient Greek Philosophy*, 2nd ed. (Lanham, MD: Rowman & Littlefield, 2015), 229–231.

[4] Ibid., 231.

[5] Bauer et al., *Greek-English Lexicon*, 445–446.

[6] Earl F. Palmer, *1, 2, 3 John, Revelation*, The Communicator's Commentary, vol. 12, ed. Lloyd J. Ogilvie (Waco, TX: Word Books, 1982), 23.

[7] See Irenaeus, *Against Heresies* 1.16; Tertullian, *On the Soul* 34.

[8] Justin Martyr, *1 Apology* 26. See the discussion on this statue in Leslie William Barnard, ed., *St. Justin Martyr: The First and Second Apologies*, Ancient Christian Writers, vol. 56 (New York: Paulist Press, 1997), 136, note 181.

[9] See Stephen S. Smalley, *1, 2, 3 John*, Word Biblical Commentary, vol. 51, ed. David A. Hubbard and Glenn W. Barker (Waco, TX: Word Books, 1984), 9.

[10] Martyn Lloyd-Jones, *Life in Christ: Studies in 1 John*, One Volume ed. (Wheaton, IL: Crossway, 2002), 30.

[11] Nathan D. Holsteen and Michael J. Svigel, eds., *Exploring Christian Theology, vol. 2, Creation, Fall, and Salvation* (Minneapolis: Bethany House, 2015), 258.

[12] John MacArthur, *1-3 John*, The MacArthur New Testament Commentary (Chicago: Moody, 2007), 26.

[13] Bauer et al., *Greek-English Lexicon*, 708.

A CLEAN LIFE (1 JOHN 2:1-17)

[1] Bauer et al., *Greek-English Lexicon*, 994.

[2] Originally published as Robert Fulghum, *All I Really Need to Know I Learned in Kindergarten: Uncommon Thoughts on Common Things* (New York: Ballantine, 1986).

[3] Robert Fulghum, *All I Really Need to Know I Learned in Kindergarten: Uncommon Thoughts on Common Things—Reconsidered, Revised, and Expanded with Twenty-Five New Essays*, 25th anniversary ed. (New York: Ballantine, 2003), 2.

[4] Ibid., 2.

[5] Bauer et al., *Greek-English Lexicon*, 766.

[6] Warren W. Wiersbe, *Be Real* (Wheaton, IL: Victor Books, 1972), 22.

[7] Holsteen and Svigel, *Exploring Christian Theology*, 2:256.

[8] See Smalley, *1, 2, 3 John*, 47.

[9] James Montgomery Boice, *The Epistles of John: An Expositional Commentary* (Grand Rapids: Zondervan, 1979), 53.

[10] For various views on John's use of these categories, see Smalley, *1, 2, 3 John*, 69–71.

[11] Ibid., 76–80.

[12] Kenneth S. Wuest, *In These Last Days: II Peter, I, II, III John, and Jude in the Greek New Testament for the English Reader* (Grand Rapids: Eerdmans, 1954), 125.

[13] Bauer et al., *Greek-English Lexicon*, 5.

A DISCERNING LIFE (1 JOHN 2:18–4:6)

1. Wiersbe, *Be Real*, 84–85.
2. For more details on the exploits of the future Antichrist figure, see Charles R. Swindoll, *Swindoll's Living Insights New Testament Commentary*, vol. 15, *Revelation* (Carol Stream, IL: Tyndale House, 2014), 188–201; Charles R. Swindoll, *Swindoll's Living Insights New Testament Commentary*, vol. 10, *1 & 2 Thessalonians* (Carol Stream, IL: Tyndale House, 2016), 124–137.
3. Irenaeus of Lyons, *Against Heresies* 3.3.4.
4. John Calvin, *Commentaries on the Catholic Epistles*, trans. John Owen (Edinburgh: Calvin Translation Society, 1855), 192.
5. Holsteen and Svigel, *Exploring Christian Theology*, 2:253.
6. Quoted from John H. Leith, ed., *Creeds of the Churches: A Reader in Christian Doctrine from the Bible to the Present*, 3rd ed. (Louisville, KY: John Knox, 1982), 35.
7. Bauer et al., *Greek-English Lexicon*, 781.
8. Smalley, *1, 2, 3 John*, 134, 136.
9. Gary W. Derickson, *1, 2 & 3 John*, Evangelical Exegetical Commentary, eds. H. Wayne House, W. Hall Harris III, and Andrew W. Pitts (Bellingham, WA: Lexham Press, 2012), 286–287.
10. Daniel L. Akin, *1, 2, 3 John*, vol. 38, The New American Commentary (Nashville: Broadman & Holman, 2001), 140.
11. Smalley, *1, 2, 3 John*, 154.
12. Ibid., 155.
13. Nigel Turner, *Grammatical Insights into the New Testament* (Edinburgh: T. & T. Clark, 1965), 151.
14. Smalley, *1, 2, 3 John*, 173–174.
15. Bauer et al., *Greek-English Lexicon*, 979.
16. Ibid., 832–836.
17. Smalley, *1, 2, 3 John*, 218.
18. Bauer et al., *Greek-English Lexicon*, 255.
19. Ibid., 708.
20. See *1 Clement* 5.3-4; 42.1-3; Ignatius, *Magnesians* 13.1; *Romans* 4.3; Polycarp, *Philippians* 9.1; Tertullian, *Against Marcion* 4.5.
21. "The Muratorian Fragment," in Bruce M. Metzger, *The Canon of the New Testament: Its Origin, Development, and Significance* (Oxford: Clarendon Press, 1987), 307.

A CONFIDENT LIFE (1 JOHN 4:7–5:21)

1. On the meaning of "propitiation," see comments on 1 John 2:2, page 42.
2. Bauer et al., *Greek-English Lexicon*, 996.
3. Smalley, *1, 2, 3 John*, 256–257.
4. Merrill C. Tenney, *John: The Gospel of Belief—An Analytic Study of the Text* (Grand Rapids: Eerdmans, 1976), 31–32.
5. Bruce M. Metzger, *A Textual Commentary on the Greek New Testament*, 2nd ed. (New York: United Bible Societies, 1994), 647.
6. Ibid., 647–648.
7. Ibid., 648.
8. Smalley, *1, 2, 3 John*, 273.
9. Metzger, *Textual Commentary*, 648.
10. See Karl Braune, "The Epistles General of John," in *Commentary on the Holy Scriptures: Critical, Doctrinal, and Homiletical*, ed. John Peter Lange, trans. J. Isidor Mombert, new ed. (Grand Rapids: Zondervan, 1976), 156.
11. Wuest, *In These Last Days*, 182.

¹² Stott, *Letters of John,* 188–190.
¹³ William Hendriksen, *Exposition of the Gospel According to Matthew,* 5th ed., New Testament Commentary, vol. 9, ed. Simon J. Kistemaker (Grand Rapids: Baker, 1982), 529.
¹⁴ See Smalley, *1, 2, 3 John,* 297–301.
¹⁵ Wiersbe, *Be Real,* 184–186.
¹⁶ See F. F. Bruce, *Answers to Questions* (Grand Rapids: Zondervan, 1972), 134.

2 JOHN

¹ Gerhard Kittel and Gerhard Friedrich, eds., *Theological Dictionary of the New Testament: Abridged in One Volume,* trans. Geoffrey W. Bromiley (Grand Rapids: Eerdmans, 1985), 38.
² Bauer et al., *Greek-English Lexicon,* 994.
³ Earl F. Palmer, *1, 2, 3 John, Revelation,* The Communicator's Commentary, vol. 12, ed. Lloyd J. Ogilvie (Waco, TX: Word Books, 1982), 82.
⁴ Smalley, *1, 2, 3 John,* 318.
⁵ Stott, *Epistles of John,* 205.
⁶ Didache 11.4-6, 8, 10; 12.1, 3-5, quoted from Rick Brannan, trans., *The Apostolic Fathers in English* (Bellingham, WA: Lexham Press, 2012).

3 JOHN

¹ Walter Bauer et al., *A Greek-English Lexicon of the New Testament and Other Early Christian Literature* (Chicago: University of Chicago Press, 2000), 7.
² Stephen S. Smalley, *1, 2, 3 John,* Word Biblical Commentary, vol. 51, ed. David A. Hubbard and Glenn W. Barker (Waco, TX: Word Books, 1984), 353.
³ 1 Clement 42.3-4; 44.1-2, quoted from Rick Brannan, trans., *The Apostolic Fathers in English* (Bellingham, WA: Lexham Press, 2012).
⁴ J. Stuart Holden, *Some Old Testament Parables* (London: Pickering & Inglis, 1934), 49.
⁵ Smalley, *1, 2, 3 John,* 360.

JUDE

INTRODUCTION

¹ Gene L. Green, *Jude and 2 Peter,* Baker Exegetical Commentary on the New Testament (Grand Rapids: Baker Academic, 2008), 1.
² Eusebius of Caesarea, "The Church History of Eusebius," in *Eusebius: Church History, Life of Constantine the Great, and Oration in Praise of Constantine,* ed. Philip Schaff and Henry Wace, trans. Arthur Cushman McGiffert, vol. 1, *A Select Library of the Nicene and Post-Nicene Fathers of the Christian Church,* Second Series (New York: Christian Literature Company, 1890), 148–149.
³ Walter Bauer et al., *A Greek-English Lexicon of the New Testament and Other Early Christian Literature* (Chicago: University of Chicago Press, 2000), 356.

4 Fritz Reinecker, *A Linguistic Key to the Greek New Testament*, trans. and ed. by Cleon L. Rogers, Jr. (Grand Rapids: Zondervan, 1980), 803.
5 Bauer et al., *Greek-English Lexicon*, 115–116.

A MANUAL FOR SURVIVAL (JUDE 1:1-25)

1 Edward C. Pentecost, "Jude," in *The Bible Knowledge Commentary: An Exposition of the Scriptures*, eds. John F. Walvoord and Roy B. Zuck, vol. 2 (Wheaton, IL: Victor Books, 1985), 919.
2 William Barclay, *The Letters of John and Jude*, The New Daily Study Bible, 3rd ed. (Louisville: Westminster John Knox, 2002), 204–205.
3 Bauer et al., *Greek-English Lexicon*, 141.
4 Millard J. Erickson, *Christian Theology*, 2nd ed. (Grand Rapids: Baker, 1998), 1197.
5 Michael Green, *The Second Epistle General of Peter and the General Epistle of Jude: An Introduction and Commentary*, The Tyndale New Testament Commentaries (Grand Rapids: Eerdmans, 1968), 181.
6 See Richard J. Bauckham, *Jude, 2 Peter*, Word Biblical Commentary, vol. 50 (Waco, TX: Word Books, 1983), 65–76.
7 See parallel in 2 Peter 2:4; see also an in-depth discussion of this understanding of Genesis 6 in my comments on 1 Peter 3:19-20, in Charles R. Swindoll, *Swindoll's Living Insights New Testament Commentary*, vol. 13, *James, 1 & 2 Peter* (Carol Stream, IL: Tyndale House, 2014), 222–225.
8 Everett Ferguson, "Lord's Supper and Love Feast," *Christian Studies 21* (2005–2006): 35.
9 Marcel Metzger, *History of the Liturgy: The Major Stages*, trans. Madeleine M. Beaumont (Collegeville, MN: Liturgical Press, 1997), 21–22.
10 Bauckham, *Jude, 2 Peter*, 96.
11 See Pentecost, "Jude," 922.
12 Sir Winston Churchill, as quoted in *Bartlett's Familiar Quotations*, 16th ed., ed. Justin Kaplan (Boston: Little, Brown and Company, 1992), 620.
13 G. F. C. Fronmüller, "The Epistle General of Jude," in *Commentary on the Holy Scriptures: Critical, Doctrinal, and Homiletical*, ed. John Peter Lange, trans. J. Isidor Mombert, new ed. (Grand Rapids: Zondervan, 1976), 29.
14 See the discussion in Bruce M. Metzger, *A Textual Commentary on the Greek New Testament*, 2nd ed. (London: United Bible Societies, 1994), 658–659.
15 Michael Green, *Peter and Jude*, 190.